Singapore Salvation

Singapore Salvation

Jennifer Burge

WORLDWISE PUBLICATIONS
QUEENSLAND, AUSTRALIA

SINGAPORE SALVATION
©2015 Jennifer Burge
WorldWise Publications
www.worldwisepublications.com
All rights reserved

Cover Design by Mike Levario
Front Cover image used under license from Shutterstock.com
Back Cover image by Jennifer Burge

Categories: Travel, Biography & Memoir,
Business Travel, Women in Business

The right of Jennifer Burge to be identified as the author of this work has been asserted by her in accordance with the *Copyright Amendment (Moral Rights) Act 2000.*

This work is protected by copyright. Apart from any use as permitted under the Copyright Act 1968, no part may be reproduced, copied, scanned, stored in a retrieval system, recorded, or transmitted, in any form or by any means, without the prior written permission of the author and publisher.

ISBN 978-0-9942449-2-5 (Paperback)
ISBN 978-0-9942449-3-2 (eBook)

Worldwise Publications
Queensland, Australia

For my husband

The road less traveled has had a higher toll than we expected, but I wouldn't have taken it with anyone else.

Contents

Prologue 1
Transplanted 3
The Koi Pond 11
Will the Real Singapore Please Step Forward? 17
Cracks in the Surface 27
Dramatis Personae 35
The Face in the Mirror 45
The Third New Year 53
Soul Seeker 61
The Rat Races In 75
Space Invasion 83
Lion City 93
One Night in Bangkok 97
Déjà Vu 105
Party Games 113
Upside Down Under 121
Superiority Complex 131
Flying the Coop 137
Sleepwalking in Tokyo 147
Miscellaneous Melbourne 155
"Home" 161
Forbidden 173
Dragon's Bite 183
Hobbies 197
Pilgrim 209
Taboo 217
Epiphany 231
Dreaming in Vietnamese 243
Thai Treats 253
Bridges 259
Aftershock 267

Author's Note 279

Prologue

Skyscrapers swayed like palm fronds in a sea breeze. Fear paralyzed me. Standing was out of the question. I had a death grip on a railing that wasn't there. My head swam as if I'd swilled a bottle of vodka. No one made a sound, but the tropical air was thick with fear and trepidation. It defied reason that the massive weight of concrete and steel dipped like a tango dancer without crashing to the ground and taking all of us with it. But it didn't. It just continued to give me close ups of the pavement before flinging me back toward the angry gray-green sky.

Chapter 1
Transplanted

Determined to eliminate the last remaining space in my suitcases, I darted from one room to the next of our historic Rotterdam *heerenhuis*. Surely there must be more I could carry with me to our next life in Singapore. Exhausted, I collapsed in a brown leather armchair in the dining room. The last rays of sunlight were reaching through the scarlet-and-gold pattern of the dining room windows.

Tears welled up in my eyes when I realized how much I would miss that view. I'd done nothing but search for an exit visa from the Netherlands for the majority of my five years here. What did I have to cry about now that my wish was about to come true? That it was finally happening? That the hell you know is better than the one you don't? I couldn't explain it.

The gold ring on the cab driver's meaty fist struck the front door as a demand. David and I eyed each other warily. This was his first international move and my third. Why *I* was the one freaking out while a burly stranger carried our most precious possessions to the warm, waiting van was anyone's guess. In slow motion, I stepped over the black sooty snow of our busy street. When we were seated and David had rattled off instructions, the driver turned up the radio. The powerful voice of Alicia Keys reached my ears, telling me everything was going to be all right. The taxi splashed down the Mathenesserlaan and my neighborhood disappeared in a blur of tears and multicolored Christmas lights.

On December 22nd, 2007 David and I were departing from the airport I'd long fallen out of love with, Amsterdam Schiphol International. The number of times I'd nearly drowned in despair upon landing at this blue-and-gold utopia of organization were eclipsed by the fact that I was about to leave the only home I knew. *Again.*

Waiting in the plush Singapore Airlines business class lounge, I made a desperate attempt to summon optimism. Our new Asian adventure was about to begin, but happiness had left the building. Confusion was king and the deep well of melancholy that had been steadily filling for the past five years finally breached its banks.

Arriving at the gate, we were quickly ushered onto the waiting plane by the eager Singapore Airlines flight crew. There seemed to be a one-to-one ratio of staff to passengers. No matter which way I turned, a smiling Singaporean offered me food, drinks, or assistance with stowing my belongings for the thirteen-hour flight.

This wasn't my first business class flight—admittedly heaven for flying more than six or eight hours—but it was my first experience with Singapore Airlines. Their exceptional standard of service was completely foreign after five years in a country which lacks a word in their language for "service." My expressionless face must have driven them crazy. *Is there no pleasing this woman?* I imagined their thoughts.

With a firm grip on a flute of French champagne and a small bowl of toasted cashews by my side, I settled in to watch the boarding circus. David was no match for the siren song of the personal entertainment system which would hold him captive for hours. No-nonsense Asian businessmen boarded and handed over their care to the beautiful hostesses who were eager to attend to their every need.

This time, there was no sideshow of frustrated travelers trying to shove oversize bags into overhead compartments or virgin travelers incapable of locating their assigned seat. It was a carefully-orchestrated dance. Despite a two-hour delay on takeoff, no one appeared ruffled or, heaven forbid, angry.

As we shuddered into the sky and began gliding soundlessly east, the performers once again took position. A gourmet feast was about to unfold. Linen napkins were spread on laps. Wine glasses and a full array of cutlery appeared. The fragrant smell of jasmine rice and slow-cooked beef was in the air and ultimately tickled my tongue.

Transplanted

Surprisingly, it was the carefully-selected wines and not the chocolate mousse that won me over. Hello Singapore Airlines and *goodbye* KLM. I was a convert for life.

Occasionally my thoughts turned to the leasing agent who would be waiting for us in our new Singapore condo. Without her mobile phone number, we'd had no way to let her know that we would be hours later than expected. Once we landed, David and I discussed the need for speed at customs and baggage claim to prevent her wait from growing exponentially. To our astonishment, arrival at Changi Airport had the same orchestrated feel of boarding the plane. When we were out the door and first in line for the taxi in just over twenty minutes, I began to wonder who was behind the curtain pulling the strings. It had to be some form of magic to get us out of there so quickly.

I didn't know then that Singapore is the model of efficiency in Southeast Asia. Before this experience I would have told you it wasn't possible to transfer luggage from the plane to the belt in record time. Because Singapore is a young nation, the airport was built with the latest technological advancements. Such advancements were unheard of in older, western metropolises. The bright-yellow 'priority' luggage tags were actually heeded at Changi too, allowing us to be among the first in line for the taxi queue as well. This method of travel came with more advantages than I'd imagined. Too bad there was no temperature control outside of the airport doors to turn the notch somewhere below the setting for "blast furnace."

Stepping into the taxi, my newly-discovered life of privilege halted, just as the car did at least ten times during the twenty minute ride to the center of Singapore. Experience counts in driving *and* airport construction. It was clear who'd done their homework and who hadn't in this equation. Despite nearly nailing the front passenger seat headrest with my face twice on a hard brake, my attention remained fixed on the exotic scenery rushing by my window.

Singapore's impressive skyline is relatively new. The oldest buildings date back to the 1970's, but it truly blossomed in the 1990's and the first decade of 2000. The view was meticulously planned so that arrivals entering via the Pacific Island Expressway would see Singapore from her best side. Finally, the familiar tingle of new territory excitement showed up. Sadness was elbowed out of the way by fascination.

In minutes, I would see my new home for the first time. David had done the footwork of viewing eight different condominiums on his last visit to Singapore. My email had overflowed with digital images of bedrooms, swimming pools, and kitchens from each of them. The Metz apartment won the prize based on proximity to Orchard Road, Singapore's main artery, and the ultra-modern Metropolitan Rapid Transit, the MRT. For us, living near the pulse of this exciting new nation felt like winning the lottery. Effectively halving our living space and gaining instant neighbors on all sides didn't enter the picture until later.

Lush green gardens of towering palms and red-orange Bird of Paradise flowers held court around the aquamarine swimming pool. A glittering chandelier hung in the living room. Our spectacular fifteenth-story view stretched all the way to Marina Bay, and a wealth of food and shopping options were footsteps away. All of this would make up for confining new quarters, right? How could this be worse than the last frustrating five years I'd spent trying to assimilate to Dutch culture? It couldn't. That was inconceivable.

My curiosity about our fascinating new surroundings had to wait. We needed to set Annie free from captivity in our new home so that she could join her own family for Christmas festivities. I had no idea that Christmas means as much to most Singaporeans as St. Patrick's Day does to Tunisians.

When we glided into the apartment carried by the private elevator, she sat barefoot on the sofa, waiting patiently. She didn't appear agitated in the slightest by the fact that we were two hours late. Ticking all the boxes on her leasing contract and handing over the keys seemed to make her happy. I was astonished that she never asked what delayed our arrival.

Looking at the polished hardwood floors and the dramatic floor-to-ceiling windows of our new posh pad, my heart skipped a beat. I stared out the living room window onto a rainbow of city lights and wondered how a small-town Ohio girl had wound up on her third continent to begin yet another new life in Asia. I'd always wanted to have the opportunity to live and work in Europe, but at age thirty-seven I'd gotten a little more than I'd bargained for with this move.

I'd never imagined living in Asia. It was David's dream materializing with this relocation. A beery late-night Rotterdam conversation started with me asking, "Where do you think we'll be ten years from now?" An uncharacteristic bit of awe crossed his face and he said, "Asia." That was less than two years earlier.

My adrenalin seemed to have gone out the door along with Annie, so we surveyed our new digs. Luckily, we were the first tenants, but despite all the checkmarks in the "pro" column, the condo came with its peculiarities. To us they were strange features, but we guessed they were normal by local standards. After all, what did we know of "normal" here?

The new amenity which we puzzled over the most was the bomb shelter. Since 1997, there has been a Civil Defence Shelter Bill in effect in Singapore requiring all residential dwellings to have them. Our own three-by-five foot space came equipped with numerous emergency power outlets and a five-inch-thick steel door that closed with a triple-bolt lock. Was I the only one who realized that if we were bombed, the fifteenth story where my feet currently stood would be rubble? That we were more likely to be crushed during the fall than safely holed up in this metal box? Soon enough I learned the hard way that in Singapore rules are rules. Logic need not apply.

Walking past the black marble guest bathroom, we inspected the master bedroom. Before we moved we'd been told that Singapore apartments didn't have generous storage space, so we chose a two bedroom. The guest room would do double-duty as storage for anything we weren't using. How naïve we were! In reality, our master closet was devoured by my wardrobe and David's took over the guest room's.

Our new bedroom had the same floor-to-ceiling windows and spectacular view as the living room. It was a smallish space, but it was stunning. There was even a little surprise waiting in the master bathroom. At one end of the shower/bathtub combination was a clear glass panel. To me it was quite funny that Singaporeans think of us as highly-sexed westerners who want to watch each other shower every day. Even funnier, they seem not to have considered that someone other than your partner might be in the bedroom when you'd like to shower. A close friend? Your mother? What if they need to use your shower when the guest bathroom is occupied? Again, logic need not apply. Call us unromantic if you wish, but we installed a Venetian blind.

There were other snazzy touches to the new joint, but nothing was more impressive than the private elevator. Admittedly, when David tried to explain this to me over the phone, I couldn't picture it. While only seeing is believing, I will try to do it justice. It isn't completely private, but it does arrive directly to the foyer of your apartment. You don't have to leave the apartment or lock the door to your place, you just have to press the button and hop in, hopefully remembering to bring your electronic key card. The elevator will only open on other floors if someone else in the same tower—there are four, one in each corner of the building—presses the button to call the elevator at the same time as you do. Otherwise it doesn't stop until it reaches the ground-floor lobby. It was impressive. Modern Asians would probably wonder what I'm rambling on about, but to me it was a big deal. Having our own elevator was beyond cool. Nothing in this new life resembled our old one.

Despite our comfy beds on the plane, we were tired after checking out the new place and marveling over every new discovery. Eventually sleep came calling, along with the revelation that our new king-size bed had no sheets. Next we realized there were no towels in either bathroom. Ten o'clock at night is a mildly inconvenient time for such discoveries. It was a stroke of luck that the guest bed had sheets and, seeing myself in that crystal-blue pool, I'd packed beach towels. Tomorrow's mission was to explore Orchard Road, but only after some rest. That was the plan, anyway. David was snoring softly within minutes, but I couldn't turn my brain off. In the blink of an eye, the sun again began to blaze, planning the day's equatorial assault on mankind.

Our Singapore condo

Chapter 2
The Koi Pond

The now-famous elevator swiftly delivered us down fifteen floors to the ground level on our first Singapore morning. David had lived six weeks in the city on assignment, so he had a vague idea where we could grab a bite and find the essentials. I didn't have a clue which direction to go. Strangely, there didn't seem to be much difference between me and the millions of Singaporeans ambling along the city streets on Christmas Eve of 2007. People wandered without an apparent destination. Okay, there were two differences. The other was that they didn't appear to have a fervent wish to flee.

A small eatery offered noodles, porridge, and rice, the Singaporean breakfast favorites. It smelled delicious, but slurping hot soup in steamy weather left a bit to be desired. A McDonald's scooter whizzed past us with a breakfast delivery logo and David raised his brow, as if to say "I didn't know that was an option!"

The next stop was the Fair Price grocery store ten minutes' walk from The Metz on Killiney Road. Killiney was home to an eclectic mix. There was a Thai restaurant, a Vietnamese Restaurant, several Chinese food stalls, a small pub and sushi restaurant, a gas station, and even a 7 Eleven. At the end of the street was a mobile phone monstrosity called Singtel. On the surface it was reassuring that everything we needed was so close. That was my thought before I walked into the grocery store for the first time, anyway.

The overpowering smell that hit me as I entered was unidentifiable. It could have been the whole fish on display ice near the entrance. But it could also be the mysterious, but beloved durian fruit. Durian has such a potent smell that it is illegal to carry it on the MRT. With watery eyes, I casually placed a hand near my nose to restrict the airflow. David appeared astonishingly unaffected. Since we were suddenly surrounded and it was impossible to say anything without being overheard, I made my way towards what I thought was the produce.

Upon closer inspection I didn't recognize any of these plants that masqueraded as fruits and vegetables. Several green and white variations of celery, or its long-lost cousin, sat side by side. A surprising array of sprouts lived in this neighborhood too. *What am I going to do with those?* Thankfully, out of the corner of my eye, I saw my familiar friends, carrots and broccoli. Never had I been happier to see them.

It might be a good time to mention that I do not cook. My demanding job in IT and associated travel had prevented me from taking the time to learn. David was a far better chef than I. We tried to share the cooking, but kitchens weren't a place I frequented. If I had, I might have known what some of these things were. *Too late now!* I wasn't known for my culinary prowess, and that seemed unlikely to change in the near future.

Pushing my cart through the remaining aisles, I searched for anything remotely familiar. A loaf of processed multigrain bread looked normalish, but made me sad. I would have to say farewell to European baked goodness too.

Eggs appeared next. In fact, it had an inordinate amount of eggs for this size supermarket. Who knew the Chinese loved them so much? *Wait a minute... are those eggs black?* How can something called century eggs be edible for humans? Next to that sat a carton of brown eggs, but the photo stopped me cold. The egg white wasn't white. It was beige. *Nope.* Not for me, thanks. David appeared and I pointed to the black ones. Finally, I got a raised eyebrow.

Slowly we continued. There! On a low shelf the familiar red-and-white Campbell's soup label jumped out at me from a sea of Chinese labels. I thought I might cry. In fact I did cry when I discovered the wine section. A quick calculation told me that a bottle of less-than-fine wine which would cost five euro in Rotterdam was now twenty-five Singapore dollars. Anything decent was over forty! I had better buy some tissues.

The Koi Pond

I was confident that I'd eventually figure out what to do with these foreign plants. I also knew that eating out was a fraction of what we'd paid in Europe. Without jet lag and a ridiculous amount of sweat pouring off me, I hoped to get the hang of this. I didn't know yet that the latter is an uncomfortable fact of life four degrees from the equator. If I couldn't manage a perspiration-free walk to grab orange juice and milk, what did that mean for the rest of my days in this pressure-cooker? I pushed the thought from my mind.

With the pantry and refrigerator full, I changed into a new t-shirt and clean shorts. For a minute I considered making the guest room my last stop instead of foraging in the great unknown again so soon. The jet lag roller coaster was having its way with me, and every bit of effort seemed a thousand times harder.

The Metz was one block from the buzz of Orchard Road with its continuous stampede of shoppers. Walking that one block felt like walking through the soup we'd had for breakfast. By eleven, the intense heat that would persist until late evening had already arrived. The accompanying one hundred percent humidity held my limited quantity of patience hostage.

Despite the generous sidewalks, Saturday morning was a challenge. There was little order to the chaos. The sweltering concrete path could be anywhere in the world, but unlike most highly-populated cities, there is no synchronized movement that keeps everyone from colliding.

If you abruptly stop walking on a Manhattan sidewalk, evil glares from your fellow pedestrians will inform you not to repeat such a move. One quickly learns to move with the crowd and step clear of the rushing masses to stop. This was not Manhattan. People moved every which way at a pace which would get you steamrolled in Chicago. There was no rhyme or reason to why one group suddenly changed direction or someone stopped to text at the bottom of an overflowing escalator. All my willpower was required to maintain civility.

My six-foot-five superhero cleared the way. I followed close behind and tried not to get distracted and commit the same crime I was mentally swearing at others about. It wasn't easy. Orchard Road is a retail circus with each bigtop holding hundreds of shops within it.

Every façade which had the audacity to mature beyond twenty years was in the process of receiving a facelift or being flattened. If it doesn't glitter it doesn't belong on Singapore's showcase thoroughfare. End of story.

David blocking the crowd in front gave me more time to notice the details. Oddly, very few people carried shopping bags. More oddly, no one appeared to have a destination. Some nibbled, many stared, but hardly anyone stopped to admire any of the hundreds of shop windows stuffed with luxury goods. Orchard Road, it appeared, *was* the destination.

Stopping for a red light, the locals taught me an important lesson. If you must stop, even for a minute, step into the shade and avoid the punishing sun at all costs. Several women carried shade with them in the form of colorful bamboo parasols. A parade of red-faced sweaty tourists showed who hadn't yet learned the lesson.

At last there was a swish of silver doors and a blast of icy air as we entered paradise, I mean Tang's department store. Calm instantly swept through me. The red-and-green replica of a Chinese temple had been beckoning me for some distance, and I was eager to see its contents. The first department we walked through was enough to make me forget that I was ready for my second costume change that day. Soft leather handbags of every conceivable color, style, and texture begged for my attention.

Not one to dawdle, David went straight to the store directory as I reached out to touch these little gems. I needed to see if this was an oasis in the desert, or if they were real. David promptly returned, forcing me to reschedule my accessory admiration for another day.

Next lesson: Driving on the opposite side of the road means that we must also walk on the opposite side. This includes escalators. Wasn't I just saying something about an annoying lack of direction when walking? I had the pleasure of eating those words when I headed for the 'down' to go up. What a rookie mistake.

We were just about to congratulate ourselves for making it to the destination when the escalator dumped us into a sea of miniature raven-haired shoppers moving every which way. It was Christmas Eve. It was

The Koi Pond

a sale. It was an absolute madhouse. Women yelled to one another from one side of the store to other, holding up different sheet patterns for approval. Harried assistants tried desperately to find matching pillow cases to meet their demands.

Due to our height, we could see above the fray. In this case it didn't feel like an advantage. The voices were much bigger than their owners, and their determination fierce. At any moment I expected a fist fight to break out over 800 thread-count linens. Sensing my intent to flee, David waded into the crowd and began pulling out random sheet sets for my review. The locals weren't tall enough to snatch them until we'd made a decision against each one. Score one for Team Foreigner.

Chapter 3
Will the Real Singapore Please Step Forward?

On Christmas Day, we watched the world go by from our fifteenth-floor windows and caught up on sleep. No one expected us to be anywhere and the mandatory supplies had been captured. It was my first chance to reflect since the barrage of activity associated with moving had begun. With my head on the pillow, I looked out over the sea of gray skyscrapers that surrounded us. I wondered about the lives that went on behind all those windows. Some of the lives were a bit close for comfort. The nearest highrise was fifty feet from the Metz and the ground on the other side of us was being cleared for another. How do people stand being cooped up all the time? There wasn't an inch of green space in sight.

For a change of perspective I padded into the living room and took a seat on the flowered rug next to the window, where I had a better view of the street below. People came and went as though it were any other day. Every shopping mall was decked out in its Christmas finest and the street decorations were the most elaborate I'd ever seen. How could a city this revved up for a holiday carry on as though it wasn't even happening?

Watching the locals pull open the carved wooden doors and enter the Chinese temple three doors down, I forgot about Christmas. My curiosity was piqued. What went on behind those elaborate doors with the fire-breathing dragons? Could we go in and see for ourselves? Would we be kicked out? I had no idea. Rolling over to stare at the ceiling, it became clear how much I didn't know about Chinese culture—or any Asian culture for that matter. How was I going to learn?

As if on cue, the following morning David described a Chinese temple he had visited on his first Singapore trip. His blue eyes widened as he talked about the exotic details of the interior, and I knew it was something I had to see. David's heightened enthusiasm was rare for my even-keeled Dutchman. I braced for the blast of muggy air that came through the lobby doors knowing I'd never get used to it. Luckily, we were across the street from the MRT stop known as Somerset. We bought cards for the MRT, a Singapore must-have without a car, and headed for Chinatown to get a closer look at Thian Hock Keng temple.

Cars are unnecessary in Singapore and, for most, unaffordable. The price tag associated with owning a car isn't limited to the outrageous amount for the vehicle itself. The taxes levied on drivers are astronomical. I couldn't believe that any place was more expensive than Europe for purchasing a car, but here it was.

Taxis are cheap and could easily be grabbed outside the front doors, but the MRT is by far the best deal in town. Not only are you in a safe, air-conditioned, underground maze, but a one-way fare to go most places is less than two Singapore dollars. Bargain! It was liberating to find this out. European public transport hadn't thrilled me in my two auto-less years there. Comparatively, it was dirty, expensive, and inefficient.

David and I traced the route from Somerset on the wall map at the station and then took the escalator down to the tunnel. I swiped my new card at the turnstile. Less than a minute later, we were carried swiftly off to Chinatown.

It was crowded and we had no chance of blending in. Not only were we taller and whiter, we were decidedly bigger all around. Singaporeans are a tiny lot. I felt like I'd walked straight out of Jennifer and the Giant Beanstalk. In an instant, I was acutely aware of what it felt like to be a minority. No one spoke on the train, so David and I just smiled at each other knowingly. As he was so much taller, he had to feel weirder than I did. He even had to duck to exit the train. There were a few covert glances in our direction, but no one stared outright. Even though the car was far from full, every exiting passenger ran for the

Please Step Forward?

escalator at once. With no reason to rush, we moved at a normal pace while several locals pushed past to get in line first. *Is this the new name of the game?* I wondered. *Me first?* Initially, I was amused.

Too large to be trampled, we emerged unscathed from the MRT into the blinding sun. The path we took to exit by following the crowd dumped us directly into Tourist Town. Since we wanted to understand the locals, the last things I expected were ten dollar t-shirts, "silk" placemats and, strangely, lots of mice. Merchants waved at us from doorways until the path narrowed—then we were face to face. An Indian merchant expertly planted a confused look on his face when David declined the offer of a custom suit at a "special" price. I was about to drop from heat exhaustion and these people wanted me to buy stuff? I had to keep moving to find air.

David pulled me along to the end of Pagoda Street where there was space to breathe. "There's a cool Indian temple over there," he said, pointing to the right. My gaze followed his fingertips to a white-walled building topped with animal figures and blue-and-green-faced gods with an above average number of arms.

"Let's go!" I said, anxious for shade in any form.

I'd never been in an Indian temple either, and I had no idea that at least one quarter of Singapore's population was Indian. This place was a cultural bonanza.

At the entrance to Sri Mariamman Temple, I saw each person remove his or her shoes before entering. Noting how dirty the street was, I wasn't thrilled to take off my Tevas, but I was in no position to refuse. I couldn't stand outside and wait because I didn't want my precious toes to touch the ground, though I considered it. What a mistake that would have been. The mysterious gods that resided within were far more exotic than what was visible from the street. Ganesh, the elephant-headed god, was my new favorite.

I scolded myself for even considering not coming in as I wandered around, silently taking photos and observing those paying their respects. Red and yellow marigolds were placed at the feet of the gods, and gold-threaded saris swished by. I snuck glances at the nose rings and abundant gold chains that decorated the women. Men wore loose-fitting white linen shirts and *dhoti*. It was the first time I'd seen men in something akin to a skirt since Scotland.

Curiosity satisfied, we collected our shoes and continued to Thian Hock Keng. I was relieved that no one had decided that my sandals were better than theirs and I didn't have to walk the sizzling sidewalks shoeless. At noon the heat was blistering. Walking a meandering route through Club Street, we came upon a quiet neighborhood that looked nothing like the modern glitz of Orchard Road. The buildings were original Singapore shophouses, each one beautifully painted with unique colors and symbols. There was hardly a soul in sight.

When the temple came into view, there was no mistaking it. The plaque outside told me that the temple was completed in 1842 as an offering to Mazo, the Taoist goddess of the sea, for the clan's safe passage to Singapore from mainland China. A high step in front leads through wooden doors with glaring lacquered guardians who protect the gods from outside evil.

Crossing my fingers that my battery wouldn't die, I snapped photo after photo of the interior details. The twisted features of the temple guardians had to be captured, as did the brass lion door knockers. Sandalwood incense wafted from the courtyard where an ornate silver censer stood surrounded by devotees. Eyes closed and heads bent, their lips moved without a sound. In the main temple, behind clear glass windows, sat the divine recipients of fully-loaded offering plates. Gifts to the heavens included dimpled oranges, cellophane-wrapped candies, pink lotuses, and full bottles of Pepsi.

David's camera got an equivalent workout. Occasionally, he snuck up and grabbed my hand, pulling me to what he wanted me to see. I did the same to him when I came across an enormous dark wooden drum suspended from the ceiling. How it made it to that position defied the imagination. Perhaps it had heavenly assistance.

As we departed, I read another placard with more information about the temple. Translated to English the name means "Temple of Heavenly Happiness," and I was under its spell. Even though I had a lot to learn about Chinese culture, I was intrigued by it. It didn't feel like effort to decode the ancient clues within each intricate pattern. It

Please Step Forward?

was a thrill. I'm sure many have left that same temple unchanged by the experience. I wasn't one of them.

David had another cultural lesson up his sleeve, something I'd often read about. He wanted to have lunch at a hawker centre. I wasn't overly enthusiastic about eating foods I'd never heard of in the sweaty food halls preferred by locals, but he wasn't taking no for an answer. Introduced to the scene by his Singaporean colleagues, David already had favorite dishes he was eager to share with me. Carrot cake? Was he serious? Didn't he know the orange cake with cream cheese frosting was an American staple? And what the hell was *laksa*? My chopstick maneuvering skills were non-existent. How was I going to pull off soup with two pencils? The short answer was, I wasn't.

As a pile of steamed rice flour and diced parsnips mixed with who knows what landed on the table, David grinned across the table. "Carrot cake!" He announced happily. While it was the weirdest carrot cake I'd ever laid eyes on, it wasn't bad. I didn't want to eat a plate of it, but it was better than I'd expected. Next came the laksa and my fear of looking like a complete idiot. The bisque-colored broth was thick. Bubbles of chili floated on top while prawns and noodles played hide and seek in the deep steaming bowl. Patiently David showed me how to hold the chopsticks correctly. I tried it. I failed. I tried again. I failed again. Covered with brown flecks, my white linen shirt gave away my chopstick incompetence.

An observant stall owner took pity on me. Out of nowhere, he ran over to hand me a fork and spoon along with an ingenious invention he called "training" chopsticks. At first I was too embarrassed to use them. Two wooden chopsticks held together with a rubber band in the middle so they wouldn't fall apart. I was pretty sure this is how children were taught, but I appreciated the gesture. The old Chinese gentlemen bowed slightly when I thanked him and disappeared again without a word.

David tried in vain not to laugh too hard. I soldiered on, letting the lemongrass and red chilies hit my tongue full force. Beads of sweat formed under my eyes and my throat closed up slightly, unused to such an assault. *How do they eat this stuff every day?* I wondered. If it were me, I'd lock myself up in a freezer compartment and eat nothing but crunchy green salads and vanilla ice cream. Then I met a frosted mug of Tiger beer for the first time at Maxwell Hawker Centre. At last, something that made sense.

The days between Christmas and New Year's Day 2008 were full of surprises. It was impossible to know what to expect anymore. This island nation was turning out to be far from what I imagined. I didn't expect the concrete jungle that greeted us. I expected Singapore Slings with tiny umbrellas on sandy beaches. Images of white bungalows, perfectly positioned to catch the sea breezes made more than one appearance in my dreams. They had to be here somewhere, didn't they? It wasn't all highways and highrises, was it?

Before we arrived I'd read about a small island off the Singapore mainland called Sentosa. According to the guidebooks, it was Paradise Found. Sentosa seemed like the logical place to search for the island tranquility that I longed for.

Numerous routes will take you to Sentosa from the mainland, each one more Disney-esque than the last. Does a cable car ride strike your fancy? Right this way! Feel like having your feet on solid ground? Take the monorail from Harbourfront Mall, along with the masses. Any notion of island tranquility evaporated before the journey began. Jumpy kids and irritated parents stood waiting for the monorail to depart. We took one look at the long queue and the cable car decision was made. Even if the wait was longer, we would have peace once we boarded. Watching passengers step into the shiny red cars that stopped before them, I noticed that the locals went in groups of four or six, but tourists went alone or in pairs. The two groups weren't mixed. Were we too loud? Too sweaty? Another mystery.

David and I stepped in, and though the line was still long, the employee shut the door and we were off. I was losing my patience with all the crowds. Looking down to the sandy coastline for the first time was exciting. There they were! The grand palm-lined resorts I'd imagined were there on the golden beach. I pictured myself with a deck chair and a coconut cocktail, looking out to see and... *wait one minute!* What's this? I could barely *see* the sea. All I could see were tankers, at

Please Step Forward?

least a hundred, floating mere feet from the shore and coughing up black soot into the sky.

After managing a scant few photos that excluded the boats laden with transport goods, we set foot on Sentosa. That was when the theme-park feeling melded with reality. Every attraction and fast food restaurant had a long queue in front. Signs directed us to the Aquarium, various restaurants, and Siloso Beach. Not knowing which side of the island we'd seen from above, I was hopeful. For the five whole minutes if took us to walk to the beach, I was hopeful.

It was a man-made beach, set up to give visitors that South Pacific feel by placing beach bars and eateries near the water. The deck chairs faced the tanker zone. Slipping off my sandals, as if to poke the imaginary wall and confirm that what I was seeing was in fact real, I walked to the water's edge. As the reality set in of what the next few years had in store, a discarded dirty diaper floated past me in the brownish water, punctuating my disappointment. Even more surprising were the groups of volleyball-playing young people who appeared not to notice the location's depressing tone. Mr. and Mrs. Bronze God Tourist took up residence on the beach chairs behind us—frothy daiquiris in hand—ready to enjoy the place as it was intended. Obviously I was the one with the problem.

The Aquarium was another story. It could have been simply my appreciation for the invention of the air conditioner, but I was sold. I touched the sandpaper skin of a stingray for the first time. Tiger sharks lurked in the shadows of a deeper tank, one I had no intention of sticking my hand into. Usually, it's the open water that calms my soul, but this time it was the fluorescent purples and striking blues of the tropical fish that flitted past. It was reassuring that there was nature somewhere, because it clearly wasn't outside. It was becoming all too clear that in Singapore, life is *indoors*.

* * *

How does one do New Year's Eve right in Singapore? Clubs offered "All Night Deals" and pubs invited us for "Free Flow Booze," but we were reluctant to get into any situation that we couldn't easily get out of.

There were so many nationalities here! Now I knew to expect Singaporean Chinese, Malays, and Indians—but there were also South Africans, Japanese, Australians, Koreans, Brits, mainland Chinese, Russians, and Filipinos. Everyone melted into the mix and I wanted to know what they were all up to. One place in town tended to draw all types, and that was Chijmes.

Chijmes is today's trendy abbreviation for the Convent of the Holy Infant Jesus. It's a church compound converted to an entertainment complex frequented by the group—which we now belonged to—called "expats." I wasn't sure how this title suddenly applied to me after I'd already lived out of my home nation for six years, but the word was everywhere.

At Chijmes menu prices ranged from high to ridiculously high if you compared them to average places in Singapore. As such, the locals were immune to its charms. There you can drink until four in the morning at Insomnia, quell your Brazilian meat cravings at Carnivore, or have an "authentic" Italian pizza. The cheesy flier that landed in my mailbox inviting us to "Disco New Year's Eve 2008!" was too delicious to ignore.

Gyu-Kaku, the Japanese barbeque restaurant at one corner of the complex, was our landing spot. Frosty mugs of Tiger were rushed to our table while we mulled over the menu options. It was written in English, but we simply didn't get it.

Our superhero waitress swooped in and removed the circular metal disc which covered our personal barbeque in the middle for the table. Ah ha! The lightbulb suddenly went on. We had to choose collections of meat, fish, and vegetables to grill ourselves. How we didn't notice the sizzling going on at tables all around us to give us a hint, I'll never know.

Delighted by the prospect of his role as grill-master, David unwrapped each foil packet like a kid on Christmas Day. Though we'd replaced the beef tongue with teriyaki chicken, it was still adventurous by our standards. Tender slices of Waygu beef were gleefully seared and seasoned Shitake mushrooms sautéed. It was more dinner fun than we'd had in ages. I couldn't imagine such a concept in Europe or

Please Step Forward?

America. Superhero supervision or not, you'd never be trusted not to burn the place down.

I worked the chopsticks as well as I could. Picking up chunks or meat and vegetables was infinitely easier than dealing with noodle soup. That was for the pros. As a novice I would have to make more careful selections if I had any hope of eating a full meal in this country.

Our superhero was waiting in the wings. She appeared the minute the foil packets had been devoured. "What kind of ice cream would you like?" she asked.

"What kind do you have?" David replied.

"Green tea or black sesame."

We stared at each other blankly. "Black sesame," I said.

"Green tea, please." David said to the waitress. "I have no idea what this is going to taste like." I just shook my head and smiled.

When she returned, a small black ceramic bowl was placed in front of me. The silvery ball inside revealed nothing, so I picked up my tiny spoon for a tiny taste. Despite the odd color, it was delicious. It tasked like sesame, toasted sesame. David's was pea green and tasted like, shockingly, green tea. We giggled at the weirdness of it. The vibe was contagious. Even the waitress seemed happier when she returned with the bill. Maybe it was because she would finally be rid of her clueless Caucasian customers.

The disco portion of our evening was less exciting. Watching a Filipino performer badly lip-syncing to tunes that should have remained in the early 90s was a sad form of entertainment. Seeing that there was no line at the bar on New Year's Eve was a dead giveaway that this would not last long. We ordered two glasses of champagne and waited in vain for improvement that never came.

Soon we were walking home. We had arrived by cab, but the night had cooled sufficiently to enjoy the walk. Well, I enjoyed it until minutes later when my strappy sandals became wearable razor blades on my swollen feet. Asking David to wait a minute, I saw the red mangled mess that was my feet and asked David to hail a taxi. Irritated, he reluctantly agreed. *Really, is that five Singapore dollars going to break the bank?* I got into the cab and was so relieved to get off my feet, I forgot to be annoyed.

New Year's Eve or not, we were glad to be home. I opened a bottle of Mumm and poured two flutes to the rim. "Here's to Singapore!" I said, with more enthusiasm than I felt.

"Cheers!" David replied.

Then we looked at each other with the "now what?" face. There was only one option—the television which had barely been switched on. I casually flipped through the channels until I struck comedy gold. The "Celebrity Spectacular!" was in full swing to ring in 2008! Just our luck.

Bad lip-synching was a national sport in Singapore. Even better, the entertainers loved to cover acts that we knew. Soon, a chubby Asian Justin Timberlake was bringing sexy back. He was followed by a petite raven-haired Kylie Minogue. We couldn't stop laughing. Chijmes was a disco bust, but this was so wrong it went all the way to right. When 2008 arrived, it came with tears of laughter.

Chapter 4
Cracks in the Surface

Reality burst our bubble in early January. David was off to his new role at a large, high-profile project and I had to find a job. My last position at a computer hardware manufacturer had been challenging and, at times, frustrating. It wasn't hard for me to say goodbye to it when the move to Singapore came up. I had been through the difficult process of finding work outside my home country once before, so I wasn't worried about starting over. My concern was my lack of a network, professional or otherwise. I was on my own.

The best place to start was the local paper. It was easy to see who the big players are in town are and who's hiring or firing. Before leaving the Netherlands I'd ordered a subscription to *The Straits Times* to begin in January.

The start date came and went without a paper in sight. For a week I checked the lobby as well, but there was nothing there either. I called the circulation desk. They were short on answers. Eventually an elderly Chinese man knocked on the door one morning. Dressed in a t-shirt and shorts, he bowed slightly when I opened the door. "Sorry lah! Could not find apartment lah!"

"Okay," was all I managed before he shuffled away on leather sandals.

Finally, I had the keys to the kingdom. I don't care if it's old-fashioned, I love newspapers. They reveal what's going on in a community in a way that online news doesn't. I immediately dug in, but was surprised to find that this newspaper actually had very little news.

The majority of each page was consumed by advertisements. In the articles that presented themselves as news, I often found a lack of substantiating facts. In a word, it was weird. Eventually, I found the classifieds and went through them in detail. I made note of the large recruitment firms and web sites of multinational firms. It was disappointing that I wouldn't be able to feast on Singapore culture through *The Straits Times*, but that wasn't the priority.

Even if the articles weren't in-depth, it was clear that the global economy was headed for a downturn. Hillary Clinton and Barack Obama were duking it out for the Democratic nomination and eight years of war in Iraq and Afghanistan had provided excellent cover for Wall Street's dodgy dealings. Stocks were plunging and no one knew how much further the bottom was. Asia hadn't caught the disease spreading through the American financial sector, at least not yet.

I turned to the internet to continue my search for work and started contacting recruiters. When no one was available to talk right away, our sparkling swimming pool seemed the ideal place to wait. Gathering my book, a tube of SPF30, and my towel, I slipped into the private elevator and punched "L" for lobby. As I was positioning my deck chair into perfect alignment with the sun, I realized. *How stupid!* The voice in my head shouted at me while the mental movie of the electronic key card I left sitting on the dining room table played.

I had to use my Dutch cell phone to send David an SMS to ask for help. He then had to cross town on the MRT to let me in the house. It was a relief that he wasn't annoyed at losing over an hour of his day. He gave me a kiss and was gone again.

The pool was long and narrow, ideal for swimming laps. It takes only minutes to overheat in Singapore, even when you're doing nothing more strenuous than reading, so I spent a lot of time in the water. Floating on my back, the palm trees waved at me and for a few minutes, I was blissfully free of the traffic noise from Devonshire Road. The blue sky was an enormous improvement from the Land of Perpetual Precipitation where I'd been living for the past five years. It's hard to imagine that the sky is going to fall on you when it's that particular shade of blue.

Cracks in the Surface

David forwarded an email invitation a few days later. It was for an orientation on Singapore culture and living hosted by his client. All partners were invited to attend. *Finally a way to get the scoop on this place.* Other "wives" had landed from various countries, so I hoped to meet new friends. The date was the following Friday, plenty of time to find something to wear and figure out how to get there.

Clothing was not my friend in Singapore. Though I wasn't a fashionista, picking out the right clothes to make an impression was important to me. Here, my wardrobe had turned against me. No matter what I went out in, if it wasn't cotton or linen, it intensified the sauna effect of the city. I could forget about wearing most of the summer clothes I'd worn in Holland. On the upside, it was an excuse to shop.

Lounging at the pool in the morning became my routine. After eleven, it was too hot to bother. Claustrophobia had set in due to too much time in the house. We couldn't open the windows in the apartment because breezes were only imaginary. Even going to the malls and checking out Orchard Road was better than being cooped up at home.

I started writing in my journal first thing in the morning next to the pool. Fresh air was a blessing in the silence before the city woke. There were few distractions. Moving from the United States to Europe had been a test of patience as my personal boundaries were invaded over and over again. Landing in Asia, that personal space was dramatically reduced a second time. No matter where I went, escaping the crowds was impossible.

The closest mall to my place was Centrepoint. If I crossed Devonshire Road, walked through the MRT station, and crossed Orchard, I was there. In ten minutes I was looking through the spotless glass window of Robinsons department store. Robinsons is a Singapore icon, the oldest retail chain on the island.

It felt like an oasis of normality to saunter through a store like this. The price tags were written in English, a first since I'd left for Germany in 2001. Walking past European cosmetics and Asian footwear, a positive feeling swept through me. Call me superficial, but the ability to shop for beautiful clothes and accessories is essential to my well-being.

Looking carefully at which escalator actually went up, I was on the hunt for women's fashion. Delighted that it consumed the entire second floor, which was now called the first floor, I began browsing. Labels of French brands I knew would never fit me were in one section. Asian brands I'd never heard of but didn't look promising either were in another. How could there be an entire *floor* of clothes that only looked terrible on me? Defeat started kicking in. *This is not the end of the world. I told myself. This is one store in one mall. There are hundreds. Just move on.* And I did.

On the below ground level of the mall, known as B1 for basement one, I found a grocery store called Cold Storage. Across from that was McDonald's. At the other end was New York Steakhouse. *It's Little America!* That positive vibe was back again.

Walking through the entryway to Cold Storage, I spied the Swiss Bakery. My favorite European breads called out to me from one corner of this massive American-style grocery store. Hurray! What else was there to discover? Anything I wanted. Uncle Ben's rice, Ritz Crackers, and Hellman's mayonnaise were all here. We hadn't had this much choice in the Netherlands. I grabbed a bag of Hershey's chocolate pieces as a consolation prize for not finding any clothes, before making my way out.

I stuffed my purchase in my backpack and continued my neighborhood reconnaissance. Emerald Hill was a pretty side street of original shophouses renovated and converted to trendy bars and hip restaurants. A shopping mecca called Paragon came next. In front, I hopped on a short down escalator and was deposited in another basement where retail oozed from every crevice. A card store, a CD shop, a Starbucks, and six or seven restaurants came into view. I couldn't believe it when I was standing in front of yet another grocery store called Fresh Market.

When I left the Netherlands, there wasn't a single Starbucks outlet in the whole country, a fact I found depressing. Not that I loved the coffee so much more than Dutch coffee, but because it was a slice of America where I could feel at home for a little while. I *understood* Starbucks when I sometimes understood nothing else.

CRACKS IN THE SURFACE

Unable to resist, I ordered a white chocolate mocha and took a seat. This mall was busier than the last one. American voices, impossible to mistake, drifted over from two separate tables nearby. One was a business meeting between two men. The other looked like Ladies Who Lunch. Obviously I wasn't the only one who enjoyed a taste of home.

While I sipped the ridiculously sweet treat I sometimes allowed myself, western mothers converged in a stroller traffic jam. I watched young Filipina girls weighted down with multiple heavy bags of groceries carried mere inches off the ground. It dawned on me that shopping on this end of town would mean a long, hot walk loaded with groceries back to the condo. Life was different without a car.

To round out my knowledge of Singaporean grocery stores, I decided to stroll through this one too. The long stems of pink and white orchids reached out to welcome me. Polished red apples and shiny yellow-green pears stood at attention. A sight for sore eyes, there was an actual deli counter! All I'd previously found were greenish looking packaged meats that had traveled for an indeterminate length of time.

In the cereal aisle I spotted familiar boxes. Cheerios? *No way!* I couldn't remember the last time I'd seen them. A bright-yellow sticker announced the bargain price tag of only ten Singapore dollars. Were they serious? *Who the hell is buying ten dollar Cheerios?* A closer look at my fellow shoppers gave me the answer—we were all from western countries.

Next I admired a fully-stocked shelf of Australian beef. "Two for twenty-two" announced the sale sign, as though it were a bargain. These weren't Porterhouse or New York strip steaks—they were average cuts of average beef. Was this the new price of "home"? I left shaking my head, relieved to find out it wasn't worth the hassle to shop there. The other part of me thought *damn! So close!*

Four more floors had to be checked out before my job was done. Above ground the prices skyrocketed. Here we had Salvatore Ferragamo, Gucci, and a host of other international brands. Knowing the pain of those price tags would never be worth it, I kept moving. There were more stores I didn't recognize than those I did.

Just when I was about to give up, a familiar logo appeared. I don't think I've ever been so happy to see a Marks & Spencer in my life. This British standby could be counted on for necessities. Thirty minutes later, I had a big smile and two overflowing shopping bags. Even though I had to sweat my way back home, I knew—just like Scarlett O'Hara—that tomorrow is another day.

* * *

When the day of the Singapore orientation arrived, I was more than ready to have someplace to be. Watching David get up for work every day had made me feel aimless and guilty. The only times I'd ever not worked were when I was laid off in the internet bust of 2000 and when I quit my American job to find a Dutch-based position in 2004. Idle and I didn't get along.

Gripping my printed Google directions, my heart pounded as I entered a room of 150 women. Not one man was present, which I hadn't expected. I thought "partners" was what you now used in English instead of "spouse" because many couples didn't marry. *Aren't there any gay couples on this project?* I wondered before taking an open seat at a round table close to the back of the room.

Five women were already seated. Surprisingly, I'd sat down next to an American. In a room of that size, what were the odds? We shook hands and exchanged names between ourselves and greetings with the others. The American was from Dallas and the others were South African and Australian. Everyone appeared roughly the same age, late thirties to early forties.

My tension began to dissipate until I heard the obvious Dutch accent of the presenter. After five years of being told how to do everything in the Netherlands, I wasn't eager to repeat the experience. Confession: she could have been the Wicked Witch and I'd still be happy to see her, if only she helped me understand this place.

Debra kicked off with some helpful information about things I'd already figured out, like the MRT and the breakdown of the four cultures who made up the majority of the population: Chinese, Malay, Indian, and Eurasian. The religions we could expect to run into were

Cracks in the Surface

Muslim, Christian, Buddhist, and Hindu. "Everyone lives here peacefully," Debra assured the curious crowd. *In a post 9/11 world, how is that possible?* Even if this was a different continent, surely some things are universal, like cultural tension in close quarters. I'd often felt hostile towards Europeans before I began understanding their point of view. Here there was the added complexity of religion—in addition to reduced personal space.

With the flip of her PowerPoint slide, Debra was on to the next topic. The slide was very simple, with the header "FACE" written in all caps. Of course I'd heard the expression "saving face," but I'd never thought twice about it. Everyone wanted to preserve their reputation after a screw up, right?

According to Debra, it went deeper than that in Asia. It was important not to look bad in an altercation, business deal, or something as simple as a sales transaction. "Westerners have a habit of blowing up at the locals," Debra said gravely, as if it were a stain on her own reputation. "Once you lose your temper or raise your voice to someone, you both lose face. In Singapore, that is very difficult to recover from. Singaporeans tend not to raise their voice to one another, or demean one another." She continued. *Is this Disneyland?* I thought. Harmonious living and happy people jammed on a tiny island? *Yeah, right.*

The consequences for losing face are indeed legendary. I understood the code of honor which forced Japanese soldiers to kill themselves, rather than live with the disgrace of failure. It was news to me that this cultural belief extended to the Chinese. The gravity of how it permeated daily life was something I'd never thought of.

Although I was frustrated with the inability to get a newspaper delivered for close to a week, I wouldn't have yelled at the slight Chinese man who came to my door. Over an issue of greater importance, I couldn't be sure how I would react. If you made me stand in the searing heat for half an hour while you dithered about how to handle something, I was likely to express my unhappiness verbally. This was advice worthy of consideration.

Without allowing the atmosphere to get too heavy, Debra was on to something else I was interested in—employment. There was one slide.

The advice we received was to go through the job board run by the American Club or to check with someone at the Dutch Club. She moved on to the topic without mentioning a word about preferred recruitment firms or even *The Straits Times*.

The next title added to my confusion. It said "MAIDS" at the top, with several bullet points below. Maids? There was more to talk about on the topic of having a maid than there was about getting a *job*? As Debra discussed in depth the step-by-step process of acquiring domestic help, her audience was rapt. Not a single question was asked about employment, but hands flew in the air as she described the pure joy of having inexpensive staff at home. "Even better, in Singapore it is completely socially acceptable!" she reported with glee.

Knowing that she was at the end of her presentation and seeing that this was the bit everyone was actually listening to, she took us into her confidence. "I have lived here for seventeen years. Recently my maid took ill and I could barely cope with my children without her! There's no way I could ever return to the Netherlands where you have to do everything yourself." *Wow.*

As this session was provided at the expense of my husband's client, I was silent. I had no idea who was who in this room, and six years abroad had taught me the golden rule of keeping my mouth shut. My tablemates chatted after the formal presentation. Some were having a "glorious time" in Singapore, while others didn't say more than a few words. The sporty blonde Texan, Leah, and I agreed to keep in touch. A tall woman with an Aussie accent dropped by our table whom Leah introduced as Sally. Both their husbands also worked at David's firm.

Sally parked her gold Prada sunglasses in her long dark hair and announced, "I was still unpacking boxes in Sydney when John told me we were moving to Singapore! I still can't believe it!" Then I recognized her as the one person who'd walked in late, profusely apologizing. Not knowing what to make of all this information, I told Leah I would call her to arrange a get-together, and said my good-byes. As I rode home on the MRT, an uneasy feeling came over me. *What am I going to have in common with these women?*

Chapter 5
Dramatis Personae

I had never had so much time on my hands. Aside from the daily swim and job search rituals, I didn't know what to do with myself. As the palm trees swayed overhead, I tried to figure out what to do with my life at thirty-seven. In recent years, my satisfaction and happiness at work had steadily eroded. I wanted to make a change in my career—but to what?

I had spent the past thirteen years in IT with increasing responsibility and salary. I'd passed the certification exam for professional project management less than three months earlier. What was I qualified for? Was I really going to kiss off a six-figure income because work wasn't *satisfying*? Is anyone ever really *happy* at work?

David seemed to be. He was part of a large team. Though he didn't show me organizational charts or talk about strategy, I knew it was big. A few hundred people would be working on this project for the next three to five years. That was all I knew about his commitment—and our future.

For him, life was already exciting. He was working with several nationalities for the first time in a leadership role. There was no reason for him to question his identity just because the scenery had changed. I knew he wouldn't be happy unless he was challenged, so I was glad for him. Because he is extremely smart, challenge isn't always part of the equation. He had an American boss and the other members of the leadership team were Australian. There were several other Europeans on the project too. Experienced consultants had been plucked from every corner of the globe. Both of us felt lucky to be part of the mix.

As soon as he left for work each day, I tried to answer the question of what would make me happy. In Holland, I'd had a difficult time at the jobs I'd held in my five years there. Before landing there, I'd loved my work in the United States and most of the time in Germany.

When the option to move to Singapore appeared, I thought it was the answer. Work and life in Europe had become difficult. "No" was the answer to every question. Immigration laws were constantly changing and eventually, I knew, my residency status would be impacted in one way or another. Singapore, the high-tech country with relaxed business laws and a low tax rate, would be my salvation. I was counting on it.

The recruiters I spoke to were very interested in my most recent experience as a regional program manager for a mobile and wireless company. Mobility was a buzzword in IT, and I decided I should capitalize on experience that few here had. I could always change direction later, but I needed to get some money coming in. Due to tax laws in Holland, we couldn't rent our house in Rotterdam, which was costing us a fortune.

About two weeks into the new year, I met with a recruiter named Bill. He was positive he would be able to find me a job, in fact he had two clients who were looking right now. Getting my foot in the door at Dutch companies had been extremely difficult, so I was relieved that this would be quick.

The first client was a European manufacturing company with its Asian headquarters in Singapore. Grateful for my light linen jacket and skirt, I hailed a taxi at the Metz and went to meet the hiring manager. "What name of building, lah?" The taxi driver wanted to know. I repeated the address. "Name! Which building, lah?" I had carefully printed out the street map showing the exact location and address. Who cares what the building is called?

He did, apparently. "Close to here," he barked and stopped the car. Stunned, I paid and got out. Desperately searching for a street number, I realized I was still at least two blocks away. *Asshole.* Sweat immediately began to pool under my pink-linen jacket as I walked.

Overheated and embarrassed, I was introduced to a crisply-dressed Frenchman. He stood before me talking about company strategy at length. After a detailed rundown, he asked about my experience. When he was satisfied with my answers, he asked how his project management team should be structured. I gave a few possibilities, but he insisted I drill down deeper into each one.

When we were thirty minutes past the scheduled end time for the interview and hadn't talked about his plans for the hiring process, I began to suspect he just wanted information from me. He didn't seem to know what type of person he needed to hire at all. I clammed up and he called the interview to a close.

The intense air-conditioning might have cooled me down temporarily, but I didn't stay that way for long. I called Bill and questioned him on the purpose of this meeting. The client and I clearly had different perspectives on that. Bill acted surprised and feigned ignorance. Eventually I decided I might be overreacting and let him arrange a meeting with the second client he'd mentioned. There was no sense in burning bridges after one meeting.

Soon after, David called to ask if I wanted to have dinner in Little India with one of the partners from his firm, John. Indian food *and* someone who knew how to open doors in this city? *Yes, please!* John lived near us, so we would take a cab together to the restaurant on Racecourse Road.

I tore through my wardrobe. I knew now that anything with synthetic fiber would overheat me in five seconds flat, so I tried on one outfit after another. I couldn't afford to look sloppy when asking someone for job connections, so I was desperate to find something decent that wouldn't be soaking wet in minutes. As I had my first meltdown over having nothing to wear, David came in and reassured me that I looked great. One of his giant hugs put the demons at bay long enough for us to get out of the house.

Sitting outside at the packed Apollo Leaf, John was nothing like I expected. He wore white socks under his leather sandals, and shorts. "It's about time we met for a good feed," he said, as if we were cattle, and that was the end of the formalities.

"What is your favorite Asian country for vacationing?" I asked.

"Laos. Strong coffee and crusty French bread for breakfast. Can't beat that." Another thread of conversation cast astray.

He and David began talking about the project and who was doing what. I occupied myself by looking around the packed restaurant to see what others were up to. The waiter placed a pitcher of cold Tiger beer on our table and proceeded to pour glasses for John and David, but not me. When he left, I served myself. Then I noticed that none of the Indian women were drinking.

They looked beautiful in their glimmering gold necklaces, nose rings, and deep jewel-toned *saris*, but they didn't appear to be participating in conversations between the men at their table. Our meals were served on banana leaves and we had to ask for cutlery. Most people in the restaurant ate with their hands.

Thankfully, the waiter's appearance at the table gave me a chance to break back into the conversation.

"Do you happen to have any tips for finding a job here, John?" I asked.

"Well, you can hit it hard now, or wait until after Chinese New Year. Nothing happens during Chinese New Year." His reply sounded ominous.

I didn't know anything about Chinese New Year other than that there is one. I certainly didn't know that the celebration lasts for over two weeks and often the business lull drags on for a month.

"Take this card and call Dominic. Tell him I sent you." He handed me a business card. I took that as a hint to get moving on the job search and thanked him for the advice.

Opening my laptop the following morning, I discovered time was of the essence—The Year of the Rat was quickly approaching. Chinese New Year would arrive on February 7th and festivities would begin well before that. Maybe that explained why resumes I'd been sending to Chinese firms were going unanswered. As disappointed as I was to delay the search, I was relieved to have a possible explanation for the silence. Clearly I wasn't going to alter the celebratory plans of billions of Chinese nationals, so there wasn't much to do but make the most of my free time.

Dramatis Personae

***

I went to meet David at his office in the Central Business District, known as the CBD. It was a short MRT ride from our apartment and it gave me an excuse to explore new territory. We went to a sushi bar near his office, a new concept for me. Multicolored plates of fish flew by on a conveyor belt sitting just below eye level.

"What's that?" I pointed to a blue plate, and David shrugged. Another one, this time red, was filled with tender pink slices of salmon sashimi. I couldn't resist. Nor could I resist the shrimp, the tuna, or the avocado crab rolls. If you happened to miss the chef carving a massive tuna right in front of you, the fresh taste in every bite was unmistakable.

We overindulged, but this was a vacation for me. *As soon as I find a routine, I'll be fine,* I told myself for what felt like the fiftieth time in weeks. Recently I had signed up for yoga classes because I didn't know what else to do in this insane heat for exercise. I'd sworn off claustrophobic gyms years ago, so this was a new start. *I'll take yoga. I'll find a job that is fulfilling, working with people who can help me learn about Asian culture. I know I will find a way forward. I always have.* My incessant internal monologue followed this script.

As if to cement my employment-finding goal, I hired a woman to come to our place every other week to clean. She was the Chinese friend of our leasing agent. She came to the apartment to meet us.

"I get one hundred twenty-five dollars every two weeks," said Angeline.

I looked at David. David looked at me.

"Okay," he said, and that was that.

After she left, I closed the door. "Do you think we should have tried to negotiate?" I asked.

"It comes to fifteen Singapore dollars an hour. That's less than ten euro. I can't imagine we would get it much cheaper than that. Let's not worry about it."

Now all I had to do was learn how to cook. Easier said than done when you've spent your adult life avoiding anything that resembles a kitchen.

One afternoon, tired of looking for jobs online and staring at the pool, I called the American woman I'd met at the cultural presentation, Leah.

"What about catching up at the Botanic Gardens for a bit?"

"Perfect. I'll call Nancy and Sally too."

I'd met Sally, but not Nancy. Both of their husbands worked on David's project and both were Australian. "The more the merrier," I said. Based on my experience, it's better to have a large network in a foreign country—more people to trade information with. Not being plugged into the local communication channels can leave you out in the cold otherwise. "It would be best to go early so we can avoid the midday heat." I suggested.

She agreed. "Yeah. It doesn't take long to heat up out there."

Shortly after, emails began flying back and forth. Nancy wanted to meet later. Eleven or eleven-thirty would "suit her better." I repeated why I preferred the morning. Finally, everyone seemed to agree.

Singapore's Botanic Gardens are a treasure, an oasis of calm in a city that never stops moving. The early morning hours were best for photos of the gardens, so I did that before meeting the others at the section called The National Orchid Garden. I was feeling more relaxed than I had been in days.

That is until I was left standing there waiting for Nancy and Sally for nearly an hour. Leah arrived at the agreed time, saying the others would be late. I found it interesting that they had been unable to let me know themselves, as I was the one making arrangements. When they finally appeared after eleven, as Nancy had wanted in the first place, I was annoyed. Is it normal that women with children begin to act like them? I didn't think so.

I didn't say anything to her. Instead I chatted with the others about our backgrounds and where we were each living, and listened to Nancy complain. She complained about the shoes she had chosen—"terrible for walking." She complained about the service in Singapore—"so much better in Australia." She complained about the heat. You name it, I heard about it.

Dramatis Personae

Still I said nothing. I had no interest in having a group bitch session about the country I expected to live in for the next few years. Sure, I was as frustrated as anyone else, but I wasn't about to hang out with a group of spoiled expats whose main activity was to bash the place we were living. I had better things to do with my time, even if it meant doing them alone. We had a brief lunch at Chijmes after sweating through the orchid display where the greenhouse effect was magnified by the intense sunlight. I couldn't get away fast enough.

At home I scolded myself for even trying. I'd learned that the most recently any of these women had a job or a career was ten years ago. All of them had children here in Singapore, and none of them were interested in exploring Asia, except for Leah. I grabbed a handful of pretzels and headed for the pool to cool off.

That night I opened a bottle of wine and called my friend in Omaha early morning her time. I had to talk to someone about what was happening, and David was working late again. The loneliness was suffocating, just like the condo. When Allison had to hang up to get to work, I called Dora. David came home around ten o'clock and I chatted on for another hour. It was a relief to confide in trusted friends about my experiences of the past month. Friends who *knew* me. Friends who were career women *like* me. Friends who helped come up with *ideas* rather than complaints. It felt immediately better to lighten the load. No one believed all that had changed, seemingly overnight. Reassured that I wasn't as deluded as I'd almost come to believe, I hung up.

Ten minutes later, I got a jolt when the phone rang. I grabbed it quickly because I didn't want David to be woken up.

A Chinese accent came over the line, "Anjlreen," said a female voice.

"Who is this?"

"*Anjreeeeeen!*"

It clicked. The voice belonged to Angeline, our new cleaner. She hadn't shown up today and I assumed that she'd gotten confused on the start date—or I had. Either way, I hadn't thought much about it.

"Went to wrong apartment! Cleaned wrong house! Thought it your house. Same house, many computer boxes. Look same."

"Huh? I'm sorry, I don't understand, Angeline."

"I thought I clean your house. Key worked, but not your house!"

How much wine did I drink? I didn't have a clue what she was trying to tell me.

"Kitchen in same place and also two bedrooms. Didn't know it was not your house!" She was insistent.

After this went on for another ten minutes, the PowerPoint presentation popped into my head with one word on it in bold black font: "FACE". She couldn't lose face by telling me she had made a mistake on the date to come to my house, so she was making up an elaborate story about having cleaned the wrong house, one above ours that was apparently an exact duplicate. It made me think of a deadpan Steven Wright routine where he says one day he went out and everything in his house was stolen and replaced with an exact replica.

"What happened here?" he asked his roommate.

The roommate replied, "Who are you?" *ba dump bump!*

Only Angeline wasn't joking. She was apologizing in her seemingly-insane way and I needed to pay attention. "No problem, Angeline. Can you please come back tomorrow?"

"Okay, lah. I see you tomorrow." *Click.*

I stared at the phone. *What the hell just happened?* My mission to understand the world I now lived in evaporated. How would I ever fit in to a place where this could pass for a legitimate excuse not to show up for work? Sleep was the only answer that came to me.

When light peeked through the bedroom curtains and David left for work, I stared at the ceiling. I didn't want to talk to anyone. I didn't want to try and understand anymore. I just wanted life to make sense again. For five years in the Netherlands, my second biggest problem after career misunderstandings was a lack of friends. It was a major sore spot. It took me a long time to understand that in Holland people tend to make friends early in life–at school or in their neighbourhoods–and then the friend quota is met. They don't need any more and they rarely socialize with people from work. Before I figured out that the Dutch and Americans were complete opposites in this respect, I took it personally and felt rejected often.

Dramatis Personae

In Singapore, along with finding a career that I enjoyed, this was what I was most eager to change. There were so many foreigners here in the same boat. I'd taken for granted that it would be easy. Since it was another reason for I'd signed up for yoga, I dragged myself out of bed and slipped on loose clothing for my first session. It took seven minutes to walk to the studio at the top of the Takashimaya building, so I didn't bother packing a bag. I could shower at home.

Smiling at the dark-haired receptionist, I signed in and waited for class to begin. The hallway began to fill with tiny Asian beauties, each one more perfect than the last. Each one more petite and fabulously dressed–even in workout clothes. I felt like a bull in a china shop, no pun intended. When class began and the Indian instructor, Sasha, with the beautiful smile and calming voice began to lead us through beginner moves, I relaxed. I gave myself a lot of space and, despite being surrounded by mirrors, tried not to worry about how I looked. The peace that came from stretching and competing only with myself was delicious. After one class, I was an addict.

With a much lighter step, I headed home. Angeline had been and gone and I was alone in the apartment again. I sat down at the dining room table with sushi I had bought on the way home. Emails trickled in. Bill had a new client that wanted to interview me. Leah was asking if I could have lunch next week. David said yes to my proposal to go to Hong Kong for Chinese New Year. Things were looking up.

Yoga was my daily medication. It was impossible to leave there in a bad mood. I'd heard about the benefits of yoga for years, but opportunities in Rotterdam to try it were scarce. My membership was a smorgasbord, entitling me to as many classes per week as I wanted.

Part of the reason I loved it was because I felt my stamina improve rapidly. I didn't have to watch what anyone else was doing, only try to take that next pose deeper. It was so satisfying to get to a place I never thought I would be able. There was only one drawback: total relaxation loosens repressed emotion. When I allowed myself to fully surrender at the end of each intense session, tears often rolled down my cheeks. I wiped them away before anyone noticed.

* * *

The next interview was at a computer hardware company. Given that my last position was three years at a similar company, I was confident. I shook hands with the female Singaporean manager and we got down to business.

Bill claimed I'd been brought in because of my experience as a program manager, but all she wanted to talk about were technical details. The kind of details that a person in a leadership position—a non-technical leadership position—wouldn't know. We were speaking two different languages and her mission was to show off her technical knowledge rather than evaluate my skills and experience. After an hour, there was nothing left to say. I thanked her. She thanked me. I left and called Bill.

"Why do you keep sending me to interviews where the client doesn't know what they want or want what I have?"

"I thought you wanted a job."

"Of course I want a job, but these interviews aren't going to get me one. Not even close."

"You just don't understand how recruiting in Singapore works."

"That's right. And it's *your job* to help me with that. All you're doing is wasting my time and theirs!"

"I guess you can find a job yourself then."

"I guess I can." *Click.*

Neither interview led anywhere. I was on my own again. I decided it was better that way. I would only respond to positions that suited me. I wasn't going to throw my resume into every pair of hands I could find just to cross my fingers and hope they needed someone like me one day.

Enjoy the time off! Everyone said. Maybe that was the best strategy until after the Chinese New Year festivities died down. *I'll do yoga. I can be a lady who lunches. I will convince David to go to Hong Kong at the peak of its glory. How can this be wrong?* No amount of self-talk helped. I felt like I was standing on quicksand.

Chapter 6
The Face in the Mirror

"When in doubt, travel." This mantra had been working for me since 2001 when I moved to Germany. No matter what was happening in my life, it would still be there when I get back. Singapore's shiny surface was losing its luster. I could now see what was under the veneer of all this harmonious living, and I was intimidated. Without realizing it I had been counting on Singapore to erase the years of career disillusionment I'd faced in Europe. With every jobless week, that wish faded. As a master of distraction, I saw Hong Kong as the answer.

We landed on Wednesday, the eve of Chinese New Year. Not knowing anything about the place, I was flying blind on my hotel search. A new luxury hotel had opened in Mong Kok, a neighborhood in West Kowloon.

Descriptions called it "daring" to place a five-star hotel in a "gritty" neighborhood away from the glitz and glamour of central Hong Kong, so of course I was intrigued. It hadn't taken long to see that Singapore is a sanitized version of its former self and I wanted to see the *real* Hong Kong, not its tourist-friendly twin. A double-decker bus, probably a British legacy, was the cheapest transportation from the airport. For a touch of irony, we passed Disneyland on the way—castle, mouse ears, and all.

A knockout Chinese woman with a crisp British accent greeted us at reception. After what passes for English in Singapore—known as *Singlish*—this was a new twist. She told us to have some lunch while we waited for the room to be ready, and handed over a map of the mall that the hotel was built into. *Next!* We were dismissed.

It was surreal. The mall was brand new, with gold everything everywhere. In the lobby an enormous pink cherry blossom tree glittered with a golden trunk. Before it stood two white mice holding golden ingots and sporting golden noses. The Year of the Rat was upon us.

Children raced to have their photos taken with the rats, and we were surrounded by the frenetic atmosphere of a circus hitting town. Laughing, David motioned me to Rat Central to get my photo taken too. Neither of us said a word over lunch, except to comment on how delicious the ramen soup was. Ramen was something I remembered from being a poor college student, but this miso-based broth was sumptuous. Strips of juicy pork belly mingled with noodles in the mocha-colored broth and I savored every bite. I even tried the beige egg that floated in it and was surprised that it tasted like any other boiled egg.

When we did get our room, I was impressed. It was nearly the size of our condo. Looking out the window was less impressive. Thick gray smog hung over Victoria Harbour and the surrounding buildings hadn't received the slick makeover of the building I stood in, or most of those in Singapore. Reality was depressing.

Fully unloaded except for cameras and necessities, we were ready to take a closer look at Mong Kok. Signs for 7 Eleven, KFC, and Starbucks leapt out at us in this "gritty" neighborhood. The further we went from the hotel, the more the landscape changed. Something unusual was tucked into every alleyway.

A waft of incense signaled a hidden temple with heavy New Year attendance. Dark-haired heads bowed and lips moved in silence as people stood shoulder to shoulder in front of seated golden gods. They moved quickly through a sequence I didn't understand. Across the street a handy fruit market sold offerings to the faithful, while unidentified liquid puddled at the side of the road. The smell told me I didn't want to know what it was.

David was intrigued. I was disgusted. The photos I'd seen of Hong Kong were gleaming skyscrapers and impeccably clean sidewalks boasting designer billboards. I'd wanted to see history, not garbage.

He took shot after shot of "everyday life" and didn't notice that I was clearly uncomfortable. I sped up the pace in the direction of the hotel and its familiar fast food outlets, while David chastised me for missing the Mah-jong game in a smoky hidden doorway. I couldn't have cared less.

That night, the mission was viewing the legendary New Year parade at Tsim Sha Tsui. I had no idea what to expect, but I was looking forward to dragons and colorful dancers, the usual scenes I'd seen on television or in the newspapers over the years. David spent decades fiddling with his camera equipment, deciding which lenses to carry with him and whether or not to take his tripod. This was his normal routine, so I made the most of it by trying to find something warm to wear. The weather was much colder than Singapore and being near the waterfront meant a further temperature drop. We left the hotel together, but felt very far apart.

The parade route was unmistakable. People already waited several layers deep. Darkness had fallen and when we stopped moving, the cold wanted to get to know me better. Bodies jostled to and fro. Children shouted while mothers handed out gloves and brightly wrapped sweets.

An elbow went squarely into my back, its owner vying for a better position. Another man stomped on my toes. Six-foot-five David stood above the ruckus looking through his lens, not noticing anything. For close to an hour I stood attempting to maintain a civil demeanor. Finally, just after the start of the parade, I hit my limit.

"Can we please try to find another spot?" I pleaded.

"Why? It just started!" David had to shout to be heard, immediately annoyed with me for wanting to change the plan.

"I can't stand this!" I didn't explain. How could it not be obvious?

He angrily packed up his camera gear, "Fine." It was not fine.

Had I been able, I would have run from where we were standing. I could barely walk, let alone flee. This crowd easily eclipsed the size of Singapore's biggest. I wasn't used to all the pushing and shoving, which for Chinese was perfectly normal. I was trying not to have a panic attack, but David clearly did not empathize. He was inconvenienced and that was grounds for annoyance. *So be it.* The parade was several hours long. Didn't I deserve to enjoy it too?

Around the corner, we happened into a row of bars and restaurants. The chance of finding a table was slim and my fears were confirmed as I looked into each packed doorway. If I didn't find something, I would never hear the end of it. That much was certain.

Finally, at the end of the row, was a quiet, overlooked restaurant.

The sign at the entry said that only patrons having meals could be seated, so that had kept most of the crowd away. Walking in, I saw an upper deck with windows looking down onto the parade route. Several seats at the bar, with a perfect view, sat empty. *Score!* I couldn't believe my luck. I skipped the wine and went straight for rum and Coke. The glass was drained before David had a chance to look at the menu. With him or without him, I would enjoy myself.

Our luck held. The parade was spectacular. Even Mickey Mouse made an appearance as the star rat, a term which he would likely have found offensive. The food was decent. No one was pushing me around or blocking my view. My third cocktail improved my mood considerably and David was taking beautiful photos even through the glass windows. The night ended with chocolate mice on our pillow and a red card with *"Gong Xi Fa Cai!"* written in fancy gold script. Yes, Happy New Year to all.

On the first day of the rat year, the temperature dropped to 4 degrees Celsius. We were not prepared in the least. The Big Buddha was the highlight of the day and we'd been warned not to miss it.

Cable cars carry you to the peak of Lantau Island for a peek at the Big Buddha. We shivered the entire thirty minutes. Despite the return of the crowds we thought we'd left behind, it was worth it. The Big Buddha wasn't just big, it was enormous. His soft features and serene smile made me wonder what his secret was.

We walked down a million stairs to reach a Buddhist temple at the base of the mountain. David snapped away and I stood watching the hive of activity around me. I nearly fainted when I saw a woman toss a stack of colorful Hong Kong bills into a fire pit until I realized something was amiss with the size of the notes. They were bigger than real currency. The next man threw in a black paper Ferrari. Apparently Chinese ancestors want for nothing in the afterlife.

That night we took a silly tourist video on the world's longest escalator and explored the famous nightlife of Lan Kwai Fong. We were finally having fun and not just pretending. Seated on a purple velvet love seat in a retro wine bar, I admitted to being completely unprepared for what we had gotten into.

"I had no idea there would be that many people."

"It's okay. I expected it, but I know it's hard for you."

"Then why didn't you say anything before we got there?"

"Because I figured you knew."

For him, crowds had never been an issue. Growing up in Europe's most densely-populated nation had cured him of that years ago. We changed the subject to the other cities we wanted to see and our luck in being close to so many. I was relieved to end the trip on a positive note.

The high note quickly turned falsetto back in Singapore. Leah told me that Nancy had complained about *my* behavior at the Orchid Garden a few weeks earlier.

"Apparently she didn't find me intellectually stimulating enough because she barely said a word to me," was Nancy's comment—parroted through enemy lines. Leah appeared to be waiting for my reaction, which would also be relayed word for word.

"Whatever," I said coolly.

Inside, I was seething. *She shows up an hour late and has the nerve to complain that I wasn't chatty enough? Who cares?* I wasn't expecting to make lifelong friends out of this group, but I'd been hoping to grow a social network. She could easily be extricated from that without any worry on my end. Briefly I wondered why she would go to such effort to make me look bad before I scratched her name off of my potential-acquaintance list.

* * *

Yoga chilled me out after lunch. I reveled in the peace it delivered. An Indian woman in her fifties struck up a conversation with me one day after noticing that I always had my nose stuck in a book before class. She too loved to read.

"Why don't we exchange books?"

"That's a great idea. I'd love to learn more about Indian authors."

"Excellent. Please tell me your favorite American books as well."

I specifically asked her to give me the names of Indian authors whom she admired—they would be new to me. In exchange I created a list of my favorite modern fiction and stuck it in one of them to hand to her.

Apparently *I* wasn't intellectual enough for *her*. I thought she was going to hurl the book at me when I saw her angry face a week later. She ranted at me that she'd started reading *Water for Elephants* and had "absolutely no interest" in reading about the lives of "degenerates."

"Okay. Well, uh… I'm sorry you didn't like it."

Abruptly, she stalked off and I was left dumbfounded by the exchange. I'd never seen anyone take personal offence to a book quite like that. If you don't like it, don't read it. To me it was a simple matter of taste. I had struggled through the long, boring epic about the Raj but I wasn't upset with her over the recommendation.

During class I considered the characters in the book I'd loaned her. It's about a circus train and the type of shady dealings that go along with it. From my perspective, that's what made the book interesting. I remembered the Indian women I'd observed at the restaurant with David and John. They didn't drink. They didn't participate in the conversation of men. Is that a lightbulb coming on?

The book I'd given her has themes of adultery, alcoholism, and elephant abuse. I couldn't have picked a worse novel for this now-hostile woman with angry green eyes that passed judgment on me anew every time we crossed paths. Sadly, I *did* consider whether or not she would like it given our difference in age, but never gave our different cultures a second thought.

Turning over on my side for a resting position, tears welled in my eyes. *Strike two.* I hurried out of the class to avoid further confrontation with the Indian woman. I didn't have the stamina to deal with it in my place of refuge. I changed quickly and hopped in the express elevator, which zoomed nineteen floors to the ground.

The Face in the Mirror

The post office was on my way home. With a birthday card to mail, I stepped into the queue. When a man approached me with a clipboard saying that he was taking a survey regarding new services to be offered at the post office after renovation, I agreed. He didn't even make it to the second question.

Tears formed rivers down my cheeks as I fled. Never more grateful for the invention of private elevators, I stabbed at number fifteen until it lit up and collapsed against the wall.

"What is your occupation?" The bespectacled Chinese man had asked. When I hesitated, he tried to help. "Housewife?" It was the last word I heard. I stood in the bathroom looking at myself in the mirror. I did look like the stereotypical woman whose stampede of children had gotten the better of her. Disheveled hair. No makeup. Baggy clothes.

Overweight.

"Who the hell are you?" I shouted at my reflection.

Yoga was building my strength, but it was doing nothing to combat the excessive calories I'd been consuming by stress-eating. My weight had steadily crept up after I'd stopped running a few years earlier. The latest bouts of anxiety had taken it to new heights and the photos from Hong Kong proved it. I wasn't just unemployed and friendless a million miles from home. I was fat too.

Mong Kok street view

Chapter 7
The Third New Year

If I wasn't at the pool, being outside after eleven was murder. The only alternative was any one of the shopping malls that blended into one another on Orchard Road. Obsession over my lack of employment had taken hold, and the last thing I wanted to do was spend money at a mall. To escape the confines of the condo, I searched online for cheap Asian getaways. I had no idea what Malaysia or Thailand were like, but they were close. All I knew of Vietnam was through stories of the war with America.

Asia was much cheaper than Europe when it came to travel. After recent setbacks on several fronts, I was grateful for that bit of good news. I looked for retreats that would help me build my yoga practice while changing the scenery. With these ingredients, the most obvious destination was Bali.

Bali, the small island off the coast of Indonesia, was the apparent home of all things yoga. The array of options was mind-blowing, everything from excessive luxury to backpacker bargains. Not fitting either of those descriptions, I chose middle ground. A six-day yoga, spa, and meditation program called "Escape the World" had my name written all over it. The accommodation was in Ubud, Bali's cultural heart, and the owners had a number of positive testimonials on their web site.

The mere thought of such an exotic trip quickened my pulse. I typed a quick email to the company to inquire about available space in the March session. The response was a lightning quick "only one spot left!" and a price tag of fifteen million Indonesian Rupiah. Fifteen million of anything sounded crazy, so I quickly converted the currency.

It came to six hundred euro for six nights' accommodation, meals, yoga instruction, and spa treatments. Compared to everything else I'd found, it was a hell of a deal. The only other expense was the flight to Denpasar, Bali's capital. In my mind, I was already there.

David was skeptical when I explained my plan that evening. I'd been traveling on my own for years by this point, so I was surprised that he didn't embrace the idea. We were both concerned about money, but I already had another lead on a possible consulting job through a connection from Germany. It was only a matter of time until something came together—and I could not sit around in that apartment waiting for it to happen or playing mind games with the local housewives.

Everyone would be happier if I were putting my free time to good use. I knew that for sure. Before I made the booking, David brought up the terrorist attack on Bali that killed 200 people in a nightclub in Kuta. I'd remembered that, of course, but with 2000 of my own countrymen killed a few weeks before I left America, I didn't think twice about it. If you stop doing what you love, terrorism wins. I'd made myself a promise long ago not to be a victim.

The trip consumed the last of my savings, but I was resolute. Looking at the photos of this idyllic jungle retreat, I couldn't wait to get there. The two weeks until my flight took forever. Every day I researched Bali and edited my list of what I wanted to see. Each day, that list became longer.

I added one night before the retreat began and two nights after for sightseeing. Jules, the owner of the retreat company emailed me once the booking was made to tell me that I would be landing on the Balinese New Year's eve, *Nyepi*. My internal radar went off immediately. *Three New Year celebrations in a year? Who gets to experience that?* Me, apparently. Jules arranged a hotel in Sanur for my first night and sent me a link about Balinese traditions. *It just keeps getting better*, I thought, clicking through the web of information.

From the eve of Nyepi until the following evening, no one speaks or goes out. The beaches are closed. The lights are turned off. Use of power by the locals is prohibited, but some allowances are made for tourists. Frivolity is frowned upon and meditation encouraged.

The Third New Year

When the sun retires for the evening, the streets are cleared for a lively procession. The *ogoh-ogohs* creep down the main streets of every village to rid them of evil. Ogoh-ogohs are large mythological demons made from papier-mâché and carried on bamboo frames. Once they frighten all evil from the island for the night, the locals keep silent so it cannot find its way back by the noise. Stillness creates the perfect environment for Balinese meditation on the year ahead. My flight was to land just before sunset the day before Nyepi. I couldn't believe my luck.

Over coffee with Leah, I couldn't contain my excitement. I told her about my plans and all the research I'd done on Nyepi and Bali. She stopped listening the moment I said I was going alone.

"Who else am I going to go with? No one I know is interested in yoga and David can't get away from work again so soon. I'd rather go by myself than stay home and wish I had someone to travel with."

"Won't you be nervous? There are terrorists in Bali." Wide-eyed Leah looked as though she might be ill at the prospect.

"Terrorism is everywhere. If you exclude every place that has had a terrorist attack from your travel list, there won't be many left."

"There is a travel warning in place for Bali for American citizens. We are advised not to go there," she continued, insinuating that I was either doing something wrong or just plain stupid.

"I won't tell if you don't!" I joked, unable to fathom why she would think I would change my plans based on this information. I hadn't thought about terrorism since I had to wait in line at the American consulate in Amsterdam where a tank sat out front in case of an attack.

"I'm going to a yoga retreat, not expat nightclubs. I'm sure I will be fine." Finishing my coffee to indicate those were my final words on the matter, I lied and said I'd get in touch when I returned.

Earlier she said that she only had a few minutes before she had to meet Nancy, indicating that she was breaking protocol by this rendezvous with the enemy. I wasn't considered appropriate company for a lunch anymore, just someone to fill the time before it. Heaven forbid Nancy would actually *see* her with me. Why did I feel like it was recess all over again?

It was a joke. What did we have in common? We were American. That was it. From my perspective, that reason wasn't enough to keep anyone around. The Americans I'd met in the Netherlands never became friends either. The US is a big country and there are many types of Americans. I was far from believing that sharing a country of birth was sufficient glue to form a friendship without any other common interests. *Enjoy your lunches, ladies. I'm hitting the road.*

I tried not to care, but without any true friends within a thousand miles, it stung. There was no real reason to be upset, but I found it odd to be passed judgment on by an entire group based on one interaction, or lack thereof. Why did Leah profess such concern for my welfare when she only wanted company for the minutes that the others were busy? Maybe it bothered them that I could do whatever the hell I pleased when they were bound by children that demanded their attention and husbands who seemed to rule the roosts?

Our conversations had made it very clear that they towed the line behind their husbands' careers, whereas David and I made our decisions together. Yes, his job had brought us to Singapore, but it was perfect timing for my desire to leave Holland. *Forget it.* Who needs friends like that?

Wandering towards home, I changed money to Indonesian currency and spent an hour in my favorite bookstore. Kinokuniya, a Japanese chain, was the most amazing literary retail world I'd ever landed in. Half the store is stocked with books in Japanese and on Japanese art, the other is for English books, maps, and artwork. It carried magazines from every corner of the globe. Though I could rarely leave without spending at least a hundred Singapore dollars, it was money well spent in diversion. The saga of Leah and Nancy vanished among the bookshelves.

Departure day arrived with a flurry of activity. I didn't know what to take, so I took everything. I gave David a huge hug and several sloppy kisses before he left for work. With a serious face, he asked me to be careful. Assuring him I would, I nearly pushed him into the elevator so I could finish packing. Yoga outfits were stuffed in with sandals,

THE THIRD NEW YEAR

sunscreen, and mosquito repellent—I was ready! I called for a taxi and stared at the clock until one arrived.

The sun was low in the sky as the plane skidded onto the Denpasar runway. The airport was a single ramshackle building with several immigration lines to accommodate the heavy tourist traffic that arrives daily. Tourists in flip-flops and shorts maintained an orderly demeanor while waiting patiently to show their identification and get on with their holiday fun. Knowing that the Nyepi celebrations would begin when the sun went down, I was anxious to be free.

A serious dark-haired customs agent flipped through my passport and gave me a hard stare. The silent message was clear: "Don't do anything stupid here." Bali has a reputation amongst western foreigners for tolerating raucous parties and drunken stupidity. Maybe the Balinese had grown tired of it. Silent understanding passed between us.

Grabbing my suitcase on the way out, I exited the airport doors. I didn't know what to expect on the other side, but I didn't expect run-down huts and stray dogs by the dozen. Where were the luxurious whitewashed villas and crystal swimming pools? Not here. A brown-skinned man with kind eyes approached. "Taxi?" Switching my gaze from him to his rusting van with a hastily written taxi logo on it, I nodded. When we had agreed on the price of the ride to Sanur, I climbed into the vinyl front passenger seat whose stuffing was trying desperately to escape.

"What can you tell me about Nyepi?" I asked, excited to finally talk to a local.

"Nyepi Day quiet. Ogoh-ogohs tonight." Those were the six words I was given. He must have been conserving his energy for the celebration.

Silence lasted the remaining fifteen minutes to Sanur. The sun wasn't about to wait for me to take my place, so I strained to see through the window. More skinny dogs scampered out of our way. The seventies-style concrete buildings of Denpasar eventually gave way to small towns. Finally I spotted the enormous painted monsters, whose job it was to rid the island of evil for the night, standing at attention. In every village, they waited patiently for their night shift to begin. My camera caught only blurred reds and hazy blues.

At the hotel I was greeted with a similar economy of words that had welcomed me to Indonesia, only friendlier. The locals were preoccupied with the evening's festivities and the following day of silence. Meals would be brought to my villa, a young man told me.

"No restaurant during Nyepi," he explained. Whether that meant the hotel's restaurant or all restaurants, I didn't know. "Parade two streets away from here. Ten minutes walking." And he was gone.

Candles waited next to the lamp on my nightstand, matches at the ready. Power outlets were covered with tape. "Villa" was a big word for where I would spend the next two nights. It wasn't glamorous, but I was *here*. I was here for *Nyepi!* By now the sky was black velvet and the air was filled with expectation. Emptying my backpack of everything but my passport, wallet, and camera, I was out the door again in minutes. I tried not to be swallowed up by the gaping holes of the dirt road in the dark. The rare bit of pavement lay in broken piles. The disposition of the local pack of strays was unknown. Streetlights are expensive, hence sparse. None of it stopped me for long.

The gamelan was the first thing I heard. That and the hushed voices of the crowd. I walked towards both, digging out my Panasonic. A typical Balinese instrument, the notes that filtered through the air from the gamelan were haunting. They set the perfect tone for a parade of giant ogres dancing through the dark.

Decorative torches appeared sporadically. Briefly I thought of the townspeople carrying pitchforks and coming for Frankenstein, but the thought disappeared when I could finally make out the smiling faces in the crowd. Tall figures emerged from the dark, faces distorted in anger or disgust. My camera clicked a thousand times during the ten minutes it took for the entourage to pass through Sanur's main intersection. More gamelan players signaled the end of the procession and I was dumbfounded by how little I knew of the corner of the world where I now stood.

Chapter 8
Soul Seeker

Rays of sunlight peeked through the cracks in the painted wooden shutters at dawn. My stirring sent a gecko scurrying up the wall and across the ceiling to beat me into the bathroom. Bird calls grew louder and heightened in pitch outside the window. I imagined their vivid feathers.

Arriving at night in a new place is something I avoid. It calms me to have a mental image of my surroundings before I go to sleep, especially when I travel alone. Lacking that information got me out of bed before coffee came to mind. Pulling my hair back and throwing on shorts, my need to investigate was stronger than my need to shower.

I walked towards the sound of the surf. Passing through an empty street market, I was grateful for the holiday, not interested in fighting to keep what little money I had in my pocket. Pastel colors painted the sunrise into a watercolor dream. Purple and pink hues complemented gentle waves of midnight blue. A Balinese temple sat at the edge of the sea, a beautiful embodiment of the thoughtful and reflective island people.

The photos I took that morning with Sanur's treasures bathed in a soft orange glow led me to believe that perhaps evil *had* been banished from the island. It certainly felt that way. Peace filled in the open spaces around me and I thought less of the potential calamity that had followed me for months.

Breakfast waited patiently on the small cement patio back at my villa. Red polka-dotted dragon fruit and glistening mango were protected by plastic from the menacing mosquitos that had already used me for their morning meal at the beach. The sweet fresh-squeezed orange juice and bread that could only have been baked that morning didn't last long. As I ate, I considered how to spend Nyepi day.

As the coffee kicked in, I realized that my options were to relax at the pool or to relax in my villa. Either way, the universe wanted me to take a breather. Who was I to argue? Picking up my guidebook, I read and nibbled until the sun was turned up a few notches.

Bali's heat is similar to Singapore's, constant and wet. The ever-present humidity discourages most activity that doesn't involve water and I was grateful for the small pool. One by one, couples appeared from the other villas and took up residence on deck chairs. No one seemed to be upset about a day of forced leisure.

It was still early when I reached my limit of sun exposure. My fair freckled skin doesn't tolerate direct sunlight for more than a few hours, regardless of the amount of sunscreen I've bathed in. On the desk my mobile phone flashed with a message. To my surprise the voice belonged to Marla from the large software firm I'd worked with in Germany. She was calling about a consulting position.

After three months of unemployment, I had to listen a second time because during the first I was numb with disbelief.

"Jennifer, would you please call me back at 9834 8777? I'll need to know your daily rate and I believe the client location is across the street from your place. Talk to you soon."

My mind went into overdrive. *Daily rate? I get to decide how much I get paid? This can't be real.*

I was destroying the suggestion of employment before it had a chance to bloom. I'd never worked as a contractor before, only as an employee. I had no idea what the going rate was in Singapore for a CRM consultant.

I called David. Level-headed and practical, he never let me down on matters like this. As a finance major, he has a much better head for figures than I do. He is also unflappable. While I was running around doing an imitation of a chicken without its head at the mere suggestion of an actual job, he calmly put across the relevant points of working as an independent. *I love this man*, I thought, making careful notes.

SOUL SEEKER

Ready with my list of demands, I returned Marla's call. She didn't answer, so I left a vague message. Wanting to gauge her reaction, I didn't give her the rate. CRM knowledge was in short supply outside the US, so I was confident she would call back. All I had to do was wait. Have I mentioned that patience is not my strong suit?

Opening the fridge, I found several chilled bottles of Bintang, the local brew. I cracked one open and read more about Bali. It surprised me to learn that the island is predominantly Hindu though the rest of Indonesia has a Muslim majority. Aside from stepping inside that Hindu temple in Chinatown with David, I knew nothing about the faith.

Before moving to Asia, I had begun to think of myself as "worldly," or at least well-traveled. In this part of the world I was an amateur. Every time I turned around another situation that I was unprepared for presented itself.

Marla called again the following morning. She explained the specifics of the project she was running—it sounded like a good fit. I had the necessary industry experience in utilities and customer management. If she was worried about my fee, she didn't show it. That was the end of the discussion as far as she was concerned. I gave her my return date to Singapore and she said she'd call with a start date and location. Just like that, I was employed.

Grinning, I hung up the phone and started packing. Jules, the director of the yoga retreat, had arranged for a driver to pick me up. My experience in Bali so far was pleasant, but it would be easier to relax under the wing of people who knew its ins and outs.

Wyan's beaming smile assured me there was nothing to worry about. He opened the car door for me and was immediately chattering about his island. Listening to his gentle voice, I thought my worries might *all* disappear.

Thirty minutes later, we arrived at Kumara. "Boys! Help the lady with her bags, please." Wyan pointed a finger towards reception and several young smiling faces appeared from nowhere.

"Welcome, Miss Jennifer! So nice to meet you." This had to be Jules, the only person I'd spoken to before arriving. He was somewhere in middle age with a twinkle in his blue eyes and graying temples.

"Thank you. I really appreciate your help with the Nyepi information. I would have been lost without it."

"Not a problem. Hardly anyone outside Indonesia understands it. Now here, take one of these." He handed me a printed schedule. "Make sure you note the times of your spa appointments. Don't want to miss those! This will also tell you what is happening day by day. Yoga begins daily at half past six in the Great Hall. Let me show you."

"I can't believe how beautiful this place is." I didn't know what else to say about the collection of villas and purpose-built rooms set into the jungle hillside.

"Thank you. Before we bought it, it was the residence of a Balinese prince."

Jules and I kept walking. Once I had the full tour of the Great Hall, the terraced lounge above the pool, the restaurant, and each unique guest villa, I believed him. The place was pure magic. Birds sang, frogs croaked, and both the setting and its residents exuded a calm that was missing in the "real world." I could definitely handle six days of this. Frankly, why would I ever want to leave?

"If you need to go into the city, just tell the boys where you want to go and give them a little notice. They'll drive you in."

"Could they drop me off at the Sacred Monkey Forest?" I asked, without skipping a beat. The official program began that evening, so I still had the whole day to myself. A place with a name like that had to be explored.

Jules nodded and translated my request. More nods followed. "Ten minutes, okay?"

"Absolutely."

I was not disappointed. The dense vegetation and three intricate temples within the Monkey Forest made me feel like Indiana Jones. I was no longer a tourist in the protected wildlife zone of a major Balinese city, I was an explorer. At least that's how I felt. Hardly anyone else was around, so the macaques and I eyed each other warily. They wanted food I didn't have.

Every mention of this otherworldly place has a second line describing the greedy nature of its 600 inhabitants. In minutes the monkeys will open backpacks and purses to take food they can smell.

Cameras, mobile phones, and anything else they can get their hands on should also be kept close at hand. I carried my bag in front of me while I tried to capture their curious faces.

Shrieking alpha males, protective mothers, and wide-eyed babies were all present and accounted for. I hadn't spotted a single monkey in Singapore and it fascinated me that I could study them here at close range. We watched each other until a busload of tourists arrived armed with bananas and I was summarily dismissed. Not wanting to be the lucky recipient of a bite laced with hepatitis B, I moved on.

It was not the wisest decision to walk the twenty minutes from the Monkey Forest to the center of town, but it was easier than hunting down a taxi or bargaining with a moto-scooter driver. I sweated my way down a road lined with stalls and small shops, trying to avoid the punishing direct sunlight.

Ducking into one stall, I found the walls staring back at me. The eye-sockets of intricately carved wooden masks lined every wall. One angry face caught my attention. The shop owner identified him as the Hindu god Barong, the king of good spirits. Carefully inspecting his fangs and wide eyes, I decided to give him a second chance when I found out he was the sworn enemy of the demon queen Rangda. *Sold!* I needed to be protected from demons and David needed a Bali present. Barong would love living in our condo.

The humidity skyrocketed as morning turned to afternoon. When I stopped in a well-known yoga outfitter to beef up my wardrobe for the week ahead, I considered making an offering to the god of air-conditioning. Bali was further from the equator than Singapore, but I actually felt worse in this heat.

The nausea in my stomach said to take cover and, having reached the center of Ubud, I heeded the warning. A café that was bustling, but somehow managed to remain quiet, appeared just after I'd passed the palace called Puri Saren. The staff pointed to a table for four and I didn't argue. All I wanted to do was sit under the swaying ceiling fan and consume anything cool.

Ordering a mai-tai, a large bottle of water, and shrimp rice paper rolls, I settled in. The dark-green canopy of the Monkey Forest, the word on the street about Barong, and my initial impressions of Ubud went into my notebook. Biting into the deliciously thin shrimp rolls, I watched a wide variety of people stroll by.

A little book called *Eat Pray Love* had recently made Ubud famous. In droves, women were replicating the pilgrimage of its author, Elizabeth Gilbert, to attempt to make sense of their lives. It was no secret to me that you have to walk your talk, not someone else's. Regardless, it was interesting to compare the physical location with the one my imagination had cooked up while reading the book. Reverie came to an abrupt halt when a gang of Russian tourists stomped toward a nearby table and began shouting orders at the waiter. *Check please!*

What fascinated me about the palace wasn't the sunburnt-peach structure itself, but the gods stationed outside. The two at the main entrance had been provided with little parasols made of bright yellow silk with orange fringe to protect them from the sun's power. Apparently even stone was affected by this evil glowering gold disc in the sky. Walking around to the side of the building, I met another guard holding his ground for eternity. He had a wide smile and a bright pink hibiscus tucked behind his ear. Perhaps he was the guardian of frivolity, forcing everyone to smile as they entered. I had no choice but to obey.

The central market was last on my required Ubud hit list. My unruly stomach spoke for me as I approached the massive wooden structure, its treasures hidden by a temperamental dark sky. The meal and my haphazard attempt at hydration hadn't been enough to compensate for the extreme heat. My visit had to be quick.

I am a big fan of markets. Their contents are both a reflection of the local flavor of humanity as well as that of the visitors. Brightly-colored handbags sat alongside polished stone necklaces. A rainbow of flower bouquets brought a smile to my face before the wooden penis bottle-openers dashed it. Sarongs and flowing white shirts promised freedom to tourists from the painful confines of their clothes ill-suited for the climate. Bali's flag rippled from the rafters in the strong breeze to announce the coming rain. When the deluge began, rain leaked from all directions, but was masterfully diverted to protect the goods from a single drop.

It rained on. I wandered and bartered, coming away with a few inexpensive tokens. My stomach declined the offer to continue navigating the maze, so I located a taxi to take me back to the Prince's house at Kumara. Ubud wasn't going to be easy, but it was going to be worth it. Those were my last thoughts before falling asleep to the music of the jungle.

Hours passed before I stirred. Despite the fact that my trip so far had been hassle free, I was nervous. *What if I don't like the others? What if I can't keep up in yoga?* The reality of spending five days and nights with total strangers crept into my worry zone. In that zone, insecurities were continuously lobbed from one side to the other. This was nothing new.

At this point, few moments of my life passed without worry. The world around me had been erased and replaced with unknown people and places. I didn't miss Europe, but the sensation of free falling in this foreign world had the tendency to intensify without notice. My stomach had tried to warn me all day that this was one of those moments.

Just before 4:30, I clicked my villa's door shut and went to the lounge for the orientation meeting with Jules, Wyan, and the rest of the retreat participants. I wasn't the last to enter, but I was close. We were four Americans, four Australians, and one Canadian. All of us were women. All of us were smiling tentatively at one another while we listened to Jules set the scene.

"Tolerance is the key word for your time in Indonesia. Life doesn't travel the same route in this country as it does in the developed western world, nor does it move at the same pace. Learn to slow down and your journey will be much more enjoyable." He paused, leaving a minute for the nervous laughter he appeared to anticipate. "Tonight after dinner we will make our way to Tirta Empul Temple in Tampaksiring. You will perform the Hindu purification ritual that has been handed down for centuries. Dressing for this is very important," he continued, handing each of us a folded white sheet and a patterned sarong.

"First, wrap the white sheet around you tightly and wrap the sarong over it. Secure both. Put a white long-sleeved shirt on over both of those and bring a spare pair of underwear in your bag."

The last few words raised nine sets of eyebrows, but no one spoke.

"See you in the dining room after you change!" Jules and Wyan disappeared while the rest of us tried to make sense of what we had heard.

"Put the sarong on first?" asked an Aussie accent. "No, the sarong goes on top of the white sheet," answered an American voice.

"Was he joking about the underwear?" someone wondered.

"It didn't look like it," I said quietly, wondering what the hell I'd gotten myself into.

We were on a schedule now, one dictated by our spiritual leaders. They looked both harmless and friendly, so this wasn't a Reverend Jimmy Jones situation. Despite my normal habit of worrying, my instinct was to trust these two. Jules wouldn't have gone to the trouble of explaining Nyepi's impact and helping me navigate it if he weren't interested in my welfare and positive experience in Bali. Would he?

Anxious to end the uncertainty, I rushed to dress in hope of getting more answers at dinner. My brain was leaps and bounds beyond my body. As I headed for the dining room, none of my substantial layers felt secure. If the intent was to make certain we were covered, I was about to blow it before leaving Kumara. Thankfully, a friendly French-Canadian named Lorraine knew more about sarongs than I did. She pulled this bit and that bit of fabric until I felt like I was wearing a Victorian corset. Later she told me she was a cross-country skier. With strength like that, I believed it.

The Aussies, Liz and Katherine, bombarded me with questions before I even sat down. I hesitated, briefly wondering if I could move to the other end of the table without offending anyone, but decided that was impossible. After saying yes to green chicken curry and vegetables, I gave several vague responses. As someone who now spent a great deal of time alone, I wasn't used to interrogation. Thanks to Nancy, I was now leery of Aussies too. Lorraine took the chair on my left and we exchanged a knowing smile before the Aussies were off on another tangent that I barely listened to.

Maybe they were nervous too. I didn't know enough about Australian culture to guess. All I had to compare them to were the wives I'd met in Singapore. Based on that interaction, I wasn't eager to know more, so I asked Lorraine where she was from and skirted the questions from Down Under. My French-Canadian neighbor was a longtime friend of Jules, the retreat director, so if anyone was likely to be "in the know" about tonight's happenings, she was the one. We continued talking on the bus to who-knew-where and my anxiety took a breather when my newfound friend and I easily connected.

As the bus shuddered to a stop at the temple grounds, I tried to make out the surroundings. Several illuminated white buildings dotted the compound. Everything in between was cloaked in darkness. The evening stars watched nine strangers disembark and play Follow the Leader with Jules at the head of the queue.

"You can leave your bags here with Wyan. They will not be disturbed. We are going to the pool next to the temple. The temple is built over a natural spring and the waters are known for their purifying ability. You will dunk your head under each of the twelve spouts on the side of the pool and say a prayer to the gods. Please follow me and watch your step." And he was off again.

Dunk my head in water that had purified the bodies of who knows how many people?

Despite my position at the end of the line, that was all I had time to think before the others began splashing into the water. *What the hell am I doing?* was the thought that jumped into the water with me. *Surely this isn't something sane people do!* The thoughts kept complaining and I kept moving, finding my brain and my body disconnected for the second time in the span of two hours. I declined to put my head underwater, but I tossed holy water from the mouth of each deity over me and said a silent prayer for everyone close to me. I thought of my mother and immediately realized she would think I'd lost it.

Soggy and shaking, I climbed out of the pool and walked towards the others. A large sarong was held up by a few of the women for cover while those of us behind it desperately searched our bags in the dim light for the dry underwear we were instructed to bring. Everyone was laughing. There was simply nothing else to do in this situation.

Regaining an ounce of composure, I tried to snap photos of the pool, but it was no use. Digital photography, limited light, and shaking hands do not an artist make. At least it gave me something to do while I tried to process the likelihood of ever finding myself in this situation.

Shepherding his lost lambs, Jules led us to a small open temple where a priest in traditional dress waited. He asked us to do something with grains of rice and our ears before mumbling a prayer in what could only be Sanskrit. I watched the others wet the rice and place some behind their ears, then more on their foreheads. *What the?* I stopped pretending I had any idea what was happening and listened to the deep rumble of the guttural voice before me. Hopefully his prayers would be absorbed without my understanding.

Confusion is exhausting. On the ride back to Kumara, nine women were quieter than I ever thought possible. Wyan announced that we should be ready to start yoga precisely at 6:30 the next morning. At this stage, I wasn't sure how much more newness I could handle. I decided not to think any more about anything.

A discovery the next morning: the jungle is an effective alarm clock. Unfamiliar voices of the feathered and reptilian varieties told me it was time to get up. Another wave of anxiety hit my stomach: *I won't be as good as the others.*

Pushing negativity aside, I showered and put on my new yoga clothes. The loose comfortable fabric made me feel more at ease—until I entered the Great Hall to see the designer mat and outfit of another American girl whose name I thought was Lisa. I smiled at her and sat on the other side of the room, admiring the huge brass gong in the center of the non-wall adjacent to the jungle.

The hall was completely open except for the roof and back wall. Despite the great height of the thick timber beams, a feeling of warmth lingered, a remnant of the rising sun behind the brass gong. One by one, sleepy women stumbled in and claimed their space.

"Please cross your legs in a seated position and close your eyes. Listen to your breath." Wyan said softly, but assertively.

I followed instructions. A moment later, the gong's powerful vibration filled my core, knocking my insides and my ingrained habits all over the place.

Wyan took the initial class slowly, with several downward dog and tree poses that beginners could do. I couldn't help feeling relieved that I wasn't the most or least flexible in the class. I was fine with middle ground. Middle ground goes unnoticed, which is where I am most comfortable.

Over breakfast I reviewed the schedule for the days ahead. Seeing the words "spa" and "flower bath" after my name that afternoon filled me with delight. Nothing was more appealing than a little peace and quiet to process the last few days.

Tomorrow was blocked out except for morning and afternoon yoga with "Day of Silence" written in. Wednesday was a field trip in the morning for yoga practice that began at 4:30 a.m. Seriously? I saw another spa session for me that afternoon. *I bet I'm going to need that Ayurveda Chakra Dahra, whatever the hell that is.* Thursday was the final day of the program with more yoga and more rituals.

I had limited experience with the spa routine, so I was grateful that it revolved around making sure I was comfortable. A petite Balinese beauty massaged oil into my skin and then scrubbed me to within an inch of my life with an exfoliant smelling of passion fruit and mango.

Next she led me to a room with a deep steaming tub. As advertised, a layer of pink, yellow, and white frangipani flowers floated gracefully on the surface of the milky water. Stepping in, I was immediately grateful for the heat that loosened the tension in my aching limbs. A large window looked onto a small waterfall bordered by brilliant red-and-fuchsia flowering bushes. *If heaven exists, this is what it feels like.*

The Day of Silence arrived, immediately nagging at me. *What are you going to do all day?* There were no televisions at Kumara. Talking was, obviously, forbidden. "Reading prohibits reflection," according to our leader Jules, who I decided might be a cult leader after all.

With a limited menu of options, I began to write. One of the reasons I'd come on this retreat was because I'd been wondering if I wanted to keep working in IT my entire life or if I should try my hand at being an author, something that had been on the back burner for years. First I wrote about that.

I kept writing. If reflection was the name of the game, I had *a lot* to say about all this ritual hocus-pocus filling my days. I thought about how much I missed my grandmother. First I cried, then I had to stifle a laugh when I considered what she would say about my present predicament.

Delicious vegetarian meals were delivered and devoured. Surprisingly, the day passed quickly, punctuated with an amethyst sunset over the swaying palms I watched from my balcony. Silence wasn't so bad after all.

Four-thirty in the morning, that's what's bad. *What the hell is this all about?* The voice of anxiety was alive and kicking after a twenty-four hour absence. Grateful for the coffee-maker in my room, I quickly downed a cup before I left to find the bus. No one was saying much, and I was grateful for that too.

Wyan, impossibly effervescent for the hour, told us we were headed to Mount Batur forty-five minutes away. There we would have our morning yoga session outside during sunrise. He casually threw in that Mount Batur was a volcano, something exotic for most of us. Anticipation replaced anxiety.

One by one we staked out territory by unrolling a mat onto the long balcony of the inn. Settled, we watched the horizon gradually appear before us like front row patrons at the theater. We were all quietly regarding the darkness, waiting for the show to begin.

Eventually Mount Batur's distinct cone shape was backlit by burnt oranges and burnished yellows. At its base was a pale blue fluffy down of fog. Clouds shot upward rather than outward horizontally. With heads bowed to Mother Nature's beauty, we meditated before yoga began. The warmth of appreciation filled me up inside. *How did I get so lucky?*

The day cut a machete path through my jungle of ordinary concerns. After yoga and breakfast, I was asked to select a bike from a line of about twenty. Once the wheels were double-checked and it was deemed in passable condition, I was flying down that same volcano mountain for twenty-two kilometers of pure unadulterated joy. Completely fearless, it was a high I haven't had since I was ten. Tears rolled down my cheeks—which could have been the wind or the relief of the respite from my adult life.

Once we reached the base of the mountain, we took a path through several villages where we were greeted with numerous smiles and waves. "Hello! Hello!" shouted small boys and girls who ran to keep up with us. I yelled back and waved like a lunatic, happy not to be me for a few hours.

My last stop of the day was a return to the spa. Grateful for an escape from the heat, I was greeted by another petite Balinese woman who asked me to take off my sandals and undress for the *Ayurveda Chakra Dhara*. Wyan had prepped me for what to expect, because once you entered the spa English was sparse.

Normally that was fine, but I was tense before this appointment. The treatment, an ancient practice, consists of dripping oil into all seven of your *chakras*, opening the body's key energy points. The final step required placement of one's forehead under the small stream of oil for a further twenty-five minutes to open your third eye and awaken your spirit. Twenty-five minutes seemed like a long time.

Dreading what could be revealed, I undressed and lay down on the massage table. I closed my eyes as the warm oil made its way around my body. It was a pleasant languid sensation which had a relaxing effect. "Breathe deep. Close your eyes." Brief instructions were whispered in my ear. At first the only change was the bright purple I saw behind my closed lids. It then morphed to dark green tinged with gold in a lava-lamp effect. The quiet spa grew noisy outside my room. The other American, Lisa, was loudly complaining about something.

When I turned over to place my forehead under the tiny waterfall of oil, the noise increased. I could no longer tell where the noise was coming from, but I thought it might be in my head. "Too much noise!" I said, loudly. "Be quiet!" I ordered to no one in particular. My eyes were still closed and the oil kept flowing.

Finally it stopped. Small, gentle hands helped me sit up slowly, but the room spun. The therapist wrapped me in a sarong and led me to a chair. When I was seated, each foot was placed in a silver foot bowl of steaming water. I pulled the sarong around me tightly, feeling exposed. She left me there feeling like a wounded animal. When she returned, I refused to give up my sarong. Too much had been revealed. I had to protect myself.

Eventually I got up and relinquished the sarong long enough to shower. I felt like I was floating. Something inside had shifted. My internal furniture had been rearranged without my consent. Not knowing whether or not to be pleased with the new décor, I was silent on the way back to my room. All I could do was sit on the bed and let the numbness dissipate. *What the hell was that?*

Even before this day, an overwhelming amount of new sensations were coming into play in my world. Things I thought were solid were actually papier-mâché. Asian life was filled with mysterious new traditions. "You will find your way," Jules told me over dinner that night. "Retreat participants often feel that the ground has given way beneath them during their time here." He told stories of grief and healing, of abuse and recovery. By the twinkle in his eye, I knew there were many more tales he wasn't about to reveal.

I wasn't the only one who had a loose grip on her marbles. Lorraine said she had experienced intense emotions associated with the loss of a baby several years ago. For her, the oil treatment bought a sense of relief from a burden long carried. We didn't discuss it further because I still didn't know how to interpret my experience. Perhaps I'd been listening to others for too long, too many voices were shouting about what I "should do" everywhere I went. *Who could possibly think with all that noise?*

Great Hall gong

Yoga view in front of Mt. Batur at sunrise

Chapter 9
The Rat Races In

Bali didn't solve all my problems, but it gave me perspective on them. I discovered that I was capable of changing gears, of not allowing myself to dwell in negativity. Despite being in a situation that I hadn't anticipated and wished was different, it didn't have to define every single moment of every day. The trip had shaken me loose from a spell cast over me by the poor economic climate and loss of control.

This wasn't the first time I'd found myself in a foreign land without the independence I held dear. Given my propensity for travel, it wouldn't likely be the last. *I will turn this around.* We were expected to remain in Singapore for years to come. There simply was no other option than success and success, in my world meant gainful, well-paid work. Four months in, the question of personal satisfaction began to lose its luster. I wanted a paycheck.

Marla appeared at the right time. She located me through a friend from my German days and I was grateful. "I can't tell you how much I appreciate this, Derek. I was beginning to lose my mind."

"It's my pleasure. Honestly we don't have enough CRM skills in house, so it's good for us too. You know, a lot has changed in the software since your time in Germany. The learning curve will be steep."

"That's never stopped me before. Can you send me the most up-to-date material you have? I'll dive into it before I meet the client."

"Sure." He hesitated. "There's something else too."

"I'm all ears."

"Watch out for Marla. I've heard she can be a real shark."

"What does that mean?"

"Just watch yourself."

"Okay. I'll do that." Butterflies appeared in my stomach. I knew I was taking a risk working as a contractor for the first time. There was no corporate wing over me anymore. I was working without a net. "Send me the documents and I'll get busy. Talk to you later."

Derek hung up and I thought about his words for a few minutes. I didn't like the sound of them, but I had to start somewhere. I had lost limbs to sharks in the Netherlands because I didn't see them coming. This time I'd been warned.

I shook Marla's hand on the steps of the Somerset building I'd be working in. The commute had taken literally five minutes from my condo. She was older than I expected, with a diminutive stature and thick glasses. "Hello, Jennifer. It's a pleasure to meet you."

"You too, Marla. I appreciate the opportunity," I said from my towering height.

"This is going to be a challenge. I hope you're up for it."

"Always."

We claimed a table in the nearby coffee shop and she proceeded to give me the lowdown after we retrieved our coffee. Once I stopped wondering how anyone drinks a steaming hot beverage outdoors in this country, I was able to focus.

"Another company has done the CRM implementation at Vos Power, an Indian firm. The client wants us to perform a quality assessment on the work they've done. We will determine the format of the assessment together and you will deliver the content."

"That shouldn't be a problem. I'll need to ask a lot of questions. How long do I have?"

"Ten days."

"Then I better get to it," I said with more confidence than I felt.

"Vos is expecting you tomorrow at 8:30 a.m. They will set you up with a badge to get in and out of the building, and a system ID so you can poke around. A woman named Bee will also introduce you to the key stakeholders and contractors you need to talk to. Let me know if you need anything."

And that was it. I wasn't used to consulting anymore, and I'd forgotten that time is money. I would be paid handsomely, but I had to perform quickly. There wasn't much time to adjust to the environment, the people, or the system—let alone analyze it—but I had no choice. If I wanted to get off the ground in Singapore, this was an open door I had to walk through. Derek's last piece of advice ran through my mind "Singaporeans are very precious. They don't take well to criticism or harsh treatment of any kind. It's not like Europe." You can say that again.

Bee was all smiles at reception the next morning. "Come this way, Jennifer, I'll take you to your desk. Once you get settled we will meet the rest of the team at nine in the main conference room down that hall on the left. See you there!" She waved as she left. The others, four very young employees in the same group of desks giggled when I said "Good morning." They didn't reply. They just giggled and covered their faces.

Rather than risk the same reaction to something with more gravitas than a morning greeting, I turned to the PC on my desk and switched it on. Quickly I reviewed my notes on the key areas the assessment would cover and entered the user name and password Bee had provided. Like my new Singaporean office mates, the cursor blinked but said nothing. I entered it again and got the same reaction.

At two minutes to nine, I walked into the conference room expecting it to be empty. To my surprise, I was the last to arrive. How a room full of people managed to stay that quiet remains a mystery. "Good morning," I said, pulling out my seat.

"Good morning," said Bee, who was clearly the designated speaker.

We went around the table and I wrote down names as best I could. In Chinese introductions, last names proceed first names. Though I'd read that, it was confusing when writing them down. Business cards were passed, always with both hands, always requiring actual reading and not just throwing into the briefcase as in western meetings.

I went to the whiteboard and drew a map of my process for the software analysis. When I asked for confirmation on the process and the subject matter, the room went silent a second time. A man from the Indian software implementation firm spoke up.

"What makes you qualified for this analysis?" he challenged.

Surprised by the question after I'd already introduced myself, I mentioned specific CRM projects I'd worked on and led. Remembering that he wasn't the one paying the bill for my efforts—and rather the one whose efforts were being scrutinized—I left it at that.

"Can anyone call IT to help get my user ID working?" I changed the subject. Four hands shot up in the air. "I would really appreciate that," I said with a sickeningly sweet smile.

Bee and I left the room and she filled me in on the weekly meetings I'd need to attend and individual sessions which were already arranged. It was a good thing they had made some plans for my time, because by late that afternoon I still had no working ID on the system.

At lunch the next day with Bee and Mara, another Vos employee working on the IT project, I was again grilled about my experience.

"You are new to Singapore?" Bee wanted to know.

"Yes, I arrived here a few months ago from the Netherlands."

"What did you do there?"

"I was the EMEA Program Manager for a mobile and wireless hardware company. Before that I was the Service Manager for a company rolling out VDS software in thirty-five countries. And before that I led VDS projects for a large consultancy in Amsterdam and the US. Should I go on?" I said somewhat snarkily. What mattered was the project at hand, not where I'd been for the last ten years of my life.

"But you did not work in Singapore?" Mara continued the party line.

"This is my first engagement after taking some time off."

"Oh," said the chorus of Bee and Mara sneaking a glance at one another.

"Let's eat. Do you like Singaporean food?" Mara wanted to know.

It should be said, I am terrible at small talk. Idle chit-chat is why I'd rather work on my own any day of the week rather than sitting in an office gabbing with my teammates. I know, I know—it sounds like I am not a team player. But that isn't the case. I just want the team to be intelligent and continually moving forward at my pace. I do not want to discuss which noodles are tastier when I have less than ten days to accomplish my goal.

The Rat Races In

My one attempt failed. I told them that I had been trying to figure out how to make some of the delicious dishes I'd tried since arriving. Out came the hands over faces to stifle the giggles once again.

"Oh no. It is much better to eat out." Bee said knowingly. "It is very difficult to do this correctly."

Had she been spying on me at the Fair Price panicking about the odd veggies and crazy eggs? Did she know I was a miserable cook? Of course neither of these things could be true. In Singapore I was merely to accept those domains that were not mine to enter—and the kitchen wasn't the only territory on the list.

At the end of day two I had a user ID and login that worked. I'd lost two full days of correspondence, questions, and system review, thinking that I would be able to get straight answers from the client team and the implementation company, MBE. I would have to uncover the facts myself, based on the agreed design documentation and the reality of what went into the system.

Bee did have something in her bonnet. I'm sorry about the pun but there is no other way to put it. She wanted to know how a future process should be designed, in the system and kept buzzing back at me to solve it for her. Later I understood that Queen Bee had posed this question to every single VDS employee who came within striking distance for the past several months. Marla had told me system architecture wasn't my role. Reviewing existing architecture was. Bee was suspicious.

Eventually I did get time with the Indian implementation team members. Every question I posed was answered with a new question. I felt like I was talking to myself. Halim from MBE wanted to go to lunch also. The only nearby place that met the dietary requirements of Halim and Josha was the Thai restaurant on Killiney Road.

"What are your results so far?" Halim wanted a preview of the assessment I'd barely begun. "I've just started, so there are no results yet."

"When you have a problem, you will come to us." It was a statement, not a question.

"Uh huh," I stammered. I wasn't only uncomfortable with the command from someone I didn't work for but also the fact that Josha was walking behind us—a pattern which persisted even when I slowed my pace to allow him to catch up.

Halim went on talking. Thankfully about himself and not continuing the interrogation of our first meeting. I found it odd that he would want to expound on where he went to school, his degree, and his certifications to a near total stranger. Why did he think I cared? Was it because I hadn't responded to his earlier questions about me with the same ones of him? Was that part of the dance now? I had no idea, but I wished timid, quiet Josha would hurry up and catch us. He never did.

The remaining days continued in a similar fashion. Bee buzzed. Halim practiced hubris. I said as little as possible and read, reviewed, and analyzed. I began formatting the presentation that I would deliver at the end of the period. In truth, though the Vos team and the MBE team appeared in a constant tug of war for authority, there was no smoking gun on this software implementation. There were no time bombs that would explode as the system gained more users and data. Sure, there were recommendations for improvement, but they were of a general nature. The things that every project suffers from.

Marla didn't want to hear it.

"The client is not going to be happy that they are paying you for ten days and you have five bullet points for them to address," she scolded.

"I would think they would be pleased to find out that the job was done well," I countered.

"I'm sure you can find more."

Do you want me to make things up? I didn't say it, but I wanted to. As I've mentioned, I don't enjoy talking about nothing. I enjoy it even less when someone is paying good money for my advice. The last thing I wanted was to water down the good result of the assessment with bullshit. The last thing Marla wanted was MDE to look good. Then there would be less reason for VDS involvement and sales for Marla.

To appease her, I created a general page of project best practices that they should employ in the next phases. These would keep them on the right track. I wasn't about to create problems where there were none. Because I didn't follow her lead, I knew there would be no further work forthcoming from Marla, even though she enjoyed frequently dangling that carrot.

What I found most amusing was the final presentation of my findings to the management team. Even though the result was predominantly positive, Halim took serious offense to my review. So much so that he burst out in the middle of my presentation to defend himself vigorously. What did he use to defend the work of his team, you ask? The many years of education and training they had combined, the big name Singapore projects they had delivered, and his deep dissatisfaction at such a personal attack. Specifics? Don't be silly.

There was no attack, but if this was the reaction from some general advice, I didn't want to see what followed the illumination of serious defects in their system. I'd been in the game long enough to know that no project is ever perfect, and the fault of that can lie with the clients as easily as the implementation partner. Did they expect to circumvent any potential improvements by merely reciting their credentials? Yes. Yes, it appears they did.

Taking back the floor, I told Vos that what they chose to do with the information was up to them, but leaving these items to fester would increase the likelihood of problems down the road. Marla didn't find a puppet. MBE didn't find a pawn. I didn't find continued employment because I wasn't prepared to bow down to win more work for myself.

Naively, I had thought I would be free of corporate politics by acting as an independent contractor. It shouldn't have been news that you can only keep working if you play the game, but it was. Is it the Buddhists who believe that you keep repeating the same mistakes in each successive afterlife until you finally learn the lesson? If so, they were definitely on to something.

Chapter 10
Space Invasion

My brief return to the corporate world was far from the illustrious beginning I'd hoped for. Within a few weeks, expectations evaporated as though they were never there to begin with. My pace slowed and I became lethargic. My ego didn't care much for what was, or should I say *was not*, happening.

With a goal to meet and clients to work with, I had felt like myself again: the go-getter, the woman who refuses to fail, and the one with all the answers. Without those things, I found less and less reason to get out of bed. The depression which was slithering into my Asian life wasn't easy to fight off.

The only time to exercise outdoors in Singapore is early morning—very early morning. By 7:30 the humidity is on the rise. I'd read about a place not far from my condo called Fort Canning Park. According to my guidebook, Sir Stamford Raffles, the founder of British Singapore, chose Fort Canning for his residence after landing in 1819. He had to change the name of the hill from Bukit Larangan because the locals feared climbing what to them was "Forbidden Hill," an ancestral burial place.

Hastily throwing on shorts and a t-shirt and pulling my hair into a pony tail, I couldn't wait to check it out. I'd rarely ventured this direction so far, and the walk would be more interesting than the glitz of Orchard Road. The neighborhoods of Oxley Road were older and filled with tiny mysteries.

The façade of old Singapore's shophouse-style home reveals nothing. Chinese characters in gold or severe black brush strokes give non-Mandarin speakers nothing to go on. A row of shoes neatly lined up at the doorstep hinted at its occupants. No movement or light beyond the front windows deepened my curiosity. Inside activities were well-hidden from prying eyes outside. I saw only one person outside his apartment—a man busily blow-drying and brushing his dog. The husky panted through a sloppy grin, reveling in the attention despite the intense heat.

At River Valley Road the area became more commercial and bland, until I happened on a row of massage parlors. Red-and-purple painted doors hung open, inviting in passers-by, but I saw no one. The pricelist hung on the door without mention of anything seedy. Color photos of busty women taped up next to it asked potential customers to use their imaginations.

Crossing the main intersection of River Valley and Clemenceau Roads, Fort Canning came into view. A sloping hill covered in lush greenery and tropical flowers beckoned. As I crossed and began looking for a way up, I found the massive concrete staircase which led to the top. A jogger ran past me and up the steep cracked stairs of death. His degree of fitness made me question my intention momentarily. *Don't be stupid.* I told myself. *You don't have to run.* It was a good thing I wasn't racing that guy because I counted two hundred and fifty moss-covered steps before I made it to the summit.

Dripping in sweat, I found two older Chinese men doing pull-ups and stretches. *If seventy-year-olds can handle this, so can I.* I walked along a winding path that circled the hill. What intrigued me most were the giant sweeping tree limbs that covered the path near the top. Their massive trunks were hundreds of years old. What they had seen of Singapore's history flashed through my mind: Malay traders from the 14th century, Stamford Raffles and his cronies, the building of a modern day high-tech metropolis.

Through gaps in their protective embrace, I looked onto buzzing Clarke Quay and a sea of concrete. Perhaps it's "forbidden" because those who stand on this hill, surrounded by the quiet jungle past, will long for it, eschewing modernity and all its trappings. At last there was silence. Occasionally, I was passed by a fellow walker or runner. No tourists were here at this early hour.

Space Invasion

Walking further, blissfully shaded by my new tree friends, I passed an enormous cannon perched on the hillside. Though it hadn't fired a shot since the days of colonial ceremony, it stood at the ready. Perhaps it too longed for the past, for its usefulness.

Fort Canning Green yawned out below. A broken path led downwards. On my left stood curious whitewashed columns and two miniature cupolas. To my right, a brick wall embedded with tombstones. Meandering down the path, I read the epitaphs of the first British settlers—mostly from the middle and late eighteen hundreds. They hadn't lived long.

What did they think of this part of the world? Uprooted from the rigid social and legal protocols of Great Britain and placed in the jungle? Was thirty-seven year old Joseph the type to attempt communication with the locals whose language wasn't his? Or did he dominate them and consider them inferior? And twenty-five-year-old beloved wife Catherine, did she love her new home or despise it during her short life?

I consumed every inch of the park within an hour, grateful for the miraculous discovery of a place where trees outnumbered people. Bird songs were the music. I picked pink and yellow frangipani flowers and inhaled their heady perfume. Not wanting to give up my newfound place of solitude entirely, I carefully placed one behind each ear and wandered home smiling.

* * *

Summer raised the temperature to something beyond my comprehension. Books were devoured in my apartment rather than poolside. When I couldn't stand being inside, I went to the movies at the cinema two streets over. The price of a matinee ticket was five Singapore dollars. Even I could afford to go often.

I met David for lunch in the CBD occasionally to give myself something to look forward to. A Japanese restaurant quickly became the favorite. The bento box was new to me. It reminded me of the compartmentalized Muppet lunchbox I carried in grade school, with vastly different contents. One section for sashimi, one section for tempura veggies, one for steaming miso, and a bowl of fat sticky rice to mix with chicken teriyaki. The small portions were fun and filling.

I looked forward to spending this extra hour with him. David's hours steadily increased and it was often after nine when he came home. When he did get there, he was exhausted. As glad as I was to see him, I resented having been stuck at home all the time. I especially resented trying to cook a dinner that went uneaten. Despite my efforts to control it, resentment bubbled over in the peaceful happy midday hour I planned with my husband.

"What do you want me to do about it?" he growled. "It's not like I have a choice."

"I don't want you to do anything other than let me know you're going to be late or you're eating at the office. Why should I waste my time cooking when I hate it and you're not even there to eat it?"

"It's not like you have somewhere else you have to be."

Ouch! He knew how badly I wanted a job. "I wish I did." Tears came to my eyes and I willed them not to fall.

As we stood outside, about to say goodbye, planes suddenly swooped low over the city. I looked up to see gray military fighter jets, three or four of them, blast across the city skyline. Once they passed overhead, I felt their vibration pass through me. "What the hell was that?" I had to yell to be heard above it.

"A guy on my team was talking about this. They're practicing for the National Day celebration in August."

It was only June.

"Oh."

"I have to go. I love you." He bent down for a quick kiss.

"I love you, too."

As I walked back to the MRT, the jets made another pass. Looking up, I saw a giant red-and-white starred flag trailing behind a military helicopter and wondered why they started practicing so early.

Hordes of suited and skirted office workers exited the MRT to return to work as I entered. Beautiful, long-haired Asian women giggled to one another in groups. Young men joked to one another. Slowly I descended the escalator, jealous of every single one of them. I could never compete with the looks of these women, and I no longer had my independence like the guys. In my sweaty cotton shirt and shorts, hair frizzed by the ridiculous humidity, I didn't even recognize myself.

Maybe it was my appalling wardrobe that led me to it, I didn't know, but I walked into one of the malls close to home. In a store I'd never seen before, I ran into the wife of one of David's clients. We'd been briefly introduced at the cultural session, but hadn't said much to one another. Marina was petite with the wiry frame of an athlete. A head full of curls on a smaller body trailed behind her, obviously lost in the racks of women's clothing taller than he was.

"Hi Marina, how are you?"

I thought maybe I'd spooked her. Her hand flew to her chest. "Oh hello, Jennifer. Nice to see you again. We are doing well, aren't we, Daniel?" She looked to her son whose freckled face opened up into a toothy grin.

"Glad to hear it. How are you handling this heat?" I was curious if I was the only one who thought I would pass out on a daily basis.

"It does seem to be getting worse, doesn't it? I thought we'd already maxxed out. My hair isn't appreciating the humidity one bit!"

She did have a lot of hair. Pretty as it was, her thick black mane had to feel like a heating blanket in the sun. "I know what you mean," I said, pointing to my own messy do.

"We should have lunch some time! I was thinking about getting a group together soon. Would you like to join?"

"Absolutely. Here, let me write down my email address. I don't have a local phone yet and I never remember the house number." I scribbled on a piece of paper.

"Great. I'll be in touch. We need to get Daniel something to eat, don't we?" The curls flopped in agreement.

"Don't let me hold you up. I'll look forward to catching up over lunch." I turned and headed out with a small wave.

I hope this time goes better than the last, said the little voice in my head. By now I had nothing to lose.

David came home early that night, at eight rather than after nine.

"We're invited to a barbeque," he announced. "Tom and Laura are having people over to their place to celebrate Tom's birthday."

I remembered them: a tall Australian guy married to a pretty blonde Canadian. We'd met in passing on a Saturday out shopping. "Where do they live?"

"On River Valley Road somewhere. The party is this weekend."

"Okay. I'll get some wine to take along." I offered.

I didn't know Tom and Laura, but they seemed nice. At least I was forming some sort of social circle. Granted, progress was slow, but in the Netherlands it was also a slow process with several false starts. Sometimes I felt like an alien who belonged nowhere. All I could do was keep trying.

That weekend we found taste of home for David. It was a Belgian café at Robertson Quay. He's not from Belgium, but close enough to have a lot of similarities. We both love Belgian beer, *frites*, and mussels. That was enough for us.

The night was cool and there was a breeze coming off the river. Stars had begun to dot the night sky and we were laughing about the million and one ways Singapore was weird. A couple came by the table, "Hey David." Both of them had red hair and he was about the same age as David. She looked a bit older.

"Hey! What are you guys doing? Want to join us?" David said. "This is John and Madeline. Guys, my wife Jennifer."

"Hi." I barely looked at them. Couldn't we have one night without the project hijacking it?

"Nice to meet you. Sorry, David, but we have dinner reservations already. I just wanted to say hi."

"Cool. Have fun then."

David turned back to me. My face was hot. "Really? You need to hang out with people from work even when you're not there?"

"I was just saying hi."

"Did you have to invite them to sit down?"

"They didn't!"

"Obviously I know that. I guess time together means a lot more to me than it does to you."

"What's the big deal? Did you want me to be rude to them?" His tone was getting louder.

"It isn't rude not to include other people in a dinner with your wife whom you rarely see. Most people would consider that normal!"

"I have no idea what your problem is."

"Then I think it is time to go." I stepped down off the chair.

"Wait," he grabbed my hand. "I like Madeline and I wanted you to meet her. I know you're having trouble meeting people you can relate to."

"It would have been much better if you had just said that to begin with."

"I know. I'm sorry. Please sit down. Relax. Let's get another beer." He signaled the waiter.

The heat sapped me of the strength to argue, and I sat down. I was glad I had put my cards on the table and that we had partly salvaged the evening. I was tired of sitting around waiting to see my own husband and even more tired of his incessant talk about work. The problem was, I didn't seem to have anything interesting to say myself.

Tom and Laura's barbeque was the following day. Twelve people lounged on the lawn and at the riverside picnic table a few blocks from where we lived. Gregarious and charming, Tom was celebrating his thirtieth birthday. We met more people from the project and chatted over cold bottles of Tiger beer and chilled sauvignon blanc.

Laura introduced me to a stylish Swiss blonde named Linda. I was surprised how quickly we hit it off.

"I couldn't wait to leave Europe, so I understand how you felt there." She looked over her shoulder to see where David was before she continued. "The Dutch really are difficult. Everyone I know who has gone to work in our office in The Hague has had a tough time."

Did I just hear what I thought I heard? Someone, a European no less, just agreed with me that fitting into Dutch culture is a near impossibility? "Please go on," I said. "Tell me how it was for others."

"Well, I didn't work there myself, but I know that everyone who goes there from another country leaves in a short period of time."

"I suppose I should be proud of lasting five years then!" I laughed.

"No really, I'm not joking. Everyone talks about it at work."

Perhaps I should be hanging out with these project people after all. I might learn a thing or two circulating in such a mixed bag of cultures, rather than having to go it alone all the time.

"Linda, you made my night." I smiled and squeezed her hand.

"Thank you for being honest about that. So many people want to smooth over the truth when it's difficult to talk about."

"You don't have to worry about that with me, Jennifer. I'm part German, remember?" She laughed too.

"Thank God for that!" Relief at being allowed to be myself for even a minute swept through me.

Laura proved to be a fantastic cook. Everyone heaped their plates and we move to a covered area to dig in. Marc, a Frenchman, introduced himself and sat down across from me.

"Personally, I think we are always being watched," He said. "Surveillance is crazy here. Have you ever noticed how many cameras there are everywhere? Just look around the MRT station next time you're there. Big Brother's got nothing on this place."

I gave David a wide-eyed glimpse as he continued.

"I also heard that many of the taxi drivers are undercover police. That's why they are always asking so many questions."

"Why would they care about us?" I jumped in. "We are nothing special here."

"It doesn't matter. What's important is maintaining the status quo. Why do you think there are fines for this and fines for that? The Singapore government likes controlling what its people do. Foreigners, with their different ideas and free speech, are a threat to that." He sounded like he knew what he was talking about, at least more than I did.

"Do you think they listen in on overseas phone conversations?" I wondered aloud.

"It wouldn't surprise me in the slightest."

That was definitely food for thought. Laura, armed with a wide grin and a layered chocolate birthday cake, rounded the corner before the conversation turned too paranoid. Tom pretended we weren't completely off key and demanded everyone sing "Happy Birthday" louder, before we were granted a fat frosted slice.

The night ended far too quickly. I had so many questions that went unanswered.

"Do you think Marc was right about the things he said?" I asked David on the way home.

"I have no idea. Honestly, it wouldn't surprise me either. It's not like people here are free to do what they want. How else would they be controlled?"

I had to agree that he had a point. We had seen Speaker's Corner, a square in town that was designated for protests and demonstrations by the people of Singapore. Every time I passed—it was empty.

Singapore National Day practice, shot from my condo

Chapter 11
Lion City

Jets continued to fly overhead periodically. When I was in the condo, I raced to grab my camera. Fifteen floors up, the view was better, though the noise more intense. No matter how hard I tried, I couldn't catch a decent shot of that huge Singapore flag flapping past our windows.

Soon after the mid-afternoon air raids began, another practice session was added. Every Saturday night, the fireworks show was rehearsed over Marina Bay. David's colleagues had told him about this too, so we were ready on the appointed evening with our cameras in the living room. Sure enough, booming vibrations thundered across the bay at eight o'clock on the dot. Red-and-white blooms sparkled in the night sky one after another. I thought since it was a rehearsal, it would be brief, but it went on for a full thirty minutes.

Who practices fireworks? It was bewildering. The sessions were publicly attended, so security and safety forces had to be implemented in full measure. The cost of the fireworks alone had to run into the millions. Was preventing a mistimed *kaboom* worth all that expense? If it meant the organizers would not lose face, yes. The idea remained incomprehensible to me.

In addition to the months of entertainment leading up to it, National Day gifted us with a long weekend too. On Saturday night an Aussie friend of David threw a birthday party at her building's rooftop common area. Champagne bottles popped like mini fireworks throughout the night and the breeze played with pink streamers and silver balloons.

The birthday girl, Jac, was an Aussie whom David had met in The Hague, along with her English boyfriend, before we'd arrived in Singapore. I didn't know her well, but she was friendly and outgoing. I was still insecure because my professional status had been temporarily revoked and replaced with "wife" status and my social interactions thus far were unsuccessful, but I tried to stay positive. Jac and Javed knew how to host a party. A friend manned the barbeque, turning out satay by the heaping platter, and drinks flowed from all directions.

The bubbly blonde birthday girl looked perfect in her flowing maxi dress and pink heart-shaped glasses. Everywhere there was pink, her favorite color. Perhaps sensing my insecurity, she pulled me by the hand and introduced me to several people. I met a Kiwi named Penny, two chilled-out Germans, and a host of other characters throughout the evening. David chatted with a fellow Dutchie, and we had such a good time that we were among the last to leave.

Sunday the champagne devil played the drums in my head, but I felt good about the night before. Finally I had met people I could relate to. As a whole, the group was experienced and well-traveled. I got tips about exciting places to visit nearby and laughed a lot. My hopes were raised for the first time in weeks.

When National Day rolled around on a Monday, we watched the celebration on television. After Hong Kong, I wasn't eager to stand in the middle of millions of celebrating Singaporeans. As expected, the orchestra performed without a single off-key note, jets cut precise swaths above the applauding crowd, and colorful explosions dotted the sky in choreographed perfection. Teary-eyed Singaporeans gleefully waved tiny red-and-white flags. Not a moment of the unpredictable surfaced.

It was strange to watch such rehearsed joviality. I thought back on the American equivalent, Independence Day, and remembered my mother grabbing up our blankets and my dad pulling me quickly to the car as fireworks at Sherrod Park went wrong when we were too close to the action. Over thirty years later, I remembering how my little heart had pounded with excitement.

Lion City

In the Netherlands, as the clock struck midnight on New Year's Eve, fireworks had exploded from every doorway and every roof.

The noise was deafening, but the sight spectacular. I'll never forget how beautifully insane *Oud en Nieuw* was. What was life without spontaneity?

After National Day was thoroughly and perfectly celebrated, Singapore was about to make history as the location for the first Night Race in Formula One racing. I was no car racing enthusiast, but give me a reason to celebrate and cheap tickets to witness history in the making, and I am there. I met Jac and David at the bar below their office for a Friday happy hour to pre-celebrate before walking to the track.

Prior to this, I had only been on the fringes of David's team at work. That was close enough. Now I walked into a sea of unknown faces dressed in work attire, revving up for the race. Jac was standing next to Penny, the pretty brunette from New Zealand I'd joked with at the rooftop party. They handed me a large glass of white wine and introduced me to other women working at the project, a Dutch-Ghanaian named Isobel and a woman from Texas whose first name was the same as mine.

David eventually wandered over to join the ladies and bring us French fries. He squeezed my hand and ordered me another drink. I listened to the girls discuss stock options and thought this was a far better place for me than the mommy crowd. Along with the glass of wine, David handed me the yellow lanyard with my F1 ticket for the night. I'd never felt so excited about anything having to do with cars.

The night was humid, but so was every night. We debated a taxi, but Friday nights are notoriously difficult for getting one, so we walked in the direction of the Fullerton Hotel to find an entrance gate. Jac pulled a pair of flip flops from her bag to replace her work heels—and I noted her technique. It was the first night the track was open, and practice rounds were starting. The entry gate wasn't crowded, but David's giant camera bag drew suspicion and had to be examined. Jac and I tried to determine the best direction while we waited.

At the turn in the road, directly after Cavenagh Bridge, we found our circuit sweet spot. We had a perfect view as cars roared one after another around the bend. The sole obstruction was the temporary fence erected to protect the crowd. David pulled out his Nikon and the shutter snapped frantically as the cars flew past so quickly you didn't want to blink. The air was electric, powered by the hum of an enormous hidden hive until the metal swarm passed us once again.

I've never experienced anything so loud, save a few AC/DC concerts in my past. On my left, I waited for the cars to come again. To the right, journalists and Asian car junkies held up camera lenses the size of small cannons. Seeing the same thing, David experienced lens envy for the first time. The little-boy longing in his eyes made me smile.

Eventually the novelty wore off and we ventured around to other areas of the track to look for a better viewpoint. At street level, it was impossible to see what was happening. Grand stands had been erected for better, more expensive viewing, and hotel rooms with the good fortune to overlook the Marina Bay circuit had dangerously full balconies. They went for a thousand dollars a night. Random viewing screens on the grounds did the trick for us.

With our three-day passes, we decided to reconvene the next night. The buzz was exciting, but I wasn't converted to a car enthusiast. Every evening ended at a waterfront bar, listening to the circuit cacophony and draining glasses. It wasn't my first choice for weekend entertainment, but it was a Singapore surprise I enjoyed far more than I had expected to.

Chapter 12
One Night in Bangkok

Late October brought our fourth wedding anniversary. David conspired with Thai colleagues for advice on where to visit. The answer was, overwhelmingly, Bangkok.

Exotic, mysterious, and dangerous were the words that came to mind when he mentioned it. All of my favorite things. I began researching online immediately to find the cheapest tickets and the best hotel. Options available in Thailand's capital are nothing short of mind-blowing. I surfed the net for hours to plan the weekend. David got a restaurant recommendation for our anniversary dinner and I picked the top of the line hotel chain, Banyan Tree.

We landed on a Friday night as the city reached its weekend fever pitch. Our first stop was Vertigo, the rooftop bar at our hotel. If I am honest, it was my main reason for picking the place to begin with. I love nice hotels, but I love saving money more—especially when I'm not making any. We changed clothes and took the elevator up sixty-one floors. As we exited, my heart leapt into my throat. Walking the path toward the bar along the building's edge was dizzying. I had to sit down.

It was already crowded, but two open bar seats came to the rescue. I looked over the restaurant to see enormous lightning rods interspersed along the edges. Every table was occupied with diners seemingly oblivious to their possible impending doom.

The bartender handed me a cocktail list the thickness of a Dostoevsky novel and we paged through it. David went for a local beer and I ordered a Cosmopolitan. I felt it fit the mood. Swinging my legs around, I took in the view behind me. It was even more overwhelming, a sea of lights that spread further than those of Los Angeles. Amazing.

David and I looked onto the metropolis and tried to determine what to do next. Hotel bars, especially this one, were too pricey and we had a lot to see. He was told of a nightspot area that was generally free of the things Bangkok is notorious for: scammers and thievery. We took a cab that direction.

The first time in any big city is a crap shoot. You need to make your choices wisely. Walking, we passed bar after bar, many of them too shady-looking to appeal. Though it looked potentially boring, we went into a British pub-style bar to have a drink and hopefully get the word on the street about where else to go.

We struck up a conversation with two young Brits sitting at the bar and told them it was our first night in town.

"You have to go to Checkers!" the blonde guy said.

"Oh yeah, you don't want to miss that," seconded the brown-haired one.

"What's that?" I asked.

"There is no way to describe it. We just have to go." Matt, the blonde, had been living in Bangkok for a year. "Are you up for it?"

I had no idea. I looked at David. "Why not?" he said.

It was weird to be heading off to destinations unknown with two strangers, but Matt and Steve seemed harmless. David and I had already wandered around aimlessly for half an hour before choosing the pub. The last thing either of us wanted was to spend the rest of the night doing the same thing.

Soon we were walking into a carpark. I expected we would be getting into an elevator somewhere, but we didn't. We just kept walking through the rows of cars. *What the hell?* For a minute I entertained the thought that we were being led somewhere we *really* didn't want to be—and then we arrived. Milk crates turned sideways to form shelves comprised the wall on one side, stuffed with the belongings of presumed patrons. Speakers thumped inside, accompanied by occasional gleeful shouts from the crowd.

One Night in Bangkok

"It's three hundred *baht* to get in and inside we'll share a bottle." Matt, our ringleader, explained.

Quickly calculating that to be ten bucks, David handed over the money. "Okay."

"Is vodka good with you guys?" Steve asked, talking to the waitress who appeared from nowhere. It was extremely dark inside, but disco lights floated by often enough for me to notice he was actually talking to her well-endowed chest rather than her face.

"Anything's fine as long as there's ice and something to mix with." I answered. David was rendered mute, shell-shocked by the extremely lopsided female to male ratio.

"I wouldn't use the ice," Matt advised.

Then I remembered we couldn't drink the water in Thailand. A bottle of Absolut arrived on the table, delivered by the woman with the massive boobs. The three guys split the bill and I poured a stiff vodka cranberry. On stage, a band covered eighties tunes and kept the crowd on its feet.

Standing taller than most of the others, David drew stares from the local female tribe. He was clearly enjoying the attention, with more than one woman attempting to pull him to the dance floor. Matt and Steve chose their dance partners carefully, but still it was always the females who approached them and not vice versa. It was expected that the dances would lead to something more.

I stood and stared, realizing we were in a carpark brothel bar. The men were nearly all foreigners and I was one of a handful of foreign women. The rest of the females were tiny and Asian, miniature despite their spiked heels. Black eyeliner and sleek hair, they prowled for prey. David went to the men's room and I watched them grab his arm as he returned. Shaking his head, but smiling, he laughed it off. A few of the women tossed me sideways glances, checking to see if I was looking for company. I wasn't.

With the bottle emptied, David and I had had our fill. Enough drinks. Enough weirdness. Enough fending off predators. Enough noise. We thanked our tour guides, who were entwined and barely noticed, and left. Walking again through the car park, there was nothing to do but laugh.

"We would never have found that place without those guys."

"I know," I agreed. "How freaky was that?"

"Definitely freaky, but I'm glad we went."

"Me too." I took his hand and we found a taxi to take us home.

Saturday morning was spent at the Chatuchak Market, a place so massive that it defies imagination. Eight thousand stalls sitting on over thirty-five sprawling acres stuffed with anything and everything imaginable. Housewares, silk goods, and flowers were among the expected. Reptiles, puppies with clothes, and unidentifiable insects were among the surprises. I was beginning to understand Bangkok's well-earned reputation for the weird and wonderful.

In the afternoon, we took the MRT to a station near Wat Pho, the majestic reclining Buddha. The heat was too extreme and the city too large to walk. Within minutes, we exited the subway into the glaring midday sun. From the station we had only to walk a few blocks to our destination, but they were very long blocks. I realized that those Asian women with the parasols weren't so silly after all, when there was no protection from the fierce rays for twenty minutes of walking.

Street vendors are savvy. They were selling chilled bottled water by the cartload to the throng of passers-by, myself included. I bought four bottles and David and I quickly chugged down one apiece. The others were stuck into our bags for later. A Thai man ran up to us as we approached the entrance.

"Closed today," he said anxiously.

"Sorry, what?" David asked.

"Holiday today. Cannot enter."

We looked at each other, both having noticed plenty of tourists entering this exact same gate only minutes before.

"You come with me and my friend," said the man, pointing to a *tuk-tuk*. "We can go to another temple close by. Easy."

Tuk-tuks are motorized steel mini-wagons that buzz across town short distances. His "friend" smiled and waved our direction. His gold tooth glinted in the sun.

"No thanks," I said as we started walking away. He didn't come after us or raise his voice.

When we were further away, I looked back to see him talking to another pair of tourists. They were laughing and getting in the tuk-tuk. As we reached the entrance, a line of people waited to buy tickets. The temple was not closed.

"What was that all about?" David scratched his head.

"I have no idea." I said, handing over my baht to the ticket agent. "There had to be something up with that, but I don't know what."

While David fiddled with his camera equipment, I watched as several teenage girls were handed shawls to cover their shoulders. Long ugly skirts with elastic waistbands could be rented to go over too-short shorts. I was grateful my khaki capris went past my knees.

Entering the temple, the hum of the crowd outside turned to a reverent silence inside. Barefoot, we tried to take in the Buddha first with our eyes. At over fifty feet high, it was a challenge. His golden face, relaxed and omnipotent, smiled down on us. The result was an internal question: *Did I deserve to be here?* I didn't know much about Buddhism. I only knew that I was impressed. The scale of devotion it took to create this and the over four hundred other *wats* that Bangkok is home to was staggering.

Lining the wall opposite the Buddha were one hundred and eight lustrous bronze bowls, symbolizing the number of positive tasks he completed to reach enlightenment. Coins were dropped into the bowls as offerings, each one reverberating loudly in the silent chamber.

How many positive tasks have I completed? I thought to myself.

Churches had a similar effect on me. I was often tempted to see if I measured up in sacred places. At least in a church I understood the general expectations. Here I had no measuring stick, but I wanted the look that Buddha had. Peaceful. I didn't expect to be all-knowing nor enlightened, but not questioning myself every minute of every day would be a start. Funny where your mind goes when you have to be quiet.

Not getting in anyone's tuk-tuk, we walked back to the MRT in another round of brutalizing rays. Finally we hailed a cab and went directly to the hotel. The previous night's action adding to our exhaustion, we needed some hours in a cool dark hotel room to rest up for Bangkok's buffet of the unpredictable.

David made all the arrangements for our anniversary dinner, conspiring with Thai friends at work. I was beyond curious what the night had in store, but ready for anything. It certainly couldn't be weirder than the previous night. He told me to make sure my sandals had a back to them, no flip-flops, and to wear "something nice." It wasn't much to go on.

The white-gloved concierge directed a taxi our way.

"State Tower, please."

"Yes, sir."

David, dressed in a dark brown linen shirt and brown pants I'd given him for his birthday, grinned at me. "This should be good." I smiled back.

Less than ten minutes later, we arrived at the gleaming front lobby of Lebua State Tower. There were people everywhere, *from* everywhere. It was definitely an international hot spot. This time David punched the button for the sixty-third floor with words Sirocco and Sky Bar in script next to it. Bangkok sure liked living in the clouds.

The hustle of activity on level sixty-three was intense. David walked to the maître d' under the sign for Sirocco while I peeked inside. Waiters in spotless black-and-white uniforms carried tantalizing trays of food. Skirted cocktail waitresses in three-inch heels glided across the floor, effortlessly carrying bottles of champagne and crystal flutes to smiling couples. All of this was outside against the backdrop of the twinkling stars.

I looked at David with wide eyes and grabbed his hand. "Wow!" I mouthed, making sure the maître d' didn't see me.

After consulting his guestbook, the man with slicked-back perfect hair said, "Please come this way, madam."

We walked to a side table, appropriately spaced to allow privacy. "Oh my God, David! This is amazing!"

"You like it?"

"How could I not?" I gushed, looking out onto the glittering city of Bangkok below. "I've never seen anything like it." It was true.

"Manee told me about it. She said it was the best place in town for a special occasion."

"Good evening sir, madam. Would you like to start with an aperitif or a cocktail?" the waiter asked.

"Two glasses of champagne, please." David answered.

"Manee was right. I can't believe this place. Thank you."

"I'm glad you like it. Happy Anniversary!" We clinked our flutes and my eyes reverted like magnets back to the view.

I was speechless. No matter who you are, this place makes you feel special. Sitting above the city looking onto the millions of lights that make the night magic was an experience in itself. That experience was all the better with a glass of bubbly in hand. Add my handsome husband smiling at me with his beautiful blue eyes to the equation and I was certain there would never be another moment like this.

After dinner we went to the Sky Bar. There was a crowd, but there sufficient space to keep the intimate feeling intact. I drank a glass of cabernet and held on to my husband while we stood looking over the rooftop's edge. The large neon bar behind us cast

Wat Pho, the reclining Buddha

us in a pink light. A female piano player played gracefully below on yet another level of sky-high indulgence. The entire crowd, transfixed by the view and the balmy breeze, spoke with a hushed tone. It was one of the most romantic nights of my life.

Bangkok delivers. Be it jeweled temples you're after or emerald Buddhas, spicy food or elegant cuisine, rooftop bars or carpark hookups —it is all there. I hadn't considered before going how long Bangkok has been a center of world trade. Given the long history of the Thai capital which began in the fifteenth century, it's no wonder you feel mystery beneath your every step. The dark, powerful Chao Phraya River was the key to its ignition, and the engine has never stopped revving. This city put Singapore's sophistication level to shame and demanded that I fall in love with it. I dutifully complied.

Me at the top of Lebua State Tower

Chapter 13
Déjà Vu

Reality bit back in Singapore. Just like my European forays out of Amsterdam, I began to dread coming "home." My stint as an independent consultant had been far from illustrious. As was also the case in the Netherlands, I wasn't willing to have my project analyses result in a forgone conclusion so someone could sell more work. Even if that someone was me, I had no intention of playing up a problem to spend weeks or months resolving a non-issue. I wasn't well-connected in Singapore which meant I was reliant on recruiters or sales people to get me in the door of a client. My new career as an independent consultant didn't look promising.

I kept looking for new opportunities. Being in a foreign country and looking for work was not a new experience for me. Finding work that didn't quite fit wasn't new either. I felt like I'd been perpetually job-seeking since 2003 when I left the multinational management consulting firm which had brought me overseas to begin with. *Perhaps I should try a new direction?* I had over ten years of project management and consulting experience. That had to of some value, didn't it?

I started thinking about how much I enjoyed school. *Maybe this is the time to pursue another degree?* It took only a few Google searches on the cost of an overseas MBA from a high-quality school to find out that wasn't an option. Even if I knew what I wanted to study, the cost was astronomical. I'd never be able to take that on without putting myself right back into the debt hole I'd finally managed to pull myself out of in the past few years. No thanks.

You could teach, a small voice distinguished itself from the cacophony of *You can't!* That was an interesting idea. Surely all that I had accomplished as a certified project manager with a master's certificate from a well-known business school was of interest to someone without their own agenda. I began looking at training companies and technology programs in American universities nearby.

I had never been a trainer or a teacher. *How hard can it be if you're the one with all the answers?* I didn't know, and as usual I didn't spend a lot of time trying to find out. I wanted to work and I wanted to work *now*. Training appeared to be my best bet, or at least a viable option.

Before moving to Singapore, I'd taken quite a few classes to get my master's certificate and I knew the training company was global. What I hadn't known was that their Singapore office was directly across the street from my apartment building, in the same building as my last client. It had to be a sign. I filled in the forms on their web site and contacted the company by phone to ask about openings.

"We are currently looking for trainers in project and contract management for a new assignment. I expect you will hear from us shortly."

"That's great to hear. Could you tell me the name of the person searching for candidates?" "Yes m'am, his name is Ari."

"Excellent. Thank you for your help."

"Good luck, m'am."

I assumed the "good luck" was something like "may the best woman win" and not a comment about dealing with this Ari guy. Time would tell.

Patting myself on the back for my masterstroke of genius, I thought about what else I could plan. Christmas was around the corner and we hadn't decided what to do with the time off. Inevitably it would be quiet during that time businesswise, and that was the best time to get away.

Recently I'd purchased an enormous new world map to consume some of the annoying blank white wall space that surrounded me. I was geographically challenged when it came to the Asia Pacific region and it was a great reference. The weird thing about it was that it placed Australia at the center of the world. Being North American, I was quite

DÉJÀ VU

used to the US owning that prime position and was now forced to look at the planet from a new perspective.

How far away *was* the land Down Under anyway? Was that a possibility for Christmas? Google and I were having a good day. The flight to Perth would take about five hours and a further five would have us in Sydney. Since Europe and America were much further from Singapore, I might actually be able to sell David on the idea of an Australian adventure.

Web sites full of turquoise water and white sand beaches did nothing to diminish my enthusiasm. At thirty-eight, the Great Barrier Reef had been on my radar for at least twenty years. Australia's Blue Mountains would provide the dose of fresh air that I so desperately needed after being confined in a tiny apartment for the better part of a year. My old friend Stan from Mass Chaos Inc. in Amsterdam had moved back to Sydney. Maybe he'd like to play tour guide? I dashed off an email. The more information I had in hand prior to speaking with David, the better.

Though I had every intention of keeping quiet, it turned out to be impossible. "What about Australia for Christmas?" The words flew from my mouth nearly as soon as David walked in the door.

"What?" Absentmindedly perusing the mail, my loving husband never had the same level of enthusiasm for traveling that I did. Hell, did *anyone*?

"I'd like to visit Australia over Christmas. We have the time and it isn't as far as going back to Europe or the US. I think it's a better idea." I hoped I was convincing.

"How much do the flights cost?" This would determine whether or not my scheme got off the ground.

"They aren't too bad. It looks like about fifteen hundred dollars total for two round-trip tickets."

"You're right. Not bad at all. It's cheaper than going back to Europe."

"And it's summer there, so we don't have to freeze."

"That would be nice. Well, if you think it's doable, then we should start making plans."

Despite wanting to dance gleefully around the condo, I attempted to remain nonchalant. "Sure. I mean, if you think you'd enjoy it, then why not check it out? We might never be this close again once we leave Singapore."

"Absolutely. We should take advantage of that."

And just like that I was making plans to visit my fourth continent. I didn't think it would ever be the center of the planet for me, but I also hadn't believed I'd ever get there. Having David agree so easily was like being handed a golden ticket. We had so many Australians around us that getting reliable travel advice would be a cinch. Living this global life so often wove threats and opportunities side by side that waiting for the other shoe to drop had become second nature. For once I would not allow myself to consider a down side.

When plotting an adventure, I have a one-track mind. I'll stare at an LCD screen for hours searching for the best deal I can get on a great hotel. I use every variation of web site and search engine to find my way. Looking at my new world map, I planned our stops. The first thing Australia had to teach me was that it is nearly equivalent in size to the United States. I'm embarrassed to say that I had no idea this was the case until I started checking distances and travel times. New information forced me to scale back on the amount of territory we would cover. It is an island, yes, but a huge one.

David worked. I planned. I also received a phone call from Ari, the manager at the training company I wanted to work for. "Could you come by and talk with me for thirty minutes or so?" he asked.

"Sure. When would be a good time?"

"Is now okay?" He knew I lived across the street.

"Ummmm well..." I looked in the mirror. Pool hair and flip flops are rarely appropriate in a professional setting. "Tomorrow would be better," I countered.

"Okay. No problem. I'll see you in the morning then." He sounded as though he was about to hang up. "What time?" I interjected quickly to catch him.

"Oh anytime is okay. Just come in the morning. I have class in the afternoon."

DÉJÀ VU

"All right. I'll be there about ten. Will you be easy to find?"

"Yep. Ask anyone. Bye!" And he was gone.

I stared at the phone. After finding most things here more difficult than necessary, scoring an interview for a trainer position had been shockingly easy. *Don't question it.* I would have to learn to roll with the punches instead of expecting every interaction to be similar to what I experienced in Europe and North America. Ari's name told me he was Indian. He didn't have to be as formal as the Indians I'd met already. Perhaps it was time that something was easy for me here.

* * *

The next morning, I took a break from my OCD planning of the Great Australian Adventure and went to see Ari. The training office could not have been closer unless it was in my own building and I was *still* damp with perspiration when I arrived. It didn't occur to me that the more I obsessed over this, the more it would drive me crazy.

Reading the placards at the doors on the second level of the building searching for ETI, I peeked through windows and doors to see what was happening at ten o'clock in the morning. Strangely, it seemed very empty for prime real estate in a city of five million people.

Eventually I spotted the indigo-and-gray logo of Executive Training International. A young Chinese woman sat at the front desk.

"Hello. I have an appointment to see Ari. My name is Jennifer Burge." I smiled at her.

"Take a seat first."

"Umm, okay. Is he here?" I wanted to know how long I was expected to wait.

"Yes." The Singaporean economy of words should not have surprised me by now.

I decided to do what I was told and sat down. Ten seconds passed.

"You can go in now. Conference room 'Kuala Lumpur.' Third door on right."

I just looked at her and then walked through the entry way. What was the point of me sitting down? My footsteps were silent on the beige non-color carpet.

"It's no problem, sir. I assure you we will have the right people in place." Ari was speaking into his mobile phone when I reached the doorway. On the table before him was a stack of resumes that had to number over a hundred. "Thank you again, sir. I will call you next week." He looked up at me and smiled as he disconnected.

"Are you Jennifer?"

"I am. Pleased to meet you, Ari." I held my hand out and he shook it vigorously.

"Welcome to ETI! You're quite local, aren't you?"

"Yes. I live at The Metz, just across the street."

"Well, work can't be handier than that, can it?" He laughed at his own joke.

"It would definitely make life easier. I haven't exactly adjusted to the heat yet."

"Gotcha. Take a seat." He indicated the one across from him.

"Thank you. I was glad to hear from you so soon after I sent through my resume."

"Well, you certainly had good timing. We have a major client that we're working with on a large training program. Have you heard of IAD?"

"No, I'm not familiar with them. I'm still getting my bearings on the local businesses."

"Ah, yes. I understand. IAD is the technology arm of the Singapore government. They take care of IT projects for all of the Singapore ministry departments."

"I see."

"They have approached us to deliver a program to all of their people on contract management. It would be a coup for us to have them as a local client, so we're looking for an A team of technology trainers with project management and contract management experience to give the courses. Would you be interested in that?"

After my recent discussion with Marc about the Singapore government and its possible surveillance tactics, I was a bit intimidated at the thought of having them for a client. "Sure. It sounds interesting. I passed the project management professional certification exam in

DÉJÀ VU

2007, so I have that background. I was also an account manager for EDS where I managed large client contracts for several years." The words flew out unbidden. I needed work.

"Fantastic! Welcome aboard then! Talk to Shun Lee on your way out the door. She has the forms to get you all set up for access to our systems, getting you paid, et cetera. We won't be ready until late January or early February because the course content is still being created. You'll have plenty of time to prepare."

Was he seriously offering me a job after meeting me less than ten minutes ago?

"Got any questions?" He started shuffling the papers before him, signaling that we had reached the end of our discussion.

"How many people are we talking about? Students, I mean?" I blurted, trying to think fast.

"A couple hundred. We're looking for four trainers in total. People with experience like yours aren't that easy to find."

"I see. And what about the rate? Is that daily or hourly? Do you have a number in mind?"

"Shun Lee will go over all that with you. We have a special rate for this client program. It's a little over the industry standard here in Singapore." "

Okay. When can I expect to have the training material to look over and prepare?"

"It will be in the new year for sure. Take your Christmas holiday and we'll catch up after." More shuffling. He was ready to be rid of me.

"All right. That sounds good. Thank you for the opportunity. I'm looking forward to it." I stuck my hand out again.

"Glad to have you, Jennifer. See you later." Dismissed.

Stunned, I wandered down the hallway towards my short-spoken new friend whose name I now knew was Shun Lee. *How can that be the end of the discussion? He didn't even ask if I have training experience. If they want an A Team, isn't that the one question to ask? Why was he in such a hurry to see me leave?*

Red flags appeared in all directions.

Chapter 14
Party Games

Before leaving on what was, in my mind, the adventure of a lifetime, David continued working at an insane pace. Having a job ready for me in the New Year and a trip to distract myself with, I didn't feel his absence quite as much. He only had time to communicate what he deemed essential information.

"There's a Christmas party on the first Saturday in December. It's for everyone on the project. You'll have to wear something fancy." He snuck a glance to gauge my reaction.

"What do you mean "fancy"? How dressed up do I need to be?" I was panicking already. This was a town for toothpicks when it came to clothing. It wasn't the kind of place to find a fabulous dress on a tight schedule.

"I don't really know, but I expect it will be quite formal. The guys are wearing tuxes." His nose was already back in his book.

I stared out at Singapore through the living room window, as though the place to get a dress would appear before me. Normally the thought of a formal engagement would be exciting. Here it felt like torture.

"I have no idea where to get something like that."

"You'll figure it out."

Yeah, and I could also look somewhere else for empathy with my plight apparently. David had no interest in my conundrum.

"Who else is going?"

"Everyone. Madeline is going. Jac will be there. There will be plenty of others you've met before. Stop worrying."

Easy for him to say! The good news was that I had developed a few friendships which made my bizarre existence easier to bear. Madeline was single and Jac's boyfriend Javed was always at work too. Linda and I had kept in touch since the party at Laura's house and suddenly I didn't mind hanging out with the project people quite so much. This was different, however—formal parties have a way of making me slightly insane, or more insane than usual anyway. I felt I could never measure up.

"I'll see if the girls have some ideas about where to get dresses."

"Good idea."

It was a good idea, but it didn't pan out. They had dresses to wear already and none of us was that familiar with Singapore yet. Instead I had to drag David shopping on a Sunday when we would both rather be doing something else. Much to my surprise, I did find a formal gown shop with something in my size on the third or fourth try. I wasn't in love with it, but it fit and looked decent. *Sold!*

We agreed to meet up with Madeline for a drink before the party. I had to quell my nerves somehow, and she was usually up for a glass of wine. She arrived at our place an hour before we were to leave and I poured the three of us a tall glass of bubbly.

"Cheers!" I said, a little too gleefully.

"Cheers to you, mate! Thank you," she said.

David clinked glasses with us and smiled. "Do you know who else is coming, Madeline?"

"I really don't. I spoke to John and he's coming. A few of the girls on my team will be there." Madeline was part of the finance team on the project. She had relocated from Melbourne shortly after we arrived in Singapore.

"I expect it will be a very large group. Everyone was invited, and that's at least four hundred people."

"It's been a long time since I went to a party of that size," I said, thinking back on the company Christmas parties I attended in Holland. Maybe that's where my dislike of them began? Always being the odd man out, so to speak, gets old fast.

Party Games

"I'm sure it will be fun." Madeline seemed to pick up on my hesitation. She knew I was having trouble finding my way in Singapore and had confided in me that she felt the same.

We continued chatting in the living room until it was time to call a taxi. I was nowhere near my required level of liquid courage, but I had no choice. My face felt hot despite the chill in our air-conditioned condo.

I hopped in the back with Madeline, and David took the front seat. They continued talking about work, which sounded more like gossip than anything I'd heard out of David since we'd been here. Was he really that interested in how people spent their weekends? He spent ten to twelve hours a day with them. Wasn't that enough? Their conversation was so animated that I guessed not. I said nothing.

We stepped from the car into the glittering lobby of the Fullerton Hotel, one of the oldest in Singapore. I felt like I was floating, like I wasn't really there. My heart was racing. It was a good thing that more golden glasses of bubbly were easily within reach inside the doors.

"Hello, Jennifer! So nice to see you again." I could hardly believe anyone was talking to me. I turned to see Marina smiling in my direction.

"Oh yes, hello! It's great to see you too. Have you met David before? And Madeline?" I turned to make introductions and Madeline had vanished.

"Hi Marina, it's nice to see you." David smiled down to greet her. They differed in height by at least a foot.

"I always feel so short standing next to anyone from Holland!" She faked disdain.

"That's because you are!" David laughed. I was mortified, until I saw her and her husband Donald laugh too.

"We can't all be giants, David," Donald grinned, shaking his hand.

"I think it's time we took a seat." Marina began shepherding everyone when she heard a call for dinner in the background.

"Oh, I told Madeline I'd sit with her," I said to David, looking around for a non-existent redhead.

"Come sit with us!" Marina motioned my way. "It'll be fun!" Suddenly I was even more nervous. I didn't know what Donald's role was on this project, but I knew he was very senior. I thought this was going to be a laugh, hanging out with David's friends, but we were about to be under the microscope of bigwigs for the duration of the evening!

"Oh. Uhhh..." I stalled a minute until my eyes landed on the redhead. She was cozily seated with everyone we knew and there wasn't one empty seat at the table.

"We'd love to," answered David, before glancing back at me with a glare.

I hadn't meant to be rude. I just didn't know these people and what on Earth would I talk about for a two-hour dinner with them?

"Great! We're up here I guess." Marina led us to a table right in front of the stage. She took a seat and Donald sat to her right. I was now in between Donald and David. Marina grinned across the table, making introductions to the others already seated. I smiled through my champagne haze.

Making conversation with Marina and Donald couldn't have been easier. They were charming and funny. I learned that Donald's family had run a travel agency in Queensland, Australia. It didn't exist any longer, but he had grown up in a city near the Great Barrier Reef. Just like that, I had my topic of conversation.

"Do you want to see the inner reef, or the outer reef?" he asked over dinner, when I told him how excited I was to visit the area.

"I didn't realize there was a difference."

"The outer reef will cost you a full day out, but the marine life is much more beautiful than in the inner reef. If I were you, I'd invest the time."

"Well then, I guess I have my answer! What do you think about Port Douglas as a base in north Queensland? It looks like a great place to spend a few days."

"Yep. I'd say if you want something more quiet than Cairns, it's the perfect place." He pronounced it *cans*.

"Is that really how you say it?"

"If you don't want everyone to know you're a tourist," he said with a wink.

Party Games

"Okay then. Thank you for the education." I smiled back.

"Good evening ladies and gentlemen! May I have your attention, please?" A male voice boomed from the microphone on stage. "I have been told you are a competitive lot. Are you ready for a cutthroat game of world trivia?"

Applause and shouts of *"Woohoo"* came from the crowd. Waiters had been delivering drinks for no less than an hour and a half and the group was primed.

As dessert plates appeared before us, photos of world landmarks flashed on the screen and we had to identify them. The room had been divided in half to form two teams. We conferred as a table before answering, but David and I had the European landmarks covered. I could also nail the American ones. Before I knew it, I was actually having a good time.

"Marina, I'd love to hear more from you about places to visit in Australia." Donald and I switched seats after the game was over.

"Of course, Jennifer. Let me give you my email address and you can give me an idea of what you're looking for. We have to take off shortly, but I look forward to hearing from you. I'm still working on planning that group lunch!"

"Thank you. I'm sorry to hear you're leaving, but I'm sure I'll see you again soon."

"I'd like that."

Once Donald and Marina said their farewells, I decided I had been sitting long enough. David was talking to someone else at the table about work, so I wandered off to find the bar. It wasn't difficult to find, I just had to follow the noise.

Standing in line, I didn't see Madeline anywhere, but I did see Jac and some of the other girls I'd met the night of the Formula One race. "What can I get you, love?" the bartender interrupted my reconnaissance.

"Oh, sorry! I'd like white wine, please."

"Bottle or glass?"

I didn't understand the question so just stared at him blankly.

Looking at me with a fading smile, "Would you like a bottle of white or just a glass?"

"A glass, please." Was he serious? People really ordered an entire bottle?

"There you go. *Next!*"

I was still stunned. I guessed that people came to get bottles to take back to their table, but I'd never been asked that question at a party before. Very efficient.

Looking over at the ladies where Jac stood in a cluster, I walked up to say hello. "What's happening? Are you guys enjoying the party?"

My question was met with several blank stares and my heart dropped into my stomach. I didn't know any of them well, except for Jac. And this was a party, wasn't it?

"Hi Jen, you remember Isobel and this is Danielle. I think you've met the others." Jac finally spoke up and the two new faces gave a slight facial movement that could have been a smile. Then again, maybe it wasn't.

I had the distinct impression I'd interrupted something, so I acted as though I had just been strolling by. "Nice to meet you. Hope you guys have fun."

What was that about? *They acted like they'd never even seen me before.* I kept walking. The hotel was so beautiful. Most Singapore buildings seemed to have sprung up yesterday, but this grand dame was from another era. I saw a few people coming and going through a side door, so I decided to see what they were up to.

I immediately regretted my decision to walk into the steamy night air in a heavy gown. A perpetual optimist, I hung onto the theory that eventually the temperature *must* drop. "Hello." An eastern European accent hit my right ear.

"Oh hello. I didn't see you there." I was too focused on my own misery!

"Hi, my name is Alexis. This is Eu-meh." The petite blonde pointed to the Asian woman standing on her left, who then smiled. It was a real smile.

"I'm Jennifer. I don't work on the project. My husband David does."

"Speak of the devil," David came up behind me. "I wondered where you took off to."

"This is Alexis and Eu-meh."

"We bought the same dress!" Alexis laughed. I laughed myself because I hadn't noticed they were dressed identically. I was looking at their faces. I liked that they were the type that laughed about such a thing. So many women would be mortified, which I think is ridiculous.

"I'm sure you aren't the only ones here that had that happen.

"Singapore is a small place!" I offered.

"We just have very good taste." Alexis nodded at Eu-meh who still smiled, but still said nothing. "I don't work on the project either. My husband is Jacques."

"Oh yes, I know him. A Frenchie. We're on the same team." David said.

"My husband's name is Darren. He's also on the project." Eu-meh broke her silence. Her accent was different from the other Singaporeans I'd met.

"Yep. I know him too. Small world!" David laughed at his own joke.

"Great to meet you both. I hardly know anyone here," I said.

"I know. It's difficult to get to know anyone when you aren't working with the whole team. We will have to meet up, Jennifer." Alexis was taking no prisoners.

"Absolutely." Who was I to turn down social interaction? "I'm a bit too warm out here. I will see you both inside." Ten minutes outdoors was the most I could handle.

"Yes. See you too." Alexis had a beautiful smile. Eu-meh waved.

"I think I've had enough fun for one night," I said to David when we were out of earshot. "What about you?"

"Yes, fine by me. It was fun, but I don't need to stay here all night."

What a relief! "There is a taxi stand at the front entrance. I'm sure we can grab one there."

"Good idea."

Sure enough, several taxis stood at the ready. We didn't even have to wait. "Did you have a good time? It seemed like you were having fun talking with Donald and Marina."

"You know what? I did. They are really easy to talk to."

"I know. Donald is a good guy. He's very funny too."

"He is. Witty. Sometimes it took me a minute to realize he was joking. And Marina was so nice to include us at their table. I didn't know where we'd end up! She has offered advice on Australia too."

"Of course—I didn't think about the fact that they are both from there. I'm glad it went so well."

"Me too." I felt silly for being so neurotic about *everything*. What I wore, who I sat with, and what I would say had all been areas of concern. In actuality I was terrified of making some grave error that would make me more of an outcast than I already felt like. When did I become so insecure?

We were both exhausted, but at the same time in good cheer. It had been a great night, one with no bickering about stupid things like whether or not to take a taxi home or who was cooking dinner. We had been a team again, if only for a few hours. I crossed my fingers we could keep it up.

Chapter 15
Upside Down Under

It's summer there now. In December, in the southern hemisphere, it is summer. *Why can't I wrap my head around that fact?* I looked at weather reports for Sydney and northern Queensland and tried to come to grips with the fact that this would be a very hot Christmas.

It seemed so weird. I'd been trained to hope for a white one. Even though I had certainly had my fill of snow shovels, landing on icy pavement, and scraping ice from my windshield, it felt wrong to be packing shorts and bathing suits. Even weirder, I was exchanging emails with the tour operator who would take us to the Great Barrier Reef and he said we'd need something called a stinger suit to protect us from both tiny poisonous jellyfish and the sun. I had a feeling this was only the beginning of the weirdness.

David was nowhere to be found in the weeks before our end-of-year vacation. He left before I got out of bed each day and came home after I returned to it each night. We barely spoke because one of us was always too tired.

In the third week of December, the project action halted abruptly. Everyone we knew left the country, either returning to their home nation or that of family to spend the remainder of the year. A "forced shut-down" at the office meant that even the most dedicated workaholics had to find something else to do until January arrived. To me, it was a relief. Given the pace of his work environment, I'd half expected to receive a call telling me to cancel our plans.

Both David and I are afflicted with the indecisive packing disease. Though I knew to expect warm weather, we lived five degrees from the Equator. It had to be cooler there on occasion, even in summer. Already a year into Singapore life, I had become intolerant of cold. One would think that since most air-conditioning is set to "blizzard" in Singapore shopping malls and businesses, that wouldn't happen, but I can testify otherwise.

By the time the 20th of December arrived, I was bouncing off the walls at the prospect of visiting my fourth continent. *Fourth!* Even the perpetual traveler I longed to be hadn't anticipated this development. Looking at the clock, I figured there had to be something wrong with it. It never moved this slowly.

My Australian friend Stan from Amsterdam now lived in Sydney. Though we hadn't seen each other in several years, he had graciously volunteered to be our Sydney tour guide. Reading *Culture Shock; Australia* in an effort not to be blindsided by the pitfalls of national identity again, I learned that the concept of "mateship" is a big deal Down Under. Aussies will go far out of their way for a "mate," a friend, or even just their fellow man, and they are well known for it.

Much to my surprise, the world was not upside down when we touched ground in Sydney. In fact it all looked rather normal. I flagged the driver I'd hired to take us to the city and he grumpily threw our bags into the back of a rusting white van. "Liverpool Street, please. We're going to the Radisson." The sliding door slammed shut in response.

David and I stared out the windows. Hardly any airport neighborhood in this world is glamorous, and these streets were no exception. Single-level square domiciles dominated, and two-storey apartment buildings claimed second place in popularity. We were driving on the wrong side of the road, which made everything seem off-kilter. The time difference was a mere two hours, but neither of us had managed much sleep on the overnight economy flight.

"May I have your name please?" said the cheery female manager at the hotel. "The reservation is in the name Dijkstra."

"I'm sorry, would you please spell that?"

David gave it to her letter by letter. He was used to it. Names like his were rare in Asia Pacific. "Here's the credit card I booked it with."

Upside Down Under

"Oh yes. Here it is! Welcome to Australia!" She scanned her computer screen. "Hmm, it's quite early. Let me check and see if there is anything available now."

I prayed silently to the God of Travel. No one gives you a room at nine o'clock in the morning. We needed a miracle.

"I do have a room. Just a moment." She smiled and fluttered off to get someone else to handle the details. "Enjoy your stay with us!"

"Thank you, I'm sure we will." Not having to wander Sydney's streets for six hours unshowered and exhausted was a major win. "We really appreciate this."

The hotel was a bit older, but we were only a few streets from the city's major tourist hub, Darling Harbour. Nothing mattered more than my head hitting a pillow anyway. "I can't believe we're here." I whispered in David's ear when we were both about to fall asleep.

"It will be great." He gave me a squeeze before he began to snore softly.

* * *

Stan left no stone unturned. He should have been wearing a chauffer's uniform because he made us feel like visiting royalty. We saw the Harbour Bridge, Sydney Heads, and The Rocks before grabbing cappuccino at Bondi Beach. Sydney and its surroundings are nothing short of stunning. I've seen a great deal of water in my day, but this deep turquoise was a new color for me.

What surprised me is that, aside from the older architecture that was clearly British in style, it felt like a cross between the US and England. The Australian accent is utterly original and it took some time to tune my ear to it so that I could understand what people were telling me. But there wasn't the stiffness, the formality that I associate with the United Kingdom. People were more relaxed here.

Right on cue, Stan took us to the Cruising Yacht Club of Australia, the CYCA in Rushcutter's Bay. I wasn't sure why we were going, because Stan didn't have a boat nor was he a member. The eastern suburbs, where the club is located, looked pretty tony to me. Large sprawling homes that reminded me of Los Angeles or Beverly Hills but with spectacular views of Sydney Harbour could not come cheap.

"Just put your name here." Stan pointed to a register at the unmanned front desk.

I looked around for the gestapo which would surely prevent me from taking up space in this posh spot, but there was no one around. I signed the book. "You don't have to be a member?"

"Of course not." Stan blew off the question at first.

"In the US you wouldn't be allowed to enter a club like this unless you were."

"Really? That's ridiculous. It's un-Australian. We are all equal here. No one is better than someone else just because you have a club membership that you probably paid too much money for." The mere thought of it cracked him up.

"It would be the same in Holland," David added.

"Just bizarre." Stan signaled the waiter for menus. "Hope you're ready for lunch. The tour guide needs a break!"

* * *

There were more stops on the Australian tour that hinted how different life is at the bottom of the planet. En route to the Blue Mountains, we stopped at Featherdale Wildlife Park. Here we found the usual suspects—kangaroos and koalas—but more mysterious creatures both feathered and furry emerged.

"What is *that*?" David asked in a hushed tone. We didn't want to be the ignorant foreigners so soon after walking through the park entrance.

"I have no idea," I answered, spying the rather large rat-like animal snoozing in the midday sun. I walked around the fence to the sign near its pen. "Cool! It's a wombat! I've heard of them."

"Me too, but at work. I heard someone in Singapore call a manager a wombat. When I asked what he meant, he said it means "waste of money, brains, and time." He laughed.

"I guess that tells us what we need to know about the guy in the cage."

We followed the path to a large empty pen with a high fence. A flash of brilliant blue feathers emerged from one of the bushes and I came eye to eye with very angry black eyes on a horned ostrich. At least, that's what it looked like to me.

"David! Come here!" I shouted, still staring down my enemy.

"The sign says it's a cassowary. They can kill you."

I didn't doubt that. I was glad for the wooden fence between us because he looked ready to lunge.

"They've got claws that'll tear your guts right out!" a tall brown-haired guy in a red and blue flannel shirt told his son. His son, about five years old, looked appropriately terrified. I could relate.

"They are wild in north Queensland apparently." David was filling me in on details he'd gathered. "Aren't we going there after Christmas?"

"Yes."

We'd been told about the number of Australian creatures that can and will kill you. The Aussies clearly enjoyed scaring the shit out of anyone who intended to visit their country. Maybe they wanted to make sure you didn't stay. Redback spiders, eastern brown snakes, red-bellied black snakes, giant crocs. Even the magpies were known to attack. Now we had a blue rhino-horned ostrich to add to the list. Had someone told me about this thing in advance, I don't know that I would have believed them.

Arriving in Cairns a few days later, we had a second round of our new game called What the Hell Is That? The ninety-minute drive from the airport to Port Douglas delivered on every single Australian fantasy I've ever had. A winding coastal road, in fact the only road, takes you past local villages too small to be called towns. Few cars passed. It felt like we were on a different planet to everyone else, after Sydney's Christmas hustle and bustle.

"Pull over!" I practically shouted at a shocked David. "I want to get a picture."

The scenic pullout at a jutting point delivered a view of the green mountains on one side, almost volcanic in nature, and the glittering blue sea on the other. Gray diamonds seemed to dance in the late afternoon waves. I had never seen anything like it. "Isn't it amazing?" I smiled at David who had since recovered from my outburst.

"It certainly is." He grabbed my hand. "Are you happy?" he asked, looking down at me when I'd finally lowered my camera.

"I could not be happier. Thank you," I said with a kiss.

"For what?" A quizzical look crossed his face and his blue eyes seemed to match the water behind him.

"For making my dreams come true." I grabbed him and squeezed as hard as I could. I was smothered with kisses in return.

* * *

Port Douglas is a charming seaside village, a striking contrast to what we'd seen so far in this country. The unimaginatively named Four Mile Beach runs the length of it to the southeast and the creek inlet which carries most of the reef traffic forms the northern border of town. Its many open air restaurants, resorts, and glitzy boutiques are best covered on foot. It was exactly the tropical paradise I'd hoped for.

For our outer reef adventure, we had to be at the marina early. Stinger suits, apparently to protect you from the minute but deadly irukandji jellyfish that are plentiful in the summer, were passed out and tried on. No one looked attractive, but if it stopped two and a half centimeters of one of the world's most venomous creatures from reaching me, I was all for it.

David, who is far from the sea lover his wife is, had taken seasick pills first thing in the morning. He wasn't used to the ocean's habit of throwing people around and he didn't want to lose the entire day "feeding the fish" as the Aussies like to say. We were both a bit nervous about how it would go for him, but I admired his ability to suck it up and not complain when it was something I had dreamed of doing for years.

As Donald had warned me back in Singapore, it's a long ride to the outer reef. We cruised for two hours before making our first stop at Opal Reef. As the boat slowly lolled, the anchor making its way to the sandy bottom, I looked at the turquoise gemstones surrounding us beneath the water's surface. I had no idea that many shades of blue existed.

Racing to slip fins on my feet, I half-listened to the explanation being given to the first-time snorkelers on board. David was taking it all in. Cautiously, I made my way to the swim ladder in the back of the boat, motioning to David that I would wait in the water.

Upside Down Under

The chill of the ocean under the scorching sun gave that simultaneous hot and cold feeling, one of the most delicious things about swimming. Licking the salt from my lips, I placed the mask over my face and looked down. The water was crystal clear and I could easily the ocean floor, ten feet below. Casting a massive shadow under the boat was the most enormous colorful green-and-blue fish I had ever laid eyes on. The guide in the water next to me told the group to take a look. It was a six foot Maori wrasse. I had been in the water less than five minutes and already I was speechless.

David jumped in with his purple noodle to help stay afloat and I pointed under the boat. His wide eyes practically jumped from the mask, but he was smiling—very difficult to do with a snorkel in your mouth. We followed the guide for a tour around the coral formation while she pointed out the iridescent beauty below. The purple giant clam had matching giant blue lips which parted then slammed shut when she poked them. Diamond-shaped black-and-yellow angelfish crossed our path, looking at us as we looked at them. Sea turtles glided across hot pink coral as we tried to capture them with the underwater camera.

I had expected this reef to be special, but what I had seen underwater before this in no way prepared me for how unique it truly is. David swam as quickly as I did, taking in one sight after the next. Not a fan of being completely underwater, he passed me the camera for close-up photos. Other than that, he was doing much better than I expected on the open ocean.

We swam on, once the guide had shown us all the creatures whose hiding places she knew. Roughly twenty others flapped about in the waves around us. Sometimes it was difficult to maneuver around people without any experience. One guy stood up on the coral right after being told never to touch it because it kills the cells. I wanted to smack him. How could people be so stupid?

I stared beneath me, trying to capture the little lightning bolts of color that flashed all around us. Then I saw something I didn't expect: a shark. Except that's not how my brain interpreted it. *SHARK! SHARK! SHARK!* That was more like it. It wasn't a great white or a bull shark, the more aggressive breeds I was familiar with. It wasn't as small as the reef sharks I'd seen in the past, either, and knew to be harmless.

I popped my head up and tapped David's shoulder. He pulled his face out of the water. "What's up?" He said in a nasally cross between someone with serious sinus issues and Darth Vader.

"Let's swim this way. Come with me." I pulled at his arm.

"Okay." He was completely calm. He hadn't seen it.

"Hurry up." I was not calm.

"What's the problem?" He was confused.

"I saw a shark, but shhh. Let it get the others, not us." I'd lost it. I felt responsible for bringing us here, and now we were going to die. We were closest to it.

"Okay." David didn't ask any questions, but that purple noodle picked up the pace.

I looked down again. The shark was there, but moving away from us. We kept swimming until we were back in the annoying crowd I'd been so anxious to flee a few minutes before.

My heartbeat slowed. Rational thought began to return. "It probably wasn't dangerous, but it was big. I want to keep all my fingers and toes."

"I understand. I don't want to be lunch." He was grinning now. I thought I detected sarcasm.

"Well you aren't used to this stuff. If something happened, it would be all my fault!" I reasoned.

"I'm so lucky I have my wife to protect me." The grin released a belly laugh.

"Yes you are! And don't forget it!" There was no choice now but to laugh at my paranoia. The air horn sounded, telling us it was time to return to the boat. My limbs had gone numb with fright and were suddenly heavy. I wasn't about to argue.

Gary, the marine biologist on board, had a flipchart out to identify the various species. "I saw a shark." I told him with all the nonchalance I could muster.

"Good for you!" His deeply-tanned face was genuinely enthused. "What did it look like?"

"It was five or six feet long with dark fins. The fins had white tips."

"A white pointer. Yeah, they are all over the reef. Nothing to worry about."

I worried that I must have looked worried. "Really? They're much bigger than the reef sharks I'm used to."

"If you're afraid, you shouldn't go in the water."

And there it was, the no-bullshit way Aussies tell it like it is.

The shark! Great Barrier Reef

Chapter 16
Superiority Complex

Waiting in my email was a meeting invitation from Ari. The ETI A Team was gathering for a discussion on the course material and expectations of the IDA program. Our vacation had been wonderful, but after so much free time, I was anxious to get to work. I was even more anxious to get paid.

I was instructed to go to the 'Phuket' conference room where I found Ari talking with three others. Lian, Greg, and Lucas all seemed to know each other. "Nice to meet you." I smiled and shook hands all around before taking a seat.

"Great. Now we can get started. I assume you've all been studying contract management over the past few weeks, right?" He was hiding a smirk, but it was clear he was joking. "I hope so because the course content isn't ready yet." This time he was not joking.

We were still three weeks away from the beginning of the program, but I was surprised the text didn't yet exist. Was this normal in the training world?

"What's going on, Ari?" Lucas wanted to know.

"Well, ETI doesn't actually have an existing training course on contract management. We are creating a custom program for IAD. They want each person to be in class for two days and we will take bits and pieces from other courses to fill those days. There will be some information on project management, best practices in contract management, etc. It's taking longer to finalize because we need to put it together," Ari explained.

Lian raised an eyebrow. "When will it be ready?"

"Soon."

"I need time to prepare the daily agenda. If we don't have the information available within the next few days, it's going to be quite difficult," she continued.

"I know. You'll be the first to know when the course is uploaded."

The two male trainers said nothing. I wasn't sure whether to be concerned or not. If the information was provided, then wasn't it a matter of familiarizing myself with it? I declined to comment.

Life went back to pre-vacation routine all too quickly. David disappeared to the office and I searched for purpose in my life. When we'd made the decision to move to Singapore, it had never occurred to me that I would be more or less trapped inside by the scorching heat. My cabin fever was rampant.

Eventually the course material did arrive, two weeks before the class date. When I reviewed the content, there didn't seem to be anything too complicated in it. My experience covered the range of the coursework and there were none of the complex project management formulas or tools that could be tricky. All I had to do was research case studies to put the theory into practice, and to talk about my own project experience. How hard could it be?

I caught Lucas outside smoking, the morning of our first class.

"Good morning, Lucas. All ready to go?"

"Yep. Not worried at all. My lesson plan is broken down to fifteen minute intervals." He boasted.

"Lesson plan?"

"Of course. Don't you have one?" That's basic training technique!"

Was he intentionally trying to knock me off kilter, knowing I was inexperienced at training? "I do, but it isn't *that* detailed. I know what we'll be doing hourly."

"Good luck." Sarcasm mixed with sincerity? Or just the first one?

'Thanks. You too." I didn't feel as confident as I had five minutes earlier bursting with caffeine. As the elevator doors slid open on the second floor, I mentally rehearsed my dialogue.

"This material is all over the place!" Lian was giving Ari an earful.

"I know it isn't perfect, but you're a pro! You'll be great!" A little schmoozing never hurt, according to Ari.

"You better hope so. The last thing you need is the government on your ass!" Lian turned her back and headed to her classroom.

What did this mean for those of us who weren't professional trainers? I had noticed that the flow of the lecture was interrupted occasionally, and we had already exchanged several emails to highlight mistakes in the documentation. But if ETI thought it was acceptable, I had no choice but to deliver it.

"Good luck, Jennifer! Knock 'em dead!" Ari said, not noticing that I had overheard his exchange with Lian.

"Thanks," I called over my shoulder on the way to my room. My confidence kept shrinking—and I wasn't even at the podium yet.

The room was incredibly noisy given only fifteen students were in attendance. I passed around the sign-in sheet. "Good morning, everyone. My name is Jennifer Burge. Welcome to Contract Management!" I tried to sound as cheery as possible.

"What time do we finish today?" A female voice piped up from the back of the room.

"We'll be done when we're done." Translation, *I have no idea*.

"I need to know. My daughter is in day care," she continued.

"I'm sure everyone here has obligations tonight. Your syllabus indicated that we would finish at 4:30. I would plan for that. If we are done earlier, then of course I will let you go earlier."

"Why can't we start earlier?"

Was she serious? Is this how it was going to be? "We might be able to do that, but it depends on whether or not everyone agrees. Please take a seat and we'll get started in a minute."

My introduction did not take long, as I don't like talking about myself. I gave them an ice-breaker to loosen them up, and we discussed the agenda.

"I have no problem starting the day tomorrow at eight-thirty if the class prefers it. Shall we take a vote?"

Several heads nodded in response.

"Okay. All those who would prefer an earlier start time, please raise your hands." There was very little need to continue as the majority was obvious. "And those who prefer to keep the same time?" A smattering of younger students raised their hands.

"Fine by me. I will see you thirty minutes earlier tomorrow."

"What time will we finish tomorrow?" The relentless female voice rang out once more.

"Thirty minutes earlier than today." End of discussion.

The morning hours flew by. We discussed project techniques and managing employees to deliver results. I gave examples from my own experience, mainly on European projects but some American ones as well. Most of the students were polite and asked intelligent questions, but two women began talking non-stop around mid-morning.

"Could you two please keep it down?" I finally asked.

"We aren't doing anything," one replied.

"If I have to ask you to be quiet that means you are being disruptive."

"Whatever. We don't need to be here. We know all this," the other one backed her up.

"If your employer asked you to attend, obviously they thought you would learn something."

The door opened and a petite woman with a mane of glossy black hair carrying a Louis Vuitton bag nearly her equal in size strode in. She made no apology for her lateness, despite the fact that we were in session.

"Welcome. What is your name please?"

"Why you want to know?" she demanded.

"Because I have already taken attendance and you weren't here. I need to mark that you have arrived."

"Mei Ching. I am a senior consultant."

"Thank you, Mei Ching."

I decided not to return to the conversation with the other two and allow them the chance to keep quiet. Unsurprisingly, Mei Ching took a seat right next to them.

"It's time to break for lunch. We'll take one hour, and you can take care of any necessary business before we begin again at one o'clock."

There was an immediate huddle among the three women. I guessed that nothing good would come of it, but I wasn't a babysitter. There were people in the room who wanted to learn. If these three continued their antics, I would put a stop to it one way or another. I left to have lunch at home. Perhaps this was not my new career after all.

"Mei Ching, there are many ways to manage contracts. This is one example that happens to be used in US government contracts. If you have a better way of doing it, please share it with us."

It felt like the second day of class would never end. It didn't matter what I said, Mei Ching had a problem with it. While I personally couldn't have cared less what she thought of me, my teaching style, or my experience, she was ruining the class for everyone else.

"Ari, it's ridiculous. She repeatedly announces that she doesn't need to take the class and she knows better how to handle every subject. What am I supposed to do with a student like this?" I caught Ari on my morning break, exasperated.

"I worried about something like this. IAD wanted everyone to attend the course, regardless of their level and years of experience. You have people who have been on the job for six months sitting with people who have been there for six years. That is what she is frustrated about."

"Then she should take it up with her boss."

"I know. Look, if it continues, you can throw her out."

"Seriously?"

"Seriously. I'll need a report detailing what happened, but she is compromising the effectiveness of the course. IAD would not want that either."

"Deal." I hadn't known that was an option. I thought I had no choice but to put up with this spoiled brat for the rest of the day.

"Who can tell me what the three types of vendor incentives are that can be used in a new contract?" I asked the class.

"It doesn't matter what they are. At IAD, we only use *one*." Guess who?

The straw met the camel's back in that moment. "Mei Ching, you can go."

"*Excuse me?*" Her black eyes were murderous.

"You can go. It is clear that you have far more experience than what is taught in this course. You are excused." The words felt so good on my tongue, although I could certainly have given her a few more.

"This is lame anyway." Mei Ching gathered her belongings and was gone, slamming the door behind her.

"Would anyone else like to leave?" I glared at the two gossipers from the day before. Silence.

"Great! Then please, let's continue. I apologize for the disruption. Now, who can tell me about contract incentives? Why do you think one method might work better than others?"

Training was not to be my yellow brick road after all. When the constant challenging from Singaporeans happened the first time, I attributed it to the corporate culture at Vos Power. I was wrong. It was quite normal that, as a country often put in first place as a prime example of Southeast Asian development, they assumed a level of superiority that was off the charts. How did Mei Ching, a twenty-something who had lived her entire life on an island less than three hundred square miles, actually believe that she knew all the methods and tools for contract management on the planet? That her experience was equivalent to someone with global career experience and a certification?

It was baffling. No matter how frustrating the experience, it had provided invaluable insight into the Singaporean mindset. As the Global Financial Crisis deepened, the locals felt increasingly threatened by the high number of multinational firms and the western-educated foreigners who came with them. I'd been told that the Singaporean public school system did not advocate reason and logic as a means of solving problems, but rather it placed emphasis on rote repetition of fact and memorization. Simply put, if placed side by side in a competitive hiring situation, the local candidate would often lose.

When I picked up *The Straits Times* from my front doorstep the next morning, a bold headline screamed, "Hire Singaporeans First!" My heart was in my throat. It was already obvious to me that civil rights and discrimination meant nothing here. Once the locals decided to publicly encourage the latter against foreign nationals, my employment days were numbered.

Chapter 17
Flying the Coop

I stopped looking for work and started looking for ways to escape my reality. I wasn't going to be a housewife, nor let my life be dictated by the comings and goings of my husband. Our time in Australia had been magic, allowing us to escape the petty arguments that had become a way of life. If I wasn't home all the time, stewing about the unfairness of the situation, then we would not return to that way of life. At least that was my logic.

March brought with it a long weekend. What better reason to plan an adventure? I trolled the internet looking for the cheapest flights from Singapore to anywhere and discovered Tiger Air. Tiger was ridiculously cheap and the fares to Vietnam were too good to be believed. *Vietnam? Don't do it!* My American mind shouted. My adventurer's soul answered *Why not?*

I began my cost analysis, knowing full well that I couldn't get away with anything too pricey after having the trip of a lifetime to Australia two months earlier. It was hardly worth the time it took to do the research. We could easily spend three days in Ho Chi Minh City, formerly Saigon, for the equivalent of what we spent in Singapore over the same period. The airfare was cheaper than the hotel room! I could have picked a cheaper one if I wasn't a wee bit terrified of what that would mean in a developing country. Hospitable nation or not, Singapore was the gold standard of Southeast Asian living. Everywhere else was a question mark until you experienced it for yourself.

David came home late and I couldn't hold back. I pounced on my unwitting victim.

"Have you ever thought about visiting Vietnam?" I asked, as though I hadn't already confirmed the where, the when, and the how in my mind.

"Ummm... not really," came his distracted reply. He'd walked in the door less than an hour before and was already checking his email.

"Is it something you would consider doing?" I pressed.

"I guess so."

"Did you know that there's a long weekend at the end of the month? We could take an extra day and see Saigon."

A deep sigh. "Can we talk about this later? I have a deadline coming up at the end of the week and I have to concentrate." His tone indicated that the discussion was closed. If there was one thing I know about David, it's that trying to get him to do something he doesn't want to do is a lost cause.

"Okay. Sure." I tried not to let my disappointment show, and turned on the TV.

"Could you please turn that down? I can't handle the noise right now."

I said nothing and turned it down. Apparently, I wasn't to speak or watch TV. The project ruled my house now, as well as my life on this tiny island. I fantasized about disappearing, but went in the kitchen to pour a glass of wine instead. It was 8 p.m. in Singapore and 7 a.m. central time in the US. Hoping to catch Alison on her way to work, I dialed. When I reached her, I closed the kitchen door and stayed there until I was ready for bed.

The next morning, head throbbing from the amount of wine I'd unconsciously consumed while talking to this friend or that one, David was ready to talk.

"Did you say it was Saigon you wanted to go to last night?" He sat down on the edge of our king-size bed next to me.

"Yeah. I was thinking about it." Although now it hurt to think about anything.

"Well, if it's something you really want to do, we can work it out. Things at work will be less intense at the end of the month."

Flying the Coop

Guilt must have worked in my favor. "Really? That's great! It's so cheap you won't believe it, and I found a lot of interesting things to do there." My brain began chugging along at the mention of travel.

"Okay. Send me some details and let's figure it out."

My reply was a giant hug. "Thank you, sweetie!"

Three weeks later we landed in Ho Chi Minh City's suffocating heat. Adrenalin coursed through my veins. I couldn't help feeling that what I was doing was taboo. Would the locals know I was American? Would they hate me on sight? Was it safe here? The visa process had been challenging enough. In the closest thing to a government racket I'd ever seen, they force you to buy a visa at the consulate where you must apply in person and pay a seventy-five dollar fee. Then they keep your passport for three to five days while the application is in process. Five days without a passport seemed too long in a country which had already denied me my professional independence.

After claiming our bags, we took a cab to the hotel in Saigon's District 1. From my research, this was the heart of the city and the place where most landmarks are easily accessible. The Reunification Palace, the War Remnants Museum, Notre Dame Basilica, and several others were on our list.

Leaving the airport, the first thing I noticed was the number of motorbikes on the road. Tourist coaches and minibuses made up some of the traffic, but as we entered the city, even those disappeared. We were engulfed in a sea of bikes. Road rules were rarer than cars. At least that's how it appeared to me. Bikes carrying multiple people swarmed in all directions. The noise was deafening.

Singapore's sterile shiny streets were a distant dream compared to Saigon's weary bones. Bones that wanted to collapse under the weight of so much activity. Hundreds of wires exploded from each electric pole. You could nearly hear the crackle just looking at them. Homespun shopfronts offered shelves crowded with bottles of beer, soda, coffee, water, and jars of brightly-colored candies. Each one had several motorbikes parked in front. Traditional conical hats, *nón lá*, covered the heads that bike helmets didn't. Women with brown sun-wrinkled faces and black ponytails carried bamboo poles over their shoulders slung with two baskets on each end. They shouted the price of their fresh baguettes, lychee berries, and red dragon fruit.

Nothing was hidden from view behind closed doors. Dishes were washed on the street in grimy plastic tubs. Babies howled while their mothers attended to customers. Men with serious faces consulted over bike engines and spare parts. Not a single street corner was left unoccupied. There was business to be done.

My head swam with all the action. While a few words were offered in French on various signs, English had vanished. Pulling up to the Duxton hotel, quite grand in these surroundings, I was grateful to be greeted with "Welcome sir! Welcome m'am! Please let me help you." David and I, looking overly large and incredibly clumsy, stepped onto the red carpet that led to the hotel. "This way please!" The miniature bellhop ran in front of us carrying two overpacked bags.

"Welcome Mr. David and Mrs. David. We are so happy to have you visiting us.

I had gotten used to the fact that David's Dutch last name was very difficult to pronounce, but "Mrs. David" was a new one. Not wanting to offend the hard-working staff, I stifled my giggle.

"You have one of our very best rooms! If you would like, Hien will show you there right away!" The female desk clerk spoke perfect English, and I had rarely encountered such enthusiasm in Singapore. She smiled, a true smile that made the corners of her eyes go up. "My name is Hanh and please tell me how I may assist you during your stay." She handed me the key.

"Thank you very much. Do you have some tour information we could take a look at?" It didn't take long to see that getting around was complicated. We needed help. "Oh, and a city map too, please."

"Yes, of course, Mrs. David! Here you go. You can book the tours here also. Please enjoy Ho Chi Minh City!"

"Thank you. We will." Mr. David spoke up.

A gorgeous bouquet of fresh flowers stood in a red-and-black Vietnamese lacquer vase. It was massive. Purple orchids shot up over white lotus flowers. Pretty pink peach tree flowers surrounded the rest.

Flying the Coop

A card inserted read "Welcome to Duxton Hotel!" Even the flowers spoke in exclamation points.

It had been a long time since I'd truly felt welcome when I checked into a hotel. It gave me a good feeling about our long weekend. David tipped Hien, and I collapsed onto the bed to take a look at the glossy brochures.

"Slightly different than Singapore, eh?" I laughed.

"Slightly!" David laughed too, and folded me into his arms. "I can't wait to check it out."

Relieved that enthusiasm had returned, we consulted our guidebooks and the hotel information before making plans with the incredibly helpful Hanh. She had a recommendation for everything, and the prices were so much cheaper than what we were used to. Before we knew it, a dinner reservation was made, a city tour booked, and a full day on the Mekong River with a guide was confirmed. We had one morning to ourselves.

That evening we strolled hand in hand across the street to an elegant French-Vietnamese restaurant for dinner. After all we'd seen on the city streets, my expectations were low. Perhaps that's why I was blown away the by beautiful hardwood décor lit by colorful silk lanterns. Oriental artwork was tastefully hung and it was practically silent, despite the many people seated. The delicate French influence on Vietnamese cuisine was heartily welcomed by my taste buds.

Saigon held us in her grip for the next three days. We attempted to cross the street in the midst of hundreds of motorbikes, not a stop sign or red light in sight. David snapped pictures of families of four on bikes, and I haggled for the best-priced jade. We cruised down the mighty Mekong to a floating village which gave me a new definition for the word "poverty," yet the residents smiled and welcomed us among them. David learned how to make rice paper from the tiniest woman I have ever seen, and I drank snake wine. My love affair with Vietnam had begun.

* * *

I was thrilled that the city was too crazy and exotic for David to keep his mind on work. I hastily made plans for another trip almost immediately. Easter was coming and friends raved about Phuket. Now that I knew how easy it was to find cheap Asian airfares, I was dangerous. Conquering my fear of third world countries made me hungry for more.

David and I agreed that what we knew of Phuket was not our kind of scene. Cheap nightclubs, tourist dives, and pick up joints could be left for someone else. We wanted to see the famous debauchery of Patong's nights, but we didn't want to stay there. Surin Beach, one of the western beaches of Phuket Island met our requirements perfectly.

The Ayara Hilltops Resort offered all-suite accommodation for adults only. Each suite came with a private plunge pool and a view of the idyllic Andaman Sea. Most places of this caliber come with a stiff price tag, so I was skeptical. Until we arrived, that is.

A deeply-tanned man in a crisp white uniform and spotless white gloves opened the door of the taxi for me. "Welcome madam, please come this way. Do you have luggage? I will bring it for you." He took my hand to help me from the jeep that had collected us at the airport. Although there were no exclamation points in his speech, I had landed on a soft fluffy cloud of impeccable service.

A smiling woman with a tight bun, not a single hair out of place, offered us a seat in the lounge. She handed David a tall glass of chilled peach-colored liquid decorated with a yellow orchid. "Your welcome drink, sir. Please enjoy." Her long golden silk skirt brushed my leg as she delivered hand towels that must have been stored in the refrigerator. Pressing it to my neck gave me a delicious chill despite the mid-morning heat.

The very business-like staff of golden clad ladies had our suite sorted out in no time. We were whisked to the truly hilltop accommodation by another transport vehicle. The ride lasted less than two minutes. Guests were not expected to lift a finger.

The room was the most beautiful space I had ever seen. The private pool, known to most of us as a large Jacuzzi tub, was between the bedroom and the veranda. Two canvas deck chairs overlooking the sea awaited our arrival. The bathroom was an open-air outdoor design, incredibly tasteful and private. Orchids and frangipani flowers were stashed throughout the room. "Paradise" was the word that came to mind.

I smiled. David smiled. We were thinking the same thing.

* * *

Vietnam was thrilling. Thailand was decadent. Singapore was suffocating. Each return to the condo brought the strangulation of newfound happiness. We weren't made of money, and David would be shown the door in short order if he didn't make the grade. He'd already told me that several of the couples we met when we arrived had departed because they could not handle either the workload or the extreme cultural difference. I had no tearful farewells for Leah, Nancy, and Sally who were among the departed.

Madeline and I began spending more time together. We had similar attitudes to life, namely She Who Sees the Most Places Wins, and she was easy going. I'd be lying if I said I didn't now have a bias against Australian females, but she was different. Her career came first. I could sing that song too, or at least I used to.

Sitting under the palms drinking red wine at the Killiney Road wine bar I liked to frequent, Madeline asked where I most wanted to visit in the region.

"Japan," I said without a moment's hesitation.

"Really. Why is that?"

"I love Japanese food. I love sake. It looks so incredibly sophisticated compared to where we live. There are a million reasons."

"Funny that you say that. I've been wanting to go too. It's so expensive to fly from Australia and I saw an advertisement on one of those travel sites the other day. Tickets throughout May are two for one on Singapore Air."

"Are you kidding? That's a bargain!" I knew the flights normally cost about eight hundred dollars.

"I know. I've been dreaming about it since I read it."

"Great. Thanks for putting that thought in my head! David will be so happy about it!" I said sarcastically.

"Sorry!" she said, but she was laughing. "Well, maybe you'll convince him that it's a deal we can't miss. You wouldn't be lying." She baited the trap for her easy prey.

"I know. We've just been traveling a lot. Let me think about it." I sipped my shiraz and wondered how I could ask David about it without pissing him off.

That weekend, David was sharing his work woes with me. He was putting in ten plus hours a day, but the workload never seemed to diminish. Instead, it grew.

"The next few months are going to be so busy. I'm afraid you'll never see me." He warned.

"What's going on?"

"We're getting ready to complete the first phase of the project. That means getting ready for the go-live, conversion, and cutover. Everything has to be ready by then, so all system bugs fixed, etc. I will probably be working weekends soon and it's likely to last all summer."

"Oh." What was he expecting me to say to that? "I didn't realize this is how it was going to be here all the time."

"I didn't either." He seemed genuinely concerned. "I'm sorry."

"You don't have to be sorry. We both signed up for this. It's just difficult because in the past I was working just as many hours. My life is so empty here."

"I know. That's why I travel with you, but I won't be able to continue and keep everything going at work. It's not possible."

Now I sensed opportunity. "I understand. I'll try to keep myself busy. The problem is that there isn't much to do in Singapore. What there is to do, we've done already. The rest is all about shopping. It's so boring. If I didn't have my mornings at Fort Canning, you'd have to put me in an institution."

"Let's hope it doesn't come to that!" he teased.

"Hey! Not funny!" I seized the moment. "What about me traveling without you. Would that be okay with you?"

Surprise registered in his blue eyes. "Where do you want to go?"

"I don't know. I thought about going to the States at some point. Madeline also mentioned a killer deal to Tokyo that she found for May."

Flying the Coop

David wasn't always honest with his thoughts, even after five years of marriage and two years of dating. I watched him carefully.

He shrugged. "I guess so. I mean, as long as it doesn't cost too much. I don't know what else you would do here. Finding a job seems out of the question in this economy." He was being logical, but I didn't think I was getting the full story.

"Are you sure? I don't like leaving you here by yourself, but I'm not sure what else to do. We don't get along when I am just hanging around waiting for you and you're too stressed to enjoy the time we do have."

"I know. It's okay. I don't blame you. I know you didn't choose this either." That remark seemed honest, so I didn't question it. Our fates were tied together, and if one of us didn't take action we would drown here.

Making rice paper

Chapter 18
Sleepwalking in Tokyo

A heavy black fog blanketed Tokyo the morning I touched down, as if the city was determined to remain a mystery as long as possible. I had chosen a hotel with a shuttle bus, because Japanese was incomprehensible. Finding the bus was a cinch, but my tension grew as we neared the city. Unable to get free of work earlier, Madeline wouldn't arrive until the following evening.

The hotel itself was just like any business hotel anywhere else in the world. Out of curiosity, I pulled out the nightstand drawer. Side by side sat *The Teachings of Buddha* and *The Bible*. Knowing I was completely covered made me smile. I stared out the window at the highways which looked strikingly American, aside from the Japanese characters spilling across the road signs. Coca-cola and peanuts were in the minibar. Some things are universal.

Early the next day, my plan was to catch the train to Kamakura, an hour south of Tokyo, to see the Great Buddha and to explore the nearby gardens. I was staying in Akasaka, which bordered the much cooler area of Roppongi. Just because airfares were inexpensive didn't mean anything else was. With the shuttle included, Akasaka was the best deal I could find. That and it was fun to say out loud.

From Akasakamitsuke Station I took the Ginza line to Kamakura after buying a ticket from a machine with English instructions. Tokyo trains were busier and bigger than the New York City subway. What struck me was how orderly people behaved. They formed queues to get on the train, waiting patiently until everyone had departed before boarding. It was nothing like New York or Singapore. People moved with precision, never taking up too much space or jostling others.

I should film a training video for Singapore, I thought to myself. It was actually a pleasure to ride this train.

Overhead a cartoon advertisement showed a man shouting into his cell phone. He was obviously seated on a train and the others around him cowered in fear and annoyance. "Do it at the office!" was written in English underneath the picture. Since everything else was written in Japanese on board the train, it didn't take a genius to figure out who the sign was talking to. Message to foreigners: Please conform.

Outside Kamakura's station, a completely different landscape awaited. The seaside town, the center of the Japanese political landscape in the 1300's, is now a bustling city of one hundred and seventy-five thousand people. Strangely, it retains its resort-style feeling. School groups of perfectly uniformed boys and girls roamed with their teachers. Tourists lingered over maps, but few I spotted were American. I felt as though I was as far from everything I knew as I could possibly be.

The Great Buddha lives up to its name. Made of bronze that has long since been transformed by oxidation, the Buddha was cast in 1252 and stands over forty feet high. His characteristic long ears, those that hear the world's worries, were six feet in length. The serenity of the large square face never failed to make me wonder, *How does he do that?* As someone constantly tormented by neurotic expectations of perfection, it was truly a mystery to me how the Buddhists exuded this calm, especially those not cast in bronze.

From there I wandered to the Hasadera Temple, which had views over sparkling Sagami Bay and gardens of loveliness at its base. The only examples of Japanese gardens that I'd seen previously were in Singapore or Disneyland. They were nothing like this. Every detail was attended to. Bonzai trees and carefully constructed mossy cliffs stood watch over miniature Buddhist statues. There were hundreds of them. I took several photos before learning that this section was dedicated to the remembrance of babies who had died. At once sad and beautiful, I could not think of a more fitting tribute. The soft gurgle of a small stream could be heard below. Even the gardens were magic.

I had one more stop to make before catching the train to Tokyo. The thousand-year-old Hachimangu Shrine. Walking the long pathway to the main hall, I tried to imagine the things that had transpired on these very grounds in all that time. More critical than retracing the past, however was a visit to the bathroom. The gardens on the shrine's grounds thankfully yielded a public toilet. When I sat down, birds began to sing. *Loudly.* Putting the toilet in use triggered an electronic noise mechanism that, to suit the outdoor surroundings, consisted of bird calls. I wondered whose sensitivities were being protected – those *inside* or *outside* the toilet? Perhaps both. There was no choice but to laugh.

Back at the hotel, I sipped champagne at the bar and waited for Madeline to arrive. Tonight's plan was a visit to Shinjuku and the mysterious Golden Gai. Golden Gai is the place where time stood still as Tokyo developed into the modern monstrosity that it is today. It is six alleys that contain two hundred bars. With streets not even big enough for cars, you can imagine the size of the bars. I would feel like a giant Alice in Wonderland surrounded by tiny chairs and miniature people, but it simply had to be done.

We collected a small piece of paper from the concierge with the list of the usual tourist haunts written in Japanese. He had placed a checkmark in the right spot so that all we had to do was hand it to the driver. *Genius!* The white-gloved driver, looking through his white-fringed curtains to see the road, took it and said, "Gorden Gai Okay!"

"Okay!" Madeline got in the Tokyo swing of things. "What is this place?"

"I have no idea. I just know it's weird and we have to see it. Apparently some of the bars do not serve anyone but regulars so we will have to try and figure out which ones to enter. Most only have five or six seats!"

"You're joking, right?"

"I am not."

The taxi halted at Shinjuku. "Over there," he said.

"Over there" looked like nothing. "Are you sure?" I asked, as though he could understand me.

"Other side." A man of few words, but I got the gist of it. Golden Gai was on the other side of a large building in front of us. That's why we couldn't see it.

"Okay." I handed over two thousand yen. "*Domo arigatou.*"

I had my routine moment of wondering what the hell I was doing. Here was a place where some of the establishments were known to dislike foreigners. And here we were, walking right in without a clue. Luckily, it wasn't hard to find.

"Look at that!" Madeline had wide eyes.

Boudoir was the word that came to mind when I looked into the first bar. Deep scarlet walls. Low-hanging silk lanterns. Fishnets. I'd seen enough. "Let's keep going."

Several of the bars were empty. It was only eight-thirty and I'd read that the action didn't get started until later. Hoping to find a bite to eat and an interesting beverage, we'd arrived too early. A karaoke bar larger than the others stood out at the end of one alley. "I'm sorry, but it is way too early for that!" Madeline spoke my thoughts.

On the outside, we were in a shantytown. Inside each tiny bar, however, there were chandeliers and mahogany. One was a library. Another had nothing but beautiful bottles of what had to be very expensive *sake*. I love sake, but I didn't want to pay a fortune for it. We kept moving.

At the end of one alley, we found Liumin. A code of conduct on the outside wall urged us in. "We Serve Everyone!" I peeked through the door to see nothing that concerned me. Eight bar stools and a few Japanese guys drinking beer seemed harmless enough.

"Let's do it," I said.

"Onward!" declared Madeline.

From there, the night was a blur. The owner and his girlfriend chatted with us in English. The words didn't always make sense, but sake is the miracle translator. Everything was understood. Beers followed the sake. A famous, we were told, comedian performed some shtick and goggle-eyed faces too weird for words. Madeline found a new friend in the gentleman sitting next to her who was, sadly, terrified of flying. Another Japanese guy in a Fedora began plucking Stairway to Heaven on the guitar, which temporarily dampened the mood. Soon the barmaid was showing us to a noodle bar. It was midnight and she insisted that we eat.

The cast—Japanese barmaid, increasingly tipsy Madeline, Businessman Who Will Not Fly—and me, crowds into a very crowded karaoke bar. The required booze level has been met. Beers are passed around.

A Swedish blonde is telling me about his "most awesome Route 66 road trip ever!" planned for next month. A giant yellow headband with a local guy under it sings badly to 'Sister Christian' but refuses to give up the microphone despite the pleas of the entire crowd. *Are those Christmas lights blinking?* Madeline is making out with the guy who doesn't fly. I'm in a cab waiting for their final farewells. We are in the hotel elevator which has a tiny chair in the corner for no apparent reason. Madeline sitting in this chair is even more hilarious. *Lights out.*

It is daylight and I have never been so thirsty in my life. Madeline is dressed. And showered. I find this disconcerting, as now I will be expected to rush to get ready.

"What time is it?" A voice comes out that sounds nothing like mine.

"It's ten. Didn't you hear anything?" She seems impatient.

"No. Hear what?" my brain cells are not firing. "Is there a coffee maker in here?"

"There isn't. We'll have to go to the breakfast room to get some. It closes at ten-thirty."

Now I know why she is impatient.

"You really didn't hear anything?" She presses.

"Not a sound. I don't normally sleep in my clothes so you can assume that I was pretty far gone. What happened?"

"I was pounding on the door."

"From *outside*?" I didn't get it.

"Yes, from outside. You wouldn't come to the door."

"As I just mentioned, I didn't *hear* you." *Is she mad at me for something?*

"What were you doing outside?"

"I guess I was sleepwalking. I woke up in my pajamas..." She trailed off.

"Oh my God! No, I'm sorry, I didn't hear a thing."

"… in the lobby." Her face glowed red.

"*Are you serious*?" I was wide awake now. "What did you do?!"

"I ran for the elevator and came up here, but you wouldn't answer the door. I had to go back down to the front desk. *I even called you!*"

"I'm so sorry, Madeline. I would never do something like that on purpose. I was out cold." I wanted to laugh so badly, but I knew it would end this friendship. "What time was this? How did you get back in?"

"It was six o'clock. The front desk guy came up with me. He had a key, but he came in first to make sure I wasn't lying."

"Wait a minute. There was all this commotion *and* another person in the room, and I didn't move?" Incomprehensible.

"You didn't move."

"Were there people in the lobby when you woke up there?" I had to know.

"Yes. I can't go back down there." Her face was still beet red.

"I'll take a quick shower so we can get some coffee. I am really sorry, Madeline. Look at the bright side, anyone who was having breakfast at six-thirty is long gone by now." I closed the door and put my hand over my mouth to laugh. Talk about one for the books!

After the Golden Gai debacle, we managed to stay out of trouble, more or less. Tokyo waits for no man or woman, as the case may be. Sunny blue skies and eighty-degree weather meant outdoor sightseeing. We compared the Meji Jingu Shinto shrine to the Senso-ji Buddhist Temple. Teenage girls in Goth outfits smoked cigarettes with others dressed like Little Bo Peep. One had cat ears, another camouflage. These were the Harajuku Girls.

Shopping in Ginza was in another galaxy from my budget. It was a more-refined Times Square, without the naked cowboys and giant Elmos. Opposite the gleaming Apple store, the largest I'd seen anywhere, stood Matsuzakaya. I couldn't resist its siren song, and found myself dragging Madeline through the spotless revolving door. Knowing that the ground level of any major department store generally holds the most expensive merchandise, I located the down escalator. Jackpot! It was the food hall.

Glass counters held every imaginable food item one might wish for. Perfectly stacked and polished fruits stood at attention. Tightly wrapped hand rolls of tuna, avocado, crabmeat, and salmon formed geometric excellence under glass. Ripe strawberries topped vanilla frosted slices of creamy cake in exactly the same place on every cake. Women in plastic gloves with white masks over their mouths and white hairnets performed the surgery, giving slight head bows as we passed each one. Nothing was out of place.

"Don't you wonder what it feels like to be average in this country?" I wondered out loud.

"What do you mean?"

"Look around. *Everything* is done with precision. What if you are the one who can't get the strawberry in the right place or, God forbid, you put an apple in the tower that has a slight blemish? Do you get fired? Have to go back to training?"

"Who knows?" Madeline was busy looking at perfect pralines.

"I mean, what does this mean for the kid that gets C's in school... or worse? Can you imagine? He's probably flogged." I was extrapolating from perfect food to academic excellence, but it was dawning on me that everywhere we went there was simply nothing average.

The New York Bar at the Park Hyatt Tokyo was our destination for the evening. Though it was also in Shinjuku, it was sure to be a less rowdy experience than the night before. Taking a seat at the same bar where Bill Murray sat with Scarlett Johanssen in *Lost in Translation* was a thrill, but the view was a heart-stopper. The Tokyo city skyline was rubies and sapphires glittering at our feet. From here I felt I could do anything.

Before getting into the taxi, I asked Madeline to wait for me while I went to the ladies room. As an old hand at Tokyo now, I was prepared for the oddities that a visit to the lavatory could produce. Glancing at my reflection in the spotless mirror, I walked to the stalls and went in. Believe me when I tell you that this time I got out my camera before attending to the business at hand. This toilet had a *flow chart* to explain its various options! I should have expected that a high-end luxury hotel would be a standout in many ways, but functions like: massage, bidet, and what could only have been a dryer button labeled "warm air" put me in hysterics.

Exiting the bathroom and laughing like an eight-year-old, "You have to go in there," I told Madeline.

"Why?" She looked dubious. Perhaps at forty-three, she was more mature than her thirty-eight-year-old travel mate.

Remembering that I wasn't the one who had recently been in the hotel lobby wearing pj's, I stood firm. "You just do."

Before long I wasn't the only one in tears. "Did you try that stuff?" she croaked.

"No, I was too busy taking photos!"

"Well, you missed out!" she grinned. "Let's get out of here before we cause another hotel incident."

You just can't predict what Tokyo will serve up, I thought to myself as I pulled open the taxi door.

Chapter 19
Miscellaneous Melbourne

Having a new travel buddy made me excited about the possibilities. David was pleased that I had a new friend, and there was never a dull moment with Madeline. She was always in motion. Perhaps I had once been that way when my demanding job gave me limited free time to do the things I wanted to do. A year and a half without one had made me forget.

"Do you want to come home with me?" The question came out of the blue from Madeline on a Tuesday evening catch-up.

"Home? You mean to Melbourne?" Even I was shocked. We had barely just returned from Tokyo.

"Yes, of course Melbourne. I get a trip back every quarter and I need to go see my mum."

Realizing she had been thinking about this for a while, I knew she wasn't joking. "Hmm. I'd need to check the financial situation. Japan blew it out of the water. Honestly, I'm not sure I can afford it right now.

"All you need to cover is the flight and some entertainment expenses. We can stay at my place and I can show you the city. I'll have to work some of the time, but there's plenty you can do on your own."

"Wow. Thank you. It's a difficult offer to refuse." I'd been thinking about Australia as a potential next home base since our Christmas trip. I had zero desire to go back to Holland and was losing patience with Singapore quickly. It was a pipe dream, but that didn't mean I couldn't feed it. "I'll talk to David and get back to you."

"No problem. I'm sure you'll love it."

For once I wasn't driving the insane travel plans, someone else was. That made it easier to broach the subject with David. I felt like I was depleting our resources constantly. On the other hand, chances like these didn't come around every day. Even he could see that.

"I don't have a problem with it. I'm glad to see you so happy."

For the second time that day, I was stunned. But not so much that I hesitated. "It's a great opportunity. I still can't believe it, but I'm not going to say no."

"I don't' think you should either. It will be fun."

***

Madeline and I flew separately. I was building up my Singapore Air miles and she was loyal to Qantas. Her flight arrived an hour before mine.

"What are you doing in Australia?" The female customs agent stood between me and the luggage carousel, blocking my path. She stared me down, waiting for an immediate response.

"I'm taking a look around to see if I might want to live here one day." I didn't take the question that seriously and she knew it.

"What exactly do you mean?"

"I'm here visiting a friend who arrived on an earlier flight. I've never been to Melbourne before and I'm here to see what it's like." I was jet lagged and tired from not sleeping on the overnight flight. All I wanted was for this woman to let me pass.

"Show me your return ticket."

Realizing this woman was without a sense of humor, I fished around in my bag for the itinerary. "I'll be here for five days," I said, handing her the ticket.

She verified what I said. "You can go."

Welcome to Australia! I thought to myself, looking for the carousel number to find my bag.

"International passengers! Please be aware that it is forbidden to bring any fruit, plants, seeds, or vegetables into Australia. You must declare any organic material or souvenirs, such as those made of wood." Loudspeakers blared with a male Aussie voice who issued the orders. "Any undeclared material may be confiscated or fines levied."

For a country with such a laid back reputation, this was anything but. As a post 9/11 traveler, I knew full well that airport security is serious business, but I hadn't experienced the brunt of it in quite a while. Flights into Singapore threatened the penalty of death for anyone caught carrying drugs, but no one said boo once you landed at the airport. At least not to Caucasian westerners, that is. I had seen Malaysians and Bangladeshis in heated conversation with Singapore customs agents more than once.

"Do you have dirt in your shoes, miss?" This time a male customs agent asked the question.

"I'm sorry?" *What the hell was he talking about?*

"You are wearing athletic shoes. Do they have dirt or mud in the tread? Have you been hiking or walking on trails?"

Lifting my foot to look, "Ummm... nope. They're clean." I showed him my right sole, then my left. *Why does he want to know what I do for exercise?*

He looked at my feet and reviewed my customs form. "You can go. Next!"

Now I was really confused. I saw Madeline in a heap on a bench just outside the door. She looked so tired.

"Thank you for waiting for me. You must be exhausted. Did you sleep?"

"Not much. Did everything go all right?"

"Yeah, fine. Your authorities ask some very strange questions!"

"What did they ask you?"

We had close to an hour in the taxi to get to her place, so I gave her the details.

"First, immigration is a hot issue in Australia, so I am sure she didn't appreciate your comment about looking for a place to live. We have so many refugees arriving by boat that it's not funny, and the government doesn't have a good answer for what to do about it. I don't know what the right answer is either." She paused a minute before continuing. "Second, yes, I completely forgot to warn you about the quarantine laws. Because we are an island, they are very strict about what can be brought into the country. If some kind of diseased plant or microorganism gets into the country unnoticed, there could be an epidemic."

This was the difference between traveling alone and traveling with a local. If Madeline hadn't explained the context, I would have believed the authorities were just rude. Well, they were still somewhat rude, but now I knew the reason. "I can't believe I told her I was looking for a new country. No wonder she was scrutinizing me, what I had on, where my return ticket was."

"I'm surprised it wasn't worse, with a comment like that. Since you don't look like you are from a poor country, she must have decided you weren't serious."

"I guess. I'm freezing! I can't believe how cold it is here." I changed the subject.

"It's almost winter, of course it's cold." Her voice was tired and exasperated.

"I knew it was winter, but you rarely see photos of an Australian winter. All you ever see are pics of Sydney Harbour and the Great Barrier Reef! I didn't know it gets down to single digits."

"Just be glad it isn't snowing yet."

Since all my remarks were coming out as complaints at this point, I decided it was time to shut up. Melbourne is a European city. No doubt about it. Corner cafés with deep rich coffee and delicate pastries. Elaborate Victorian architecture sits side by side with buildings of modern design. Award-winning Greek, Spanish, and Italian restaurants dominate the gourmet scene. You would hear no further complaints coming from me. Madeline's day at the office gave me the opportunity to wander and play tourist.

The Melbourne Gaol, from the original Old French spelling, the city's oldest jail, opened in 1845. The tour was given by a diminutive woman in a police uniform, even though the building was now a museum. "There are so many stories in here. Can't you feel it?" she was saying enthusiastically. Based on the death masks on display in each holding cell, I didn't think they had happy endings.

"Ned Kelly was executed in this very place!"

If someone's hanging made her that excited, I didn't want her around when I kicked the bucket. "Who is Ned Kelly?" I asked.

"Who is Ned Kelly? Where are you from?"

"I'm American."

"Well that explains it. Ned Kelly is the most famous bushranger in Australian history. He assaulted people, including a police officer. He was the leader of a gang that held up banks. One time they did it dressed as cops! He committed all kinds of crimes until they caught him and sentenced him to death in 1880."

"Good to know." I wasn't about to ask what a "bushranger" was. It had to be the same as an outlaw.

"His death mask and fake suit of armor are at the end of this floor. You can see where he was hanged a little later." She was still a little too cheery for my liking.

Over tapas and sangria that evening, Madeline told me that Ned Kelly was a bit like a Robin Hood figure, someone who was known to be a criminal but was loved anyway. "He often made fools of the police and people like that."

Another interesting Australian trait. I thought it, but I did not say it.

"Tomorrow we'll leave early for the Great Ocean Road. It's a long drive, but it'll be worth it."

I nodded between bites of *patatas bravas* and Serrano ham. "Sounds great indeed! I looked up photos online. Hard to believe it's as good as it looks."

"You won't be disappointed."

The Great Ocean Road began as a project to put returning veterans back to work after World War I building a memorial to those who had not returned. Initiated in 1918, it winds for two hundred and forty-three kilometers along the southeast coast of the state of Victoria. Completed and opened as a tourist attraction in 1932, it finally linked several isolated coastal villages to Melbourne and created the largest war memorial in the world.

The photos didn't give an accurate view of just how narrow the road is, and Madeline liked driving fast. Already nervous on the "wrong" side of the car, my nails occasionally dug into the leather armrest of her black Toyota sports car. A gray wintry mist blew across the black asphalt, turning it into a writhing snake. The view from the passenger window was no consolation. Down below, *very far* down below, the angry sea thrashed white against razor-sharp cliffs. I could see why this area is known as the Shipwreck Coast. English explorer Matthew Flinders is known for saying, "I have seldom seen a more fearful section of coastline."

"I'm not sure exactly where we should stop. The weather will make it difficult to get any decent photos." She was thinking ahead, oblivious to my escalating anxiety.

"Whatever you think is best. I'm sorry I'm not up for sharing the driving. I've never driven on the left and this doesn't seem like the place to start."

"That's true, mate. This road is tricky in places. The turns come up on you quick."

"I see that."

There was little need for further conversation. The dramatic views held my attention until we reached Port Campbell, the home of the Twelve Apostles. Parking at the visitor lot, we had no choice but to put our faces to the lashing rain and biting wind to experience the Apostles, the crown jewel of Ocean Road tourism. Happy that I had a raincoat with a hood, I held my camera inside my pocket. *Why do I do this to myself?* I wondered. And then I knew.

Looking down from the wooden viewing platform was what the Aussies call being "gobsmacked." Think of it as being made speechless, but you have to agree it's a far more colorful expression. Even the absolutely terrible weather couldn't diminish the beauty of this landmark. The Southern Ocean is known for its extreme weather, hence my earlier reference to the Shipwreck Coast of Australia. Limestone erosion originally drilled caves into the coastline and when those eventually collapsed, it left only stone pillars. People pilgrimage by the thousands to photograph the Apostles with a sunset backdrop.

Having taken some very unremarkable photos, we dashed back to the car to continue the drive. When the rain subsided, a staggering variety of turquoise shades appeared in the water below. At the shoreline, slim black rocks glistened like death's fingers luring ship's crewmen to their demise. It was simultaneously beautiful and fierce.

Chapter 20
"Home"

Is it possible for this place to get any hotter? I'd often wondered just how much the summer would change the temperature this close to the equator. The first summer we spent in Singapore, I was too preoccupied with finding gainful employment to worry about what season it was. Now that I had a great deal more time on my hands, I found that the answer is *yes* it can get hotter. Not only that, the storms ratchet up a few notches to make sure any time spent outdoors is an adventure.

Lazy days next to the pool were no longer interesting. If I spent any time there, it was swimming. I worked up to swimming a mile a day in that pool. It was one of the few things left that I enjoyed about Singapore. That and five-dollar admission to the matinee at the cinema. David was oblivious to everything at this point.

"I don't think you should go out there just yet," I said to him one morning as water poured from the sky in astonishing quantity.

"I only have to cross the street, and I have a meeting." He neatly tied his coffee-brown leather shoes and zipped his laptop into this backpack.

He wasn't even looking at me. "Have you seen how high the water gets when the rain is coming down this heavy?"

"I'll be fine."

"Good luck," I said sarcastically. There was no way the storm would keep up the pace for long. Generally, taking shelter for five or ten minutes was sufficient to be able to move on.

"Bye." A quick kiss and he was in the elevator.

I looked down to the street. Normally the smattering of umbrellas would tell me when it was time to go. This time, there were none. The locals didn't feel like swimming to work.

Three minutes passed and the elevator doors swished open again. A sopping David squished out. "Would you please bring me a towel?" A puddle immediately formed at his feet.

My hand flew over my mouth to stop the laughter that wanted to escape. "Mmph... sure." I ran into the guest bathroom to grab a stack of them. One was not going to be sufficient. "Here you go."

"Even my laptop is wet! I can't believe this!" he ranted.

I said nothing.

"I'm sure it will stop soon," I offered.

"My shoes are ruined." The hit parade continued.

"What did you expect? You can see how fast the rain is coming down." I couldn't take it anymore.

My outburst was like a pin pushed into a balloon full of hot air. He collapsed onto a kitchen chair, deflated. "I know. It was stupid. I was in a hurry because this meeting is important. Now I don't even know if my laptop will turn on."

"I'm sure it will be okay. You were only out there for a second. Look, it's already letting up." *Why can't I keep my mouth shut?* I didn't want him to feel worse.

David sloshed into the guestroom where his closet was and closed the door. I mopped up the trail of water he left behind.

"There was a Singaporean girl on the other side of the street. The water was nearly up to her waist! On me, it came to here. He pointed to a spot below his knee. I thought she might get washed away!" Now he was laughing.

"She didn't, did she?"

"No. She made it to higher ground." He looked at his watch. "Shit! I have to go. I'll get a taxi downstairs." Another quick kiss and he was gone.

I turned back to the window. *Nope.* I wasn't going anywhere.

* * *

"Home"

The brutal summer looked more and more like the perfect time to escape. David was always at the office and a mile in the pool didn't consume a great deal of my day. I couldn't imagine being trapped inside for the next two months. Visits from Angeline to clean the condo were the only thing that forced me outside now. If I stayed, she wanted to talk. *A lot.* The three to four hours she took to clean turned to five.

As part of the package that David received for working overseas, we were entitled to trips to our home country. Since we still owned a house in the Netherlands and he was part of the Dutch practice, Holland was "home." I didn't know what I would do in the Netherlands for all that time, so I went to the States. David couldn't go anywhere.

I hadn't been back to America for a visit in two years, and I hadn't lived there in nearly eight. My parents now lived in different houses with different people in the same city. My friends all lived in various places on the east and southeast coasts. I stayed with my mother and felt like an intruder in a house where there was a daily routine that my presence disrupted. She was glad to see me of course, and we tried our best not to irritate each other but being an adult in the house of a parent is difficult no matter how old you are. We hatched a plan that gave us both some peace.

I took a road trip to see my friends in Florida and Georgia, borrowing my mother's car. She flew to North Carolina later and we visited my aunt in Charlotte. For six weeks I roamed the US looking for the person I used to be, because I no longer knew who I was. No matter where I went, I was uncomfortable. I lived in an exotic place but had nothing to show for it. There was no longer a high-flying career or my own identity of any kind. I was someone's *dependent*. Returning to America depressed me more than ever.

Needless to say, my state of mind wasn't rosy when I flew back to Singapore in August. I had expected the familiarity of friends and family to provide some respite from my complete lack of purpose. It didn't. They were a mirror for everything I used to be and a painful reminder of what I no longer was: successful. Landing at Changi Airport was a far cry less exhilarating than the first time. Even being with David again felt foreign. Since I moved to Holland in 2003, we had never spent this much time apart.

He, on the other hand, seemed happy. "I can't believe you're finally home!" I was pulled into a bear hug and squeezed until my arms hurt.

"Yep. It's me. Seems like a long time, doesn't it?" I called over my shoulder, walking away. I *had* to get the clothes off that I'd worn now for over twenty-four hours.

"It *was* a long time." He shouted after me.

"Let me just take a shower and then I can think." Getting the airplane grime off of me could not happen fast enough for my liking.

"How was it?" he asked when I walked back in ten minutes later in a towel.

"Weird." How could I even explain it all?

"How do you mean?" Concern put creases in his forehead.

"I didn't feel comfortable anywhere. It's weird to be in other people's houses for that long after having your own. I mean, I was happy to see my friends, but I couldn't relax. Since I always feel tense with the constant noise in Singapore that was all I really wanted." I hoped I was getting my point across.

"I wondered how that would go." He knew me better than I knew myself sometimes. That hadn't changed. "Come in here and I will help you relax." He grinned and grabbed my hand. I pretended to resist. It lasted about one minute.

* * *

"The project Go Live date was delayed. It will be in early September." David looked sheepish, knowing I had left town for so long to give him all the room he needed to finish this phase of the project.

"You're joking, right?" I didn't want to believe I had heard him correctly.

"No. Unfortunately not. But I have a great idea!"

"Lay it on me." I deadpanned.

"We're going to Bintan for four days before everything gets crazy at work." A big smile lit up his handsome face. He knew he had me.

"Oh we are, are we?" Now that I wanted to believe him, I wasn't sure I could.

"Home"

"Yes. I already arranged the Banyan Tree and the ferry tickets for next weekend." Clearly very proud of himself. "Doesn't that sound nice?"

I had to admit that it did. Bintan is an Indonesian island off the coast of Singapore. It is the closest possible escape from city-state captivity. A forty-five minute ferry ride across the strait will have you at any one of several beautiful resorts. Sweaty Singapore can quickly be a distant memory when you're surrounded by rainforest bordered by palm-lined beaches and crystal swimming pools. There was no way I could be upset about this and he knew it.

"That sounds perfect. Thank you, sweetie."

"I'm sorry about the project delay. It isn't up to me, but of course you know that. Once everyone agrees to the new schedule and milestone dates, no one can make changes."

"You sure pulled a rabbit out of a hat though! I'm already excited about Bintan. The Banyan Tree will be gorgeous. What a way to unwind." I gave him the fat kiss he deserved with this winning attempt to diffuse yet another annoying argument before it happened.

* * *

"Are you all right?" I asked, even though I knew the answer.

"Yes, I'm fine." David lied. His pale face turned greener with each passing moment. "I'm going to sit on the outer deck to try and get some air."

"Okay," I replied to no one. He was already gone.

The ferry rolled over another huge wave and I was silently grateful that the ride was less than an hour. David hadn't forseen the afternoon storm in enough time to take seasick pills and he was paying the price. Peering through the plastic sheeting that stood between me and a saltwater facial, I looked for a clearing horizon. It wasn't there.

The weather became inconsequential when we saw our private villa. It was white stucco with deep-brown wood and plaster trim. Our view of the sea was blocked by nothing. A Jacuzzi was strategically placed on the deck to take in the sounds of the waves below. Mosquito netting draped from the four poster mahogany bed and a bowl of fresh bananas and lychees sat on the nightstand.

"Will there be anything else, Mr. David?" the driver asked.

"No, thank you. We're fine for now."

"Yes, sir. Please call us to let us know when you would like to have dinner." The door closed softly behind him.

"This is unbelievable!" Of course I acted very nonchalant when the driver was with us, but now I wanted to inhale every inch of our lush surroundings.

"I'm glad you like it." His reply came with a sly grin, as though he'd known all along how perfect it would be. "Let's get room service tonight."

"I totally agree. There's a table on the deck and we can soak in the Jacuzzi after. It's going to pour down again tonight, so we might as well enjoy where we are. God, this is paradise. You'll never get me out of here."

The weather delivered what we needed for the first two days, forced relaxation. We read. We slept. We found other ways of entertaining ourselves in our stunning villa. But when the sun finally showed herself, Bintan was transformed. The black sea returned to blue and the sand to brushed gold, as though Midas had been up for an early morning walk.

"Get your suit on!" I started tickling David, my one superpower that could get him to do anything I asked.

"Stop it! STOP IT! Okay, I'm getting up!" He couldn't stop laughing.

"I've been dying to get down to the beach and the pool. There's a restaurant down there too. It's perfect today." I was all action.

We dropped our things on two lounge chairs and took our cameras to the beach where David promptly became transfixed by a coconut. He was trying to shoot the perfect artsy photo of the waves washing over it. I waded knee deep in the sea to find live creatures to photograph.

I didn't have to wait long. Black-and-yellow-striped fish flitted past my legs. Silver ones shimmered in schools nearby. A trail of large rocks that originated on the beach looked too inviting not to sit on. Splashing around with my feet, I spotted movement over my shoulder from the corner of my eye. As I turned, I lifted my camera to zoom in on the largest lizard I had ever seen in my life. It was no less than five feet long, its blue forked tongue zipped in and out of its mouth. Our eyes met. For a moment I panicked. Would it attack?

It turned and ambled toward the beach restaurant. Apparently I was uninteresting, and for once I was glad. "David!" I shouted. He didn't look up. "DAVID!" Louder this time. I hated doing it, but I didn't want him to miss this thing.

"What?"

"Come here!"

He looked back at his cherished coconut for a minute before deciding that I might be onto something more interesting and walking my way.

"Get OUT!" a man behind me yelled. He was waving a broom around. I hoped he wasn't talking to a guest.

"WOW! Look at that thing!" David saw that Godzilla had attempted to penetrate the sacred beach kitchen, and the chef was having none of it.

"Monitor lizard," said the chef when he saw us with our cameras. "He like chicken!" he continued.

I wondered if that thing was gulping them down whole before I heard a woman's shrill scream. David and I looked at each other before running up to see what the commotion was about. We arrived in just enough time to see the lizard swim past three women. They'd been drinking cocktails with their backs to it before one of them looked over her shoulder. Godzilla suddenly had the pool all to himself. Perhaps that was his master plan?

"I didn't know lizards could swim…" I said in awe.

"Me neither," David agreed.

"Nowhere is safe!" I mocked terror, grabbing him and pushing him to the other end of the pool. Godzilla decided there were too many noisy tourists around for his liking and headed toward the bushes. David and I jumped into the chilly water to relieve our pale burnt skin. In all the excitement, I had completely forgotten about sunscreen.

That evening we had dinner on the terrace overlooking the ocean. A bottle of white wine sat in a chiller next to the white-linen tablecloth.

Our fish was being prepared. From my perspective, the evening was perfect. Until it wasn't.

"There's one more thing I have to tell you." David was obviously choosing his moment, which meant it was something I wasn't going to like.

"If it's going to spoil everything, can you just save it for now?"

"No, I don't think it will. We finally got new neighbors."

We owned the upper floors of our Rotterdam building and the lower level apartment had been for sale for some time.

"Oh we do?"

"Yes, Roland and Yvette are going to be moving in at the beginning of September."

"I guess it's quite lucky for them that we are never home!"

"We're the perfect neighbors. Definitely." He stalled.

"So what's up?"

"Remember what I told you before that when you share a building with another family in Holland, you have to open a bank account and jointly finance all the repairs and maintenance?"

"Yeah, I remember. We used to pay into it with the people that lived there before."

"Right. Well, the new neighbors want to paint the outside of the building."

"Okay. It's mostly brick so it can't be that expensive." I was wondering what the catch was going to be.

"It isn't. Roland has already gotten quotes. The problem is that the painter will need to be in and out of our house."

His concern was suddenly clear. Dutch people thought nothing of handing over their keys to handymen and neighbors they had never met. It was an argument that we'd had in the past. Someone was going to have to be there or we would have to deliver a key to strangers.

"I see. How much is it going to cost?"

"I think about five thousand euro."

"It seems like someone ought to make sure we are getting what we want in this picture as well, right? I mean, why should we let them decide everything? It's our house too."

"Home"

"I agree." David waited for me to decide what I was going to do.

"Don't you have a free ticket back to Holland that hasn't been used?"

"Yes. I was thinking the same thing. We should meet these people and since you have the time…" he trailed off.

"All I have is time," I sighed. "Okay, I'll do it. You are going to be slammed at work anyway."

"At least the weather should be great in September!" He was trying to make me feel better.

"That's true. It will be better than here!" I brightened to the idea. We couldn't ask the neighbors to put it off for the unknown number of years we would be in Singapore, and it was the chance to change the scenery once again. I would have been a lot happier about it if I hadn't just been away from my husband for six weeks, but I guess this was the life I signed up for.

"I think I'll have some more wine." I held out my glass and David filled it. "At least that's much cheaper in Holland." It was a tarnished-silver lining.

* * *

Pink was sitting three rows up from me. I was sure of it. There wasn't an empty seat in business class on the KLM flight from Singapore to Amsterdam. *He's Just Not That Into You* was playing on the screen in front of me, the soundtrack coming through my Bose headphones. I sipped champagne and tried not to be obvious.

"That's Pink, isn't it?" I asked the stewardess who refilled my flute.

"Who?" her accent was Dutch.

"The short-haired blonde in the first row. She's an American rock singer." I was intrigued. I'd rarely ever spotted anyone famous.

"I don't know. She is American, but I'm not sure of her name. I will find out."

I went back to the movie. My glass was refilled several more times by the same stewardess. "All I know is that she is a celebrity." She told me on her last stop after dinner. "Would you like to try this port? The pink one? It's new."

"Sure. I'll have some." I said no to a new drink about as often as I spotted a celebrity. "Thank you."

She smiled as she handed over the glass. I thought she was about to say something else, but she didn't. As soon as the port kicked in, which was quite tasty if I remember, I fought to keep my eyes open. I lost the fight.

The announcement that we were about to land woke me. Quickly I ran to the bathroom and grabbed a disposable toothbrush. My reflection frightened me. My hairbrush was no match for bedhead. The red light came on to tell me I was out of time and I went back to my seat. I drained the bottle of water that the thoughtful stewardess had left me.

Suddenly she was bending down to whisper in my ear. "I thought you might like to have this as a present." She handed me a bottle.

This is the last thing I need. I smiled at her and then looked more closely at the label. It was the pink port that I had tried earlier. "Thank you." She patted me on the shoulder.

It took me a minute to remember that Pink was a few seats away. I'd forgotten all about it. This was confirmation that she was who I thought she was. Apparently I was being thanked for not annoying the special guest or making a scene. I laughed to myself. It was a nice thought, but I'd never have said anything to her anyway.

The house was cold. It was early morning in Rotterdam and even though the days were warm, the overnight temperature was not. At least not compared to Singapore. After sitting empty for so long, the air seemed stale and the house lifeless. My neighbors could wait to make my acquaintance. Thinking about my appearance, I realized they would be grateful if I showered first!

It was strange to be alone in so much space. One of my favorite things about my Rotterdam home was the bedroom. It was huge. I'd always joked that all we needed was a disco light and a dance floor because the room could certainly accommodate it. Four tall glass windows and cream colored carpet lit up the space with sunlight. The full tree outside was beginning to show hints of orange. The only drawback was the lack of internet and cable TV.

"Home"

I called downstairs and spoke to Yvette.

"Could you stop by for a drink this evening?" she wanted to know.

Grateful for the few hours reprieve, "Yes. That would be lovely. What time?"

"After dinner, I think. What about seven?"

"Perfect. I'll see you then."

Roland was a man of medium build with a kind face. He was a bit older than me, but I couldn't tell how old. "How do you like Singapore?"

"It's a great base to explore the rest of Asia." My standard response to anyone who asked.

"I have never been there, but my brother lives in China. He's been there for years and I did have the chance to visit once."

"Really, that's interesting. We have been discussing a trip to China later this year. Where does he live?"

"I can never remember the name, somewhere in the south. But he took me on an amazing trip to the Great Wall when I was there. We slept in one of the guard towers on the wall. A local guy took us there and cooked for us. The whole thing cost nothing, maybe one hundred dollars US?"

Immediately I was intrigued. "How long ago was this?"

"Just last year." He looked at Yvette. Yvette nodded to confirm.

"Wow. That sounds fascinating. If you think you would still have the details, I would be delighted to have them. It sounds amazing." In my mind, I was already there with Allison and David on the trip we had been planning for October when she came to visit.

"I'm sure I do. I will send them to David by email. Now, shall we look at paint colors?" He was more eager to change the subject than I was.

That was the most exciting moment of my week in the Netherlands. In the evenings, I walked down to my favorite café for a Duvel or a few glasses of wine with dinner. They had wifi so I could stay in touch and surf for details about travel in China. My South African friend Marlena and her husband lived north of Amsterdam and I went to spend the night with them. As wonderful as it was to see their smiles and talk about old times, I felt as uncomfortable as I did in Ohio. The feeling didn't even dissipate when two other friends took me to Antwerp for the day—and I love going to Belgium for *any* reason. Now I was nobody. These friends had known me as someone with a great job and a bright future. What could they possibly see now?

Chapter 21
Forbidden

The Killiney Road post office, scene of my initial branding as "housewife," had been undergoing a transformation for the better part of a year. I'd seen twenty-story buildings go up in a shorter period of time, so they had to be up to something serious in there. Though the great unveiling happened in August of 2009, I didn't get a good look until a few weeks later.

Singapore was determined to be a trendsetter. This neighborhood, which was a block from fancy Orchard Road, was a combination of western foreigners living in nearby condos and locals working in any one of the establishments nearby. I can only assume that this post office was carefully constructed to appeal to both. It had a bar in it. That's right, a bar.

It wasn't a local watering hole that happened to post letters and packages on occasion. It was a full-service post office on one side and modern trendy café and bar on the other. The café had a digital display to update customers drinking in the bar, telling them when their number came up. *Might as well have a pint while I wait to send granny's birthday gift.* Singapore was all about money, and once again they capitalized on a captive audience. It was impressive. Even more impressive when I visited the roof bar a few days later.

Madeline and I were sitting on bar stools on the upstairs deck of the hip and trendy KPO, as the building was now called. The bar, called Chivas, was packed on a Tuesday night and there was that rarest of all Singapore weather occurrences—a breeze.

"It's just so difficult to meet anyone here..." Madeline was talking, but I was busy people-watching.

"Mmm... yeah, I'll bet."

"You would think in a place with this many expats, the chances would be higher. Asian guys rarely catch my eye." She went on.

"Aren't there any hot guys at the office? I mean, that's where David and I met in Germany." It seemed to me that with the hundreds of people working there, there must be *someone* who struck her fancy.

"I went out with John a few times, but he's been flaky. There are plenty of guys around, but most of them are married." Her blue eyes scanned the audience as well. At forty-three, Madeline had never married.

"That's a bummer." Who was I to offer dating advice?

"In fact, the only ones that hit on me are the married ones."

Now she had my attention. "What do you mean?"

"It's happened at least six or seven times. They want to confide in me for some reason. I don't know. It's weird."

"I'll say it's weird. Don't these guys have families here who packed up and came with them? Are we talking about people that I know?" Most of the time, I tuned out to what went down at the project because I was forced to hear about it all the time. Scandal was a horse of a different color.

"Do you know Paul Lansing? Or James Bates?" She tossed out the names she thought I might recognize.

"No, never heard of either one." It was a relief. I really didn't want to hear something like that about a friend.

"Then probably not. Paul's wife is here. When I asked him why he wasn't spending his time with her, he said all he does is pay the bills. There's nothing left between them."

"God, that's sad."

"I know. I didn't know what to say."

"I really don't know why you would stay married if that were the case. Divorce must be better than sneaking around."

"Oh well, it would certainly be better to find someone single. But then there's yellow fever."

"Yellow fever?"

"You haven't heard that?" She was incredulous.

"No, but I could probably guess."

"Yes, you probably could. It's a terrible expression, but that's what they call all the white guys going crazy after Asian girls."

"Honestly? Now you're just depressing me. Because of how they look or because they are more submissive?" I was so out of touch.

"Both." Madeline shook her head. "It's rough out there, that's for sure."

I waved to the server passing by our table. "Sounds like we need another round." It hadn't occurred to me that Madeline was unhappy being single. I had been out of the dating game for over five years and didn't think about it anymore. "I guess you're right. I can't say I'm attracted to Asian guys either, except for some of the Japanese men. Wow, there were definitely some hotties there. They seem more masculine to me than Chinese men."

"Yes there were. Should we go back?" She grinned and we clinked our wine glasses.

* * *

One of my favorite travelmates, Allison, arrived in October. Our strategy was to let her get her bearings in Singapore for three days before we left for China with David. Except I didn't let her get any rest to ease the jet lag. It was her first time in Asia and I was determined to show her as much as possible.

The Singapore Zoo is one of the most amazing zoos on this planet. There is a complex about thirty minutes outside of Singapore's busy center that houses the zoo and the Night Zoo. There's much more land out there than the European zoos that were my most recent benchmark and the animals are given much more room to roam. There are also decent restaurants there and, as everywhere in Singapore, ample retail opportunity.

Another morning we toured the Botanical Gardens and went for pedicures.

"I don't know, Allison. It's hard to explain." Finally there was someone here I could actually confide in—and I was having a great deal of trouble doing it.

"Take your time, Jen. You've got me for two weeks!" She laughed, not knowing what had been in the back of my mind for weeks.

"I just feel like something's missing, like… like we don't connect anymore." It was hard to say the words. "I worry that he could be cheating on me."

"What gives you that impression?" As always, Allison was practical. "Is he acting differently towards you?"

"I can't even put my finger on it, to be honest with you. It's more of a feeling than anything else." *A nasty gut feeling* was what I wanted to say.

"He might just be distracted at work. That would be my guess."

Logic, a true Allison trait.

"Yeah, you're probably right. Hey! I know where we are going for Happy Hour. You won't believe our post office!"

Allison looked at me as though I had finally lost it.

The girls rallied early at KPO that afternoon to meet Allison. Penny, the kiwi I had met at Jac's birthday party the year before, was the first to arrive. Full of energy and quick wit, she injected adrenaline into our casual gathering. Madeline showed up shortly afterward, more conservative in a group than in our recent escapades overseas. Wine and conversation flowed easily.

"I don't know if it's true or not, it's just a theory I read recently and I was curious what you guys thought about it." I was always testing the thought process of my friends, sometimes to their chagrin. In this case, the resistance was telling.

"Say it again," Penny demanded. "I didn't get it."

"The psychologist's argument was that there are only two types of expats: runaways and adventurers." I looked at the women in front of me to gauge their reactions.

"So, a runaway left something behind that they don't want to deal with?" Madeline looked concerned.

"That's the idea."

"Bollocks." Penny had her hand in the air to signal another round.

"I started studying Spanish when I was eleven. I don't think I had much to run from. I just had big plans!" I laughed. The chardonnay went down like water. I traded my empty glass for the full one already on the table. "Thanks, Penny."

"What kinds of things were people running away from?" Madeline's blue eyes were watery.

"I don't know. It's just some random psychologist. I don't even know where he claimed to get his expertise or research on the matter, so it's a theory unless we decide otherwise. I just thought it was interesting and was curious what you guys thought."

"It's bollocks!" Penny gave us the Aussie expression for bullshit once more. "There are all kind of reasons why people move to another country."

"What made you move?" Allison asked her.

"My job! Both times. I moved from New Zealand to Australia first, and then Singapore. But it was all work related." Penny thought the conversation was pointless.

"This is my second move as well. I was in Hong Kong for a while before Singapore. I'm not really sure what started it. Curiosity I guess." But Madeline looked anything but convinced.

"I think you're all brave women and it doesn't matter why you did it." Allison sought to smooth over the emotions I had inadvertently unleashed.

"The only reason I mentioned it was because I found it ridiculous to try and place people in two groups. It's old-fashioned! There are many reasons why people leave their countries. What about love, for example? That's a big one. I went to Germany for work, but I stayed in Europe because I fell in love with David." I gave my two cents after I'd heard from the others.

"I've never left the States to live, but I'd venture a guess that there are generally a combination of reasons behind the decision."

I nodded at Allison in agreement. "Yes, that's my point. It's a rather narrow-minded statement."

"Who cares? What matters is making the most of it while we're *here*!" Penny was all about living in the moment. You could ask her to do just about anything and she was game. "What are we going to do tonight? Little blondie here needs a night on the town!" She winked at Allison.

"I was thinking about the Four Floors." There was enough wine in my blood to raise the level of crazy.

"Four what?" Allison wanted to know.

"Ha! Really? You want to show her *that* dump?"

I nodded.

"Okay. I'm in, provided we make a stop at Harry's first." The plan was in motion.

"Four what?" Madeline this time.

"*The Four Floors of Whores*," Penny clarified, a little too loudly.

"Oh Jesus," Madeline whispered.

"I don't even know *what* to say to that! What is it?" Allison needed facts.

"The real name of the place is Orchard Towers, but no one calls it that," I said. "It's off of Orchard Road near the Hilton, a building that has several bars and four floors where prostitution is legal."

"You're joking, right?" Allison questioned further.

"Unfortunately, I'm not."

"I've heard of it but I haven't been there," Madeline said. "People are always talking about it at work."

"If you want to see it, we'll go." I looked at Allison.

"Sounds too weird to miss. I'm in."

Penny signaled another round. "One rule: we *cannot* go there sober."

"I don't think that's going to be a problem." Madeline looked at the full glass of merlot in her hand and the other on the way.

"Me neither." I snuck a look at my watch. It was barely six o'clock. "The guys should be here soon."

"Who's coming?" Madeline wanted to know.

"David will be here for sure. I think Zander and Bob will probably come too."

"Bottoms up!" Penny was already dangerously close to breaking out into the Haka, a New Zealand warrior dance that she was known to perform when she got drunk.

FORBIDDEN

Harry's Bar, the Singapore institution that it was, had a location across the street from Orchard Towers. Several glasses were emptied again in short order for courage. The patrons of this location were decidedly different from the ones in David's office building. Grizzled older men made up the majority. Tiny Asian women were the next largest representation. Mid-thirties foreigners without a clue were last. That was us.

"I know the way."

Everyone turned to look at Zander. "Oh! Are you a regular?" David joked.

"Of course!" Zander replied, giving no further information.

"Lead the way!" Bob signaled what I was thinking. "Let's get this show on the road."

Apparently not drowning in chardonnay, the butterflies were rampant on our way up the escalator. Allison, in front of me, turned to look back. Her wide eyes said it: *really?*

Really, I nodded in return and swallowed hard. My throat was dry.

"Hey! You sure you know where you're going?" Penny yelled up to Zander, the leader of the pack.

He silenced her with a look.

There were so many bars. Country music, surprisingly, came from one side. Techno from another. Zander walked toward the entrance that had rock bellowing from the speakers. Women paid nothing. The guys paid five bucks each to get in. Neon lights kept you in the dark, except when the flashing blues and greens matched the bass of the music. Impossible to talk, we were now communicating in a game of charades.

Zander lifted his fist to the side of his mouth and pretended to drink an imaginary beer. David and Bob nodded.

"Rum and diet!" I shouted to be heard above the music.

"Whiskey!" Penny called out.

Allison and Madeline walked to the bar with Zander, presumably to avoid shouting, or to contribute cash. I looked around, taking in everything but afraid to see too much. Girls, very young Asian girls, walked through the crowd, smiles plastered on their faces. One placed a hand on David's shoulder and I threw her a glare. Penny looked for a dance floor. Perhaps the whole bar would get to see the Haka.

We moved like islands, everyone in his or her own world. My nose was assaulted with traces of vomit and overpowering cheap perfume. I moved next to David and Allison, sipping my drink.

"What do you think?" I yelled in her ear.

"Pretty tame, actually." Allison yelled back.

She was right. I hadn't known what to expect, but on the surface, it was harmless. Zander was talking to one of the girls, one that looked very masculine. Bob sat on a stool smiling and drinking his beer. Everyone was getting steadily drunk. It was easy to tell, because our singing got louder with every round.

"We have to go up higher!" Zander shouted.

"What?" said the chorus.

"There are more bars to see. Let's keep going!" The tour guide was back.

Allison looked at me and I shrugged, *Why not?*

She nodded.

My legs were no longer taking orders. They wobbled instead of striding. Another cover charge was paid and we herded in like cattle to a bar that was very similar to the last one, except the tables were longer and the dance floor had disappeared. The number of Asian girls attending to patrons multiplied. "I'll get this round!" I yelled, even though I didn't need anymore. Allison joined me.

We sat at the bar to order. This one was only attended to by women. In fact, the only guys that worked here were at the door.

"A rum and diet, three beers, whiskey, a glass of red wine..." I trailed off and looked at Allison.

"Captain and diet coke," she finished the order.

"Wait please," said the bartender.

Allison and I looked at each other, then surveyed the room. The music was quieter. We were now on the top level. At least I thought we were.

"This must be the pickup place." I could whisper now.

"Yeah. Easier to make a deal in here." Allison agreed.

FORBIDDEN

Two western guys, they could have been European or American, overweight in their sixties, sat with petite Asian women. It was impossible to tell how old the females were but they could not have been older than twenty. I guessed much younger. A waitress delivered drinks and shots to the table. The guys clinked glasses and the girls' shrill laughter was anything but happy.

"Seventy-eight fifty," the bartender was back.

I swung the bar stool around and handed her my credit card. She gave me a hard stare before walking to the cash register. Allison carried off some of the drinks.

"*Help me,*" a small female voice on my right near the seat Allison had just vacated. I couldn't see anyone.

"What?" I said to no one. "*Help me please,*" a silhouette in the dark said a second time. "Sign here!" the bartender squawked at me, a long black fingernail pointing at the signature line.

I signed and looked to the right. An Asian girl, maybe eighteen or nineteen, stared at me and said nothing. The bartender barked at her in Mandarin. Visibly rattled, she ran off to follow orders. I sat there stunned. *Did I hear that right?* I looked around for someone to confirm, but Allison had rejoined the others.

Silently I handed out the remaining drinks. My heart was in my throat. "Maybe it's time to go." I whispered in David's ear.

"Yes. After we finish these, it's definitely time," he agreed.

Allison came with us. The others left in stages and some went on to other clubs. Suddenly sober, I was ashamed for patronizing a place that provided women as a service. *Who were they? How did they end up there? Were they held against their will?* My head began to throb in the taxi. I couldn't decide if I had heard someone beg me for help or if I had imagined it.

Chapter 22
Dragon's Bite

We boarded the Malaysia airlines flight on the night of October 4th. Allison would stay just over a week in China, before flying back. David and I had a return to Singapore on the 18th. We had to change planes in Kuala Lumpur, but it was a quick stop.

Arrival in Shanghai was a very slow process. We stood outside immigration for over an hour. Our visas had been arranged in Singapore in advance. All the paperwork was in order. None of us spoke Chinese, however, so we had no choice but to wait. Uniformed officers came and went. Five or six western tourists waited with us. There was nothing to do but stand and wonder what exactly they were checking out on each of us.

A small man in a red-and-green uniform came out and handed Allison and me our passports.

"What about his?" I pointed to David.

In return, I received an arm pointing towards the next queue.

"Just go ahead," David said. "I'll catch up."

Allison and I passed through customs without any drama. I marveled at the size of the baggage hall. The airport had to be new or at least recently renovated—and the ceilings were sixty feet high at least. Already I was forced to re-examine my assumptions about China. I had expected an airport with a more communist flavor, nothing too fancy. The bags were already waiting for us.

David walked up to take control of the baggage cart from me, giving me a quick kiss. "What did they say?" I asked. "Not a word. I was the last one standing there, but I have no idea why." David looked puzzled and very tired.

Our hotel shuttle had a pickup point just outside baggage claim. The temperature was chilly, but I could feel the sun up there somewhere. The haze didn't give up any immediate answers, but I didn't care. It was good to be free of the plane, even though a night with interrupted sleep left everyone off balance.

The Radisson Shanghai looks like a column with a spaceship on top, an attempt at modern architecture gone slightly awry. We had chosen it based on its location close to the city's main pedestrian thoroughfare, Nanjing Road. As we unloaded our bags from the shuttle bus, I stopped to stare at the amount of people everywhere. There was hardly a spot of pavement to be seen in the sea of Shanghainese.

Our room wasn't ready because it was barely ten o'clock in the morning. "*Xie xie,*" I called after the young man who carried our bags to storage. The three of us stood in the lobby looking at each other.

"Now what?" David said.

"I have no idea," I said.

"Me neither," Allison agreed. "Let's step outside and see what we can see."

People. Everywhere. They were laughing, joking, singing, laughing, wearing costumes, marching in uniform, and talking a mile a minute in a language none of us understood. Slowly it dawned on me that the language barrier here would be the highest yet. On my left a blue-and-white street sign gave information for all directions. In Chinese. I just started laughing. "Go stand under that, David."

"Why?"

"I want to take a photo."

Allison and David began to laugh too. David stood dutifully under the sign and added some extra flair. His arms went up in the air and he struck a clueless pose that made me laugh harder.

"Let's cross," he said, pointing toward Nanjing Road where the human river was flowing.

"There's a Starbucks!" Allison was excited to be able to read at least one sign.

Carrying massive doses of caffeine, we found a bench on Nanjing Road. It was the perfect place for viewing the insanity. Fueled by coffee, my brain began to work again. I remembered an article I'd read. October first had been the sixtieth anniversary of the People's Republic of China. The celebration was still happening and we were sitting in the middle of it. Why a woman sold bunny ears to several enthusiastic customers still didn't make sense, but the rest came together.

* * *

Shanghai has multiple personality disorder. Your impression of the city and its modernity varies with every step. Walking the stretch of the Haungpu River known as the Bund is an international history lesson. Originally established in 1846 when China became a British trading settlement, the Bund grew into a mini United Nations of commerce. By the time World War II began, trading houses existed for the UK, the US, France, Belgium, Russia, Italy, and the Netherlands, each one seeking access to China's massive trade market.

Gothic, art deco, and Victorian buildings maintain their elegant stance today only to stare across the river at the miracle that had grown out of farmland in the 1990's, Pudong. Pudong is the ultra-sexy collection of highrises that sparkle onto the river traffic below. There is no question that this is the new home of Shanghai Finance, including the addresses of the stock exchange and Shanghai World Financial Center.

Allison, David, and I walked along the river to a stunning bridge dressed up with multicolored lights that flashed in changing colors. It was an iron chameleon meant to attract the masses that come to photograph the Bund. For a while we attempted decent photos of the bridge and the electrifying scene that is Shanghai's riverfront. Then we gave up and went for beer at a small riverside restaurant that had small private tables overlooking the view.

I could only stare. *How did I get here?* The thought that came back to me often in places I would never have expected to find myself popped up again. "We are in CHINA!" I said to David and Allison.

They looked at me, oddly, given that this information wasn't exactly news. Neither one reacted.

"I can't believe it! Did you ever imagine you would be sitting here with me?" I directed my question to Allison.

"No," she laughed. "I can't say that I did."

"Exactly!" I wanted them to be as excited as I was. "Did either of you guys see a restroom?" We had walked a fair distance and I hadn't seen one anywhere.

"No," said David. "We can ask the waitress when she comes back."

Easier said than done. She had no idea what we were talking about. "Ladies room?" I tried.

Nothing.

"Toilet?" David tried.

She shook her head.

"Powder room?" Allison gave it a shot. She looked confused and gave a signal that she would return. "I have a new app on my phone for translation," David offered.

"Let's try that."

I rolled my eyes. I was sick of hearing about this wondrous new invention, the iPhone. David typed the word into his screen and waited for the waitress to return. Then he pressed enter.

Her eyes lit up and she smiled. "Yes!" She motioned for me to follow her.

I gave David a giant hug and a kiss first. "I was wrong! I bow to the master of technology!"

The next day Allison wanted to go to the Hard Rock Café. She had looked it up previously and we got the concierge to write out directions in Chinese. David bowed out, wanting to catch up on sleep.

Since most things in Shanghai were close, I was becoming alarmed after sitting in the taxi for over twenty minutes.

"Are you sure you had the right address?" I asked Allison.

"I think so," she said.

The taxi jerked to a halt. The driver pointed into the distance, but said nothing.

"Where is it?" I asked.

He didn't understand.

"I don't see anything," I said to Allison. "This doesn't even look like an area where the Hard Rock would be." Everywhere around us were students. The buildings were residential. I was sure the people at Hard Rock Inc. had not chosen this as their ideal site.

"No," Allison said, looking worried.

Showing him the paper from the hotel, I said "This is where we want to go."

All he did was shake his head and point the same direction.

"I guess we have to wait for the police then," I threatened. My guidebook had warned of this and advised to stay put.

His eyes widened. He started yelling at us in Chinese.

"I'm not paying you for a ride to the middle of nowhere. We will wait for the police." It took everything I had not to freak out. He was scaring the hell out of me, but it was daylight and we outnumbered him. I took a pen and piece of paper from my purse and wrote down his taxi ID number.

"Is there a problem?" A handsome young student wheeled up on his bicycle. His English was perfect.

"Do you know where I can find a cop?" I asked him.

"I'm sure we can figure this out without the police," he calmly replied. He squinted behind his wire-rimmed glasses because of the sun, but his eyes were kind.

I explained our side of the story. He listened patiently and then spoke to the driver who immediately began yelling again. Allison and I looked at each other.

"You can get out here and take another taxi," our bicycle angel told us.

"Okay, but I'm not paying for a ride that went on forever and took us nowhere."

He translated. There was more yelling.

"It's okay. Just get out. We will find you another cab. You don't have to pay. The driver wants no trouble with the police."

I smiled at Allison. The driver glared at us in the rearview mirror and tore off the moment I pushed the door closed. It's a hollow victory when you still don't know where the hell you are.

***

China Eastern carried us to Beijing a few days later. The Communist Party celebration was still in full swing. Everywhere we went, we were the few Caucasian faces in a sea of Chinese.

Tiananmen Square was where the real party was. The formal anniversary parade had taken place a week earlier, but the floats were kept intact in the square for the common people to have a chance to visit them. Ten thousand soldiers had marched in the parade, later inspected by President Hu Jintao. One hundred thousand carefully-selected civilians had also taken part in the parade. An enormous screen in Tiananmen Square repeated the highlights continuously.

To stand in that square was one of the more surreal travel experiences I've ever had. In 1989, the week before I graduated from high school, hundreds and perhaps thousands of innocent protestors were murdered on this spot. Now here we were surrounded by cartoonish floats with rainbows and communist heroes in poses of golden glory. Walking through the spot where one million people gathered to protest the actions of the party before so many of them were mowed down by tanks, my heart was beating fast. *What's to stop that from happening again?*

Just before I turned to locate David, who thankfully stood out as a giant amongst all the Beijingers, I spotted one more float. It was the planet Earth, ringed with golden halos and white doves of peace. Written in English across the rings, it said "Harmonious World." If seeing that while standing in the middle of a communist birthday party in Tiananmen Square doesn't top the list of Great Moments in Irony, I have no idea what does.

* * *

It took about a week for my prejudices about China to fade. I had heard so many business horror stories about the theft of intellectual property, hacking, and unfair business practice that it was difficult to look upon the nation with an open mind. The Tiananmen Square tragedy had only been the start of a parade of negative press over the past few decades.

Beijing was another planet compared to Shanghai. It is tradition and history on an unimaginable scale. The opening ceremony of the 2008 Summer Olympics put the city on my radar for the first time. The dazzling spectacle and display of humans as an art form was unlike anything the world had ever seen. For years the press shouted that

Dragon's Bite

China was taking the world stage as a superpower, and I decided then I needed to see it for myself.

Perhaps because of its name, The Forbidden City was a magnet. I'd heard the name for many years without fully understanding the magnitude of its importance. For nearly five hundred years it was the residence of Chinese power, the home of the Emperor. It was "forbidden" because no one in the kingdom could enter or leave the grounds without the emperor's permission. The fact that it is surrounded by a wall over twenty-five feet high was handy for reinforcing that law.

Walking through the main gate with Allison and David, I felt the enormity of China for the first time. The Forbidden City occupies one hundred and eighty acres of central Beijing real estate. The deep red walls of the Meridian Gate put you on notice that you are on sacred ground, but nothing prepares you for the hundreds of various buildings—temples, residences, and halls—that make up the city. Nine thousand employees, servants, concubines, and advisors lived here under the thumb of one man.

These vast rooms of ceremony and education have the most amazing names. I could only dream of having a place in the "Hall of Literary Glory" or the "Palace of Tranquil Longevity." The emperor's throne, a grand golden vision decked-out in yellow silk and embroidered with dragons was originally installed in the "Palace of Heavenly Purity." Who wouldn't want to live there?

Each courtyard was built to hold millions of devotees and worshippers. Main entrances, painted in red and embellished with golden hinges and lion door knockers were easily fifteen feet high. Every single tile, step, and gateway was decorated with Chinese symbols. Envisioning this place in full throttle defies the imagination. It was difficult to take it all in and impossible for my camera lens to capture.

We exited the main structure onto a large courtyard filled with both communist party revelers and tourists. From the map we found we were close once more to Tiananmen Square, so we walked that direction. David the Giant was easily a foot taller than the majority of the crowd, which made him easy to follow. I got behind him and Allison behind me. Looking around David's back to see where we were going, I noticed the gaping mouths and wide-eyed passersby. His height was inconceivable to most Chinese. I started giggling.

"What are you laughing at?" David was focused on finding the square. He hadn't even noticed what was happening down below.

"Their faces!" I laughed. "You are a freak here!"

"I'm not a freak!" He yelled back, but he had begun to notice the reaction he was getting and started laughing as well. "A little respect here please, or I'll make you walk six paces behind!"

"You're impossible to lose. That's the best part!" Allison was closer to the locals in height.

By the time we reached Tiananmen Square, we were all laughing. Watching us made the locals laugh. Suddenly we were one big happy family rather than the circus freaks we often felt like, based on the way people openly stared. Unsure of our next move, we stopped for a minute underneath the portrait of Chairman Mao. I couldn't help but notice a family studying Allison.

"You take photo!" the woman said to Allison.

"I'm sorry, what?" Allison's brow creased in confusion.

"Take photo! Baby!" with that, she thrust her two year-old into Allison's arms.

"WHAT?!?" Allison found her vocal cords. "WHY?"

I started to laugh at the insanity of it. David let out a hearty chuckle. I snapped a photo of Allison holding a very confused little girl. Allison couldn't help but laugh too. The family was laughing. We were having a fabulous time, but had no idea why.

"Here you go," said Allison, handing over the woman's daughter.

"What, you don't want to take her home?" I joked.

"Very funny," Allison was waving at the family, trying to escape. "What the hell?!" she said when we were a few feet away.

"Blonde people are special here," David told us. "There aren't any naturally-blonde Chinese, so you are unique. I think it's also a status thing for people to have photos with blondes."

"Thanks for the warning!" Allison shouted, still laughing.

"I don't think we could have predicted that one," I said, wiping my eyes from laughing so hard I cried. "Only in China."

"Only in China is right!" Allison agreed.

* * *

It became our new mantra. The next morning, riding in a stunted purple minivan to an unknown destination two hours from Beijing, I thought it again. Green trees and brown terrain blurred together outside the windows. I looked at Allison's face and tried to read it. David's was inscrutable as well.

"Where else would we get in a car with people we don't know and can't communicate with in order to spend the night at an unknown destination?" I whispered for no reason, because they didn't understand English well anyway.

"Good question," Allison responded.

The late afternoon sun was barely on top of the trees when we arrived in Jinshanling. The jagged mountain backdrop provided the perfect scenery for our first glimpse of the Great Wall of China. We drove through the village, nothing more than a few stone houses and shops, and stopped at the landmark for the Jinshanling section of the wall. I ran into a public restroom to find a hole in the floor to squat over. There were definitely some things I did not love about China.

"Up those stairs," Adam, Mr. Sun's sidekick, directed. At the top of the stairs, I could see the wall and one of its famous guard houses.

We all looked at each other. David threw on his fleece. The autumn air had made a steep decline in the mountains outside Beijing. David went first, Allison followed. It was getting dark and the stairs looked precarious. I hesitated. One of our hosts, Adam, handed me a flashlight.

The twenty-minute climb nearly consumed the last moments of daylight, but we managed to capture the golden-orange sunset on the wall in a few photos before it evaporated entirely.

"I can't... believe... I'm standing... here." It takes a while to get the words out while gasping for air.

"Amazing." One word was enough for Allison.

The wall snaked up behind us to the first guard house, its curves electrified and glowing in the last light of day. There were no other tourists around. No people period besides Mr. Sun and Adam. Our visit to Jinshanling was arranged by one of David's colleagues who spoke Mandarin. Mr. Sun was the man who had given my Dutch neighbor Roland the tour of his life the year before. A number of tiny miracles had fallen into place for us to be standing on this ancient ground.

"Dinner!" cried Mr. Sun from down below. We followed his orders to come down.

"Is that where we are sleeping?" David asked Adam, pointing to the guard house.

"Not that one. Different one." Adam replied.

"In here. Meet Mrs. Sun!" Mr. Sun held the door open and a smiling woman gave us each a small bow.

"You like noodles?" she said.

"Yes," we replied in unison.

"Good. Sit. Sit." She pointed towards a picnic table that could not be missed. The building was their home, their shop, and their dining room. It was tiny.

We did as we were told. Mountains of steaming dumplings were placed on the table before us. "Coke? Coke light?" Mrs. Sun asked. We each chose one. The room was freezing and the steam felt good hitting my cold nose. Soon there were so many bowls and so much steam that it was difficult to see each other anymore. I'd forgotten that most buildings have no heat.

The dumplings kept coming until we declared defeat. I kept wondering how all this was going to work, but Adam told us soon enough to follow him. This climb was steeper. Everyone was given a flashlight. A few stairs crumbled beneath my feet and my heart raced again with each step.

Adam stopped outside the first level of the guard house. I panicked when I saw the open windows all around. One sleeping bag was on the concrete slab.

"I sleep here," he told us. He then turned again and climbed up to the next level. A huge padlock was on the guardhouse door. Adam fumbled with the key and his flashlight before the lock popped open.

Dragon's Bite

Behind the door a clothesline was strung across the room. Several sleeping bags hung over it. At the back of the room were three stacks of cans: coke, beer, and water. It was cold, but the windows were blocked. I felt slightly better. That is, until he showed us our bathroom. It was a large blue-plastic bucket outside in the corner of the stone railing. I looked at Allison. Neither of us said a word. It wasn't as though we could ask for a better room.

"You keep door locked all night. If someone knock that isn't me, do not answer. If you need help, call to me. When sun rise, we bring breakfast. You can have all the drinks you want." He pulled three sleeping bags down before he said, "Goodnight. Sleep a lot. Long walk tomorrow." With a wave, he was gone.

"This is crazy," I said.

"Who would come to the door?" David wondered out loud.

"They must be paying someone off. This can't be legal." Allison volunteered.

"No, it can't. Maybe that's who they are worried about. Guards or police?" I ventured.

"Maybe" David said. We didn't analyze it further. "I'm going to get my camera."

"I'm getting a beer. Does anyone else want one?"

The night passed slowly and coldly. It was impossible not to think about where we were and how bizarre it all was. I tried to be happy, but I was nervous about the climb. We knew it would be at least an eight kilometer walk. The other photos I had seen of the wall were very different than where we had walked today. Out here, original jagged rock replaced the smooth renovated trails I'd seen in tourist photos. That hadn't been part of my mental equation, nor had the mountains.

I must have slept at some point because the first silver light that slipped through the cracks of the guardhouse was a surprise. I got up and tried to deal with my hair before going outside, though it was obviously a wasted effort in the middle of nowhere. David was close behind me. Allison was too. We each set up in the "best" location to catch the sunrise.

An orange hue gave notice that the sun was nearly ready for her entrance. Magenta came next. It wasn't until the sky turned yellow that we could finally get a view of our entire surroundings. The giant snake rolled over each neighboring mountain and through every guardhouse. There was hardly a cloud in the sky. The best part about it was the total absence of tourists around us. Sunrise was a magnificent private show from a fourteenth-century Ming Dynasty guardhouse balcony. *How could it possibly get better than this?*

After breakfast we began our hike to Simatai. The first few kilometers of the wall had been resurfaced, but the longer we walked, the harder going it was. David was a machine, climbing every mountain to take in the views. Allison and I moved at a slower pace and skipped some of the steeper climbs. At one house, a local vendor sold drinks from a card table. The trademark-yellow of a bottle of Veuve Cliquot champagne made me laugh out loud. "Only in China!" I said.

At lunch afterwards, we pondered our adventure in silence. The experience we had just had was one of the most magnificent of my lifetime, perhaps *the* most—but it had been far from easy. I didn't help myself by worrying about every step I took. It was a metaphor for my entire encounter in China—difficult to maneuver but delivering unexpected rewards in return. All my preconceptions about China were wrong. This was a place that could make dreams come true if you were willing to let it. The problem was I didn't know how.

Our sunrise view from the guardhouse

Ming Dynasty guardhouse on the Great Wall of China

Chapter 23
Hobbies

As with every return to Singapore, depression greeted me like an old friend. It was worse this time because Allison had gone home and my grand adventures were over. Back to my pointless existence. I couldn't lie around feeling sorry for myself, so I tried to create diversion.

When Marina sent an email asking if I wanted to join a group for lunch, I didn't hesitate. She was easy to talk to and struck me as a truly genuine person. I knew I could be wrong again, but I wanted to widen my circle of friends. I suggested we meet at the Orange Lantern, a Vietnamese restaurant close to my place on Killiney Road.

There were five in attendance, all different nationalities. Marina, the token Aussie, introduced her friends.

"I met Kate in South Africa and she lives here now. Janneke is Dutch—where exactly are you from again, Janneke?"

"We have a house in The Hague. I travel back and forth between the two countries to manage my business there." Janneke, a pretty blonde, smiled at everyone.

"Right. You and Jennifer might have something interesting to talk about then. Jennifer is American but married to a Dutchman and you lived in…? Sorry, I don't remember." Marina threw her hand to her forehead, as if to will the information to the forefront of her mind.

I smiled at everyone, too. "Rotterdam."

"And this is Melanie," Marina pointed to the woman with chin-length brown hair in a headband. "She and her husband lived in London. Phew! I think I've got everyone then, right?"

"Yes. Nice to meet you all," I said.

The Orange Lantern is a casual place, not the kind of place you would linger over lunch. I chose shrimp rice paper rolls and a bowl of beef *pho* and waited for the others to decide.

"What kind of business do you have?" I asked Janneke.

"I do media and public relations in Holland," she said. "I've been building the business for a few years now and I can't let it fall apart while we're over here."

"Absolutely not. It sounds interesting." I was thinking more about not having to live here full time than the details of her business.

"Jennifer, I didn't have the chance to tell you, but I found a job!" Marina had been debating working and not working since she'd arrived in Singapore. I was impressed that she found something in this ridiculously-difficult economy. "That's wonderful. I hope it's doing something you like?"

"It's nothing big, just a few days a week, but will be helping out at an accounting firm. The people seem very nice." She looked hopeful that their niceness translated into people she could relate to and work with.

"I'm glad to hear it and I'm officially jealous," I joked. She knew of my difficulties in the employment arena.

"Don't be. Where is your next adventure taking you?" Marina wanted to know.

"That's a good question. We've only recently returned from an amazing trip in China. The next one isn't on the books yet. I'll have to get working on that!"

"Do you have children?" Kate, a middle-aged woman who seemed to have lost the ability for small talk, if she ever had it, directed her question at me.

"No, I don't." I had long since given up explaining to people why I don't have kids. It was a choice, not a painful regret.

"Oh. Whatever do you *do* with your time then?" Kate continued.

"I seem to find plenty to keep me occupied." My tone was a bit too sharp, but the implication was irritating—if I wasn't rearing children, I must be wasting my time on frivolous things.

Hobbies

"Melanie, how are you getting along in this heat? It must be a huge change from London." Diplomatic as ever, Marina made sure the conversation between Kate and me went no further.

Lunch was quick once it arrived. I'd say it was painless, but I kept mulling over Kate's remark. Why on Earth would you say something like that to someone you just met? And why did it bother me what a complete stranger thought? Because she had made me think: *Am I wasting my time?* My annoyance wasn't about the kid thing. I was facing my thirty-ninth birthday and was long past that debate. She had hit my Achilles Heel: no job and no purpose.

Halloween was coming up. I decided that would be my new purpose. Our place was small, so I booked an area at the pool to host a barbeque. I invited everyone I could think of and told them to wear costumes.

When I had the idea for a party, I hadn't thought about lugging the supplies to our apartment with no car. I also decided to forget how crazy hot it was outside and that costumes would increase it tenfold. Penny came to the rescue with several neon wigs, devil horns, and pitchforks. At least I could hide my hair.

The minute we got the cooler down to the pool area of our building, she had it open and was popping the sparkling wine. I wanted to kiss her. Nothing eases one into a social situation like bubbly. Along with the champagne, we got busy hanging spider webs and pumpkin lanterns in the poolside shrubs. It was then that I noticed that the sky was inordinately black for six o'clock.

"Oh shit..."

"What?" Penny followed my gaze. "Oh shit! That will hit any minute!"

We ran around gathering the decorations we'd just hung. I yelled out greetings to those arriving.

"Hi! Sorry, we're going to have to delay!" I said. The sky delivered warning drops before opening the faucet full blast.

"Into the carpark!" David yelled, picking up the cooler. "Follow me!"

Ten of us stood in the garage in various stages of wet. "I don't believe this." I shook my head. "Not exactly the kind of weather we worry about on Halloween in Ohio!"

"Give me your glass," Penny ordered. She filled mine and hers before sharing with the others.

"I'm not sure what to do. We could wait, but sometimes it takes a while to stop." I was thinking out loud.

"The problem is that even if it does stop, it can always start up again," David reasoned.

"Hi guys!" Laura and Tom got out of a cab that had just rolled up. "What are you doing in here?" Laura asked.

"Oh, this is the new place to party! Didn't you know?" Penny acted like we were planning a garage rave all along.

"We're trying to figure out what to do," I said, looking at David. "It will be tight in the condo, but I'm not sure what else we can do."

"Let's just move upstairs," he replied. "We'll be fine."

We rolled everything into the elevator and set up again inside the condo. Everyone understood, but I was still frazzled. Linda the vampire arrived along with her ghoulish friend Amy. Captain Jack Sparrow and his sexy high-heeled witch, the Germans we'd met at Jac's party, came next. Madeline showed up without a costume and Alexis and Eu-meh had crazy wigs and feather boas.

We sat on the floor most of the night, taking turns wearing the wigs and feather boas. The drunker we got, the funnier it was. David's friend Carlo arrived late from his flight from Santiago. He carried limes, bitters, pisco, eggs, and sugar syrup: the ingredients for pisco sours. I'd never heard of that before, but they pack a hell of a punch. Soon Carlo had on the wig and feather boa too. People came and went, but the party continued until the wee hours of the morning.

The problem with a party as a diversion is that one day later you're back where you started. It was fun and the gang had a good time, but it was a lot of effort for one night. It wasn't something I could continue doing, so I started a club instead—The Singapore Supper Club was born. If there's one thing Singapore excels at, it's eating. There are so many great restaurants that I thought it would be fun to organize a group to go out and try new ones every month. Everyone could raise suggestions and we would vote on the winner.

The first dinner went off without a hitch. An upscale Italian restaurant called Oso had a table for twelve in their wine cellar, away from the noise of the main dining area. Six couples who loved good food and wine could not have been happier. Wine selections were made jointly and though the restaurant was known for fine dining, it wasn't outrageously expensive. Several people made suggestions for the next gathering, and I was pleased with my new hobby.

It didn't cover the majority of my days to plan a monthly dinner, so I still had a lot time on my hands. I received notice that my residence permit in the Netherlands had to be renewed. Though I had no desire to return, it was still "home"—and we might not have another choice. I checked the airfares and discovered luckily that November wasn't overly expensive. David and I had been having a lot of trouble communicating, so I was sure he wouldn't mind me leaving again. My only dilemma was whether or not to invite Madeline.

She had mentioned several times that she wanted to go to Holland and Belgium because she had never been. Because she had invited me to Melbourne and gone to a lot of effort to show me a good time, I felt somewhat obligated to bring her along. *We could go to Heidelberg.* I thought about my former home in Germany where this travel extravaganza had begun in 2001. It would be great to see Bruges again too. I was sure Madeline would love it. It was impossible not to.

"Of course I'd like to come!" She was thrilled at the thought.

"I have to go collect my Dutch residency card. They insist that you do it in person, so if you want to join me, we can make a road trip to visit some nearby places I like."

"Yes! Just let me take a look at my schedule and flights and I'll get back to you. It sounds great."

I knew she would be quick because that's the kind of person she was, but I was surprised to get an update that night. Madeline's flight was booked. We were going to Europe.

It was shockingly cold when we arrived. I had bought a new North Face coat with a lining in Beijing, but I hadn't felt single digits in a long time. When we arrived at my Rotterdam home, I discovered it was just as cold inside.

"I turned the heat up, but I didn't hear it kick on." It was alarming. Our heat was normally very reliable.

"I'm sure it will be fine," Madeline said through chattering teeth.

"I'll ask the neighbors if they have any space heaters." I went downstairs to talk to Roland.

"Hmm… we have been doing some remodeling on our house. I wonder if somehow your wiring was affected." Roland scratched his head. "Come in. Come in. We have some heaters we used during the renovation. You are welcome to them. Did you enjoy the trip with Mr. Sun in Beijing?"

I thanked him profusely for the heaters and his tip on Mr. Sun's accommodation at the Great Wall of China and went back upstairs. "I'll have to call David when Singapore wakes up. I don't have any internet here and even if I did, all the web sites for electricians and tradespeople are in Dutch." I placed a space heater in the guest room for her and switched it on. "I'm so sorry about this. I had no way of knowing."

"I understand. We'll be fine."

She kept saying that, but I didn't know how we were going to be fine. "Worst case scenario, we'll go to a hotel," I said, but hoped that wouldn't be necessary. I wasn't exactly flush with cash after all the traveling I'd been doing. "I'm going to take a shower. The hot water heater doesn't seem to be affected and I feel gross."

I went into the shower and tried to figure out what to do. We had only planned to be at my place two days, and then we would pick up a rental car to drive to Germany and Belgium. I had to get someone to check into this right away or we'd have to cancel everything.

"There's nothing I can do about it from here." The response from David when I finally reached him did not make me happy.

"What the hell do you mean there's nothing you can do? You *know* these guys don't speak English, and I don't even have a way to look them up! You're sitting in front of a computer that has all the information you need!" I thought it was logical. He did not.

"I don't have time for this."

HOBBIES

"This is your house too. I didn't plan for this to happen but we're talking about a maximum of thirty minutes to make some phone calls. FIND THE TIME!" I hung up on him.

I was beyond furious, stomping up the stairs to my room to dry my hair.

"What's going on?" Madeline stuck her head in my bedroom door.

"David is refusing to help. That's what's going on! He doesn't have time. He doesn't know what to do. And every other excuse he could think of!"

"Oh."

"Don't you think that's ridiculous?" I asked her. "I can't even speak the language properly and have no way to find an electrician but he can't make a few phone calls." The more I talked about it, the angrier I became.

"I guess you'll sort it out," she said and walked away.

Too upset to speak, I turned the hair dryer on. *What the hell does that mean?* Was I crazy to expect some help from my husband in his native country and language?

My phone rang. "Yes?"

"I found a guy to come tomorrow. He'll be there before three is all he could say." David gave me his name and mobile number.

"Thank you." I didn't know what else to say.

"I hope you have a good time in Bruges."

"Me too. I'll talk to you later." I disconnected.

I waited all day the next day, but the guy never showed up. Finally, I called to see if we could pick up the car a day early and get out of the freezing house.

"I don't know who this guy is, but he doesn't answer the phone and he never showed," I told David that afternoon. "We're leaving. Please see if you can find someone for a week from now."

"I'll try."

"Good-bye," I practically threw the phone down. *I'll try?* Why was he being so difficult about this? It's not like there were electricians on my street and I was refusing to go talk to them. Rotterdam is huge. I had no idea where to go.

"Get your stuff, Madeline. We're out of here. The hotel extended our trip for another night in Bruges. We can't stay here."

I was grateful that the drive was barely over two hours. Even after five years of it, driving in Europe makes me edgy due to the narrow roads and parking spots. I find it especially challenging in Belgium and France because road signs don't seem to be obligatory, often disappearing without a trace. There wasn't any snow yet and we still had daylight, so the trip was quick.

Bruges is one of my favorite European cities. Eating and drinking are sport in this town full of indulgence, and the city simply could not be more picturesque. I wanted to show Madeline everything.

The Straffe Hendrik Brewery could not be missed. The canal ride is non-negotiable. Sipping wine at a bistro? If we must! The only problem was that I didn't realize when Madeline was over her alcohol limit. I only understood it later when she tried to leave with a scruffy-looking guy that she had been chatting with in line for Bruges' famous *frites*. The guy was obnoxious, shouting at his friends and insulting me when I tried to pull her away.

"Get lost *bitch*!"

I couldn't believe my ears. Madeline just stood there like a droopy doll. "She doesn't want to go with you. She's leaving with me." But Madeline's dopey smile wasn't making it easy. I pulled her away and held her up on the cobblestone path. The sudden confrontation was such a shock that I strode off without looking where I was going.

Bruges is famous for the many things I mentioned previously, but it has its less desirable traits as well. At the top of the list is the spider web of one-way streets that all look the same. Before I knew it, I was completely lost.

"Just stand here a minute." I tried to get her to stand on her own two feet while I pulled the map out of my pocket.

"Okay," she mumbled. Immediately she crumbled into a heap on the street curb.

Great... that's just great, I thought. The map was only useful if we knew where we were. "Do you see a street sign anywhere?" I knew it was useless, but I was trying to get the point across that we were in trouble. Her head slumped and she began crying, quietly at first before gearing up to a full-blown wail. *I don't believe this is happening.*

"Sir! Sir, please. I am completely turned around. Would you please show me on this map where we are?" I was practically begging. My embarrassment took a back seat to my desperation.

"Yes. We are here." The man pointed at the map, unable to resist a sideways glance at the weeping Madeline. "Is she all right? Do you need help?"

"No. We will be fine. I just lost my way and she's had too much to drink." I tried to explain why I was standing on a dark empty street at nearly midnight with a hysterical friend who had just collapsed. Even I knew how bizarre it looked. "Thank you for your help." I smiled

"Get UP!" I whispered loudly in Madeline's ear, and pulled her up by her forearm. Now she was covered with dirt. The man had vanished through a nearby doorway.

* * *

"I'm so sorry." A red-faced Madeline was apologizing up and down when I woke up. "I don't know what happened. I didn't realize how much I had to drink."

I said nothing. Taking a shower in my forty-degree house and walking around with a wet head had been a very stupid idea. I was having trouble breathing. The last thing I wanted to do was rehash the night's events.

"I'm going to go out and have a look around so you can have some space." She already had her coat on and was pulling on gloves.

"Fine. I'm going to find a doctor. I'll find you later." I rolled back over. It was too early and too cold for me to consider getting up yet.

The doctor confirmed that I had a respiratory infection and gave me antibiotics the size of horse pills. I texted Madeline when I was finished, and we met for lunch at a cozy restaurant in the Grote Markt. Pulling out a chair near the fireplace, I was relieved to get rid of the chill that I'd thought might be permanent.

"Let's just forget it," I said. I really didn't want to talk about it anymore. "Lunch is on you though." I smiled.

"Deal." Madeline's blue eyes began to twinkle again. I knew she was embarrassed. What was the point of analyzing it?

* * *

The weather reflected the return of our good humor. Sunny skies followed us all the way to Germany. In contrast to my dislike of driving in southern Europe, I love the *autobahn*. Perhaps because it was the first road I'd driven on when I landed in Europe in 2001, it felt more natural. Granted, the roads were still slim compared to American highways, but they were familiar. Germans drive with precision and they mark absolutely everything with a sign. It was good to be back.

Hanna, my former German office-mate and cultural mentor, met us for dinner at Café Rossi in town. My golden-haired diva friend had not changed in the slightest. Well, perhaps she had a little.

"I asked my angels to give me a place to park because it's always such a pain in the ass to park in Heidelberg—*and there it was!* Right in plain sight. That never happens here." She gave me two German kisses and a big hug. Then she handed me a giant bag of German marzipan and holiday cookies. "I was afraid you might have missed them! Take some back for David. There's tea in there too, very special tea."

When she took a breath, I introduced her to Madeline. "Nice to meet you," Madeline said. "I've heard so much about you."

"I hope it was good!" Hanna had a very loud laugh. It was one of the things I loved about her.

"Of course," Madeline said, not understanding it was a joke.

"Jennifer, you won't believe what I have been through! I have to tell you about the past life regression I did." Hanna was off and running.

"Go on," I said, as if she needed any encouragement.

"Well, I have always been afraid of fire. Very, very afraid, *ja?*" She slipped a German word in for emphasis. "It turns out that I was burned at the stake in a past life! That's why I'm terrified!"

Clearly she was thrilled to have uncovered the mystery. I wasn't going to be the one to tell her that most people are afraid of fire. Hanna has always been one to make up her own rules—she didn't care what people thought of her. It was another thing I loved about her and why I had kept in touch with her for so many years.

HOBBIES

"It's good that you know that now," I said. "It must make your feelings easier to understand." I played along. Madeline's wide eyes took it all in, but she said nothing.

"Absolutely. It has changed everything for me. It's so good to see you." She beamed. "Now, what are we going to eat?"

The trip was a whirlwind, but I didn't care. I had time to relax at home after Madeline flew back to Singapore and I no longer felt indebted to her for showing me Melbourne. We arrived early in the morning and returned to the drama of the non-existent heating.

"This guy had better show up," I said, referring to the second contractor David had found. "I was so pissed at David's attitude when we arrived. How could he be so thoughtless?" I asked her.

"I don't want to be a part of it," she shot back.

"I'm sorry?"

"I don't want to be part of your marriage problems," she stammered.

I didn't get it. "I'm not asking you to participate in it. It's already over."

"You want me to take your side against David and he's my friend. I'm not going to do it."

We stood in my living room and I searched her face for a hint of irony or humor, but there was none. "Let me see if I understand this. I've just taken you all over three countries to my favorite places with a serious respiratory infection, even picking you up off the street when you acted like a complete ass—*and I'm the one who is being unreasonable?*" My face grew hot as I glared at her.

"I didn't tell you to sleep with a wet head in a frozen house." Her words dripped with sarcasm.

Not a millisecond passed. "Is your bag still packed?" If looks could kill, she would have hit the floor.

"Yes." She answered.

"Good. I'm taking you to the train station. You can go to Amsterdam from there, and it's very easy to take the train to Schiphol Airport when you're ready." Stomping down the stairs, I held the door for her to carry her bag. My hands shook with rage. The train station was less than ten minutes from my house. If I wasn't sure she'd screw it up, I'd have made her take the tram.

Chapter 24
Pilgrim

I didn't see Madeline again. I had no reason to. Asking someone's opinion about an argument didn't constitute a request to play a part in my marriage. And what "marriage problems" was she talking about anyway? I hadn't told her anything about what went on between David and myself when she wasn't around. Allison was the only person I'd confessed my fears to.

Another "friend" gone. Why was it so difficult to find people I could trust? I'd never had this problem in the States. Sure, I might have had friends that didn't turn into lifelong buddies, but I didn't often misjudge people so much.

Still, I felt the problem was within me. Why was I allowing people into my life who would treat me this way? In my search for deeper meaning, I landed upon a very interesting article about a Buddhist monastery in Taiwan. This place, normally such a mysterious cloistered society, was open to visitors. One could even stay the night. I thought that if I could just look deep enough inside, I'd know what to do with my life and things would stop coming apart.

Fo Guang Shan Monastery was in Kaohsihung outside Taipei. I wrote to the contact email address on their web site and waited for a reply. It came swiftly. Yes, they could accommodate me on November 29th. The beginning of my thirty-ninth year on the planet seemed the right time to take inventory of my soul. I didn't know if it would make any difference one way or the other, but I had nothing to lose.

The real mystery was why David wanted to join me. I told him I was staying in the Buddhist monastery by myself for a night, but he insisted on flying to Taiwan with me: we weren't getting along and he did not enjoy spending time in a foreign place alone. I didn't get it, but I didn't fight it either.

I wasn't expecting Taipei's sophisticated style. Taipei 101 was the tallest building in the world and I'd never heard of it. It was now officially the Christmas season so I posed in front of the trademark-blue Tiffany Christmas tree for a photo. The shopping, if one was in the mood for it, was world class. The dining area included a Maxim's of Paris, truly an unusual sight anywhere else in the world.

We went out for drinks and dinner on the first night. It was anything but comfortable. I could keep changing the scenery all I wanted, but nothing changed how I felt on the inside. David made an attempt to be jovial, which wasn't his natural state as of late. He was generally stressed, annoyed, or overtired—possibly all three. Outside the work environment, he was able to lighten up.

"Happy Birthday!" He lifted his flute of golden bubbles to me, indicating that I should do the same.

"Thank you." The crystal clink ran hollow. "I wonder what I've gotten myself into," I said, thinking about my voyage to the inner sanctum of Buddhism.

"Me too," David replied. "I hope you find what you're looking for."

"Me too." My reply sounded sarcastic, but I was serious. Was I crazy? Why did I think that running off to Taiwan to meditate with monks and live with nuns was going to solve anything? I wasn't religious. I barely understood the tenets of Buddhism.

The trip from Taipei to Kaohsihung is a four-hour drive. Thankfully the high-speed rail cuts it in half. I still had plenty of time to contemplate my situation. Buddhism was magnetic. I wanted even the tiniest slice of that peaceful existence which seemed forever out of reach. If I went to a place like this and asked questions of someone who had it, perhaps I could understand why I was so unsettled all the time.

As directed by my contact Linda, I took a taxi from the train station to FGS. My guide had short black hair cut very close to her head and she wore round light-purple glasses. Her smile lit up her face and her pale-yellow pajama-like outfit looked supremely comfortable.

"You must be Jennifer! Hello!" She closed her eyes and made a slight bow. "Welcome to Fo Guang Shan."

"Thank you. It's nice to be here." I smiled back. "And thank you for all your help with the directions. It made my trip easier."

"Good. Good. Please come this way. I will show you to the pilgrim's quarters." Linda led the way down a path to our left.

Is that what I am? A pilgrim? I am on a "pilgrimage"? I hadn't thought of it that way. Fuchsia and bright-yellow flowers bloomed everywhere. Tiny Buddha statues with brilliant smiles were stashed in quiet corners for contemplation. At the top of the hill overlooking the compound, a large golden Buddha stood with his open hand welcoming visitors in peace. It wasn't exactly a temple, but the decoration and feeling were similar, like a temple that people lived in. On the other side of the compound were the student dormitories.

In Taiwanese, Linda told the desk clerk who I was, and she left me with a promise to collect me for dinner in a few hours. Until then I was free to go anywhere I liked.

"Is it okay to take photos?" I had to know.

"Of course. Take as many as you like." She smiled and waved farewell.

The room could have been that of a budget hotel anywhere in the world. There was no real décor, just basic wood and tile. I had a telephone and even a television. Perhaps I could watch Beautiful Life TV, the Buddhist programming that was made on site. I was insanely curious as to what was on there.

For those who don't know the story of Buddha, it goes something like this. He was born Siddhartha in India in the sixth century B.C. to a royal family. The family was visited by a soothsayer who prophesied that Siddhartha would either become a great king or a great holy man. Not knowing anything of the world outside the palace until he was twenty-nine, everyone believed he would become king. When he made contact with the outside world and understood the great suffering of humanity, however, he renounced all of his wealth and privilege to become a compassionate holy man.

There is more to the story about how he sat under a Bodhi tree until he became enlightened and what that enlightenment meant, but ultimately Buddha's teachings are all about "right living." That means living compassionately, harmlessly, not being deceptive, and making an effort to improve yourself. I think that's what made it so incredibly attractive to me: its simplicity. How could living a good life be so easy, when other religions seemed to make it so incredibly complicated?

I have never been drawn to organized religion, but I was intrigued by the concept of using the power of one's mind to defeat the ego or self-sabotaging tendencies. Was that really the secret? I didn't know, but I thought this might be a good way to find out.

At dinner I received instructions to be at the prayer hall just before dawn. For a minute I thought Linda was joking, but that was followed by directions to the building where meditation took place. Afterwards she would give me a tour of the compound and answer any questions I had.

We ended the day at evening meditation. I sat amongst the nuns, listening to the vibration of a group chant. Occasionally I opened my eyes to sneak a peek at the others. Everyone was in full concentration. I looked at the sheet of paper I was handed along with a pillow to sit on, and tried to follow the chant. When I kept missing the rhythm, I just closed my eyes and smiled. Though I felt out of place, I didn't feel anywhere near as uncomfortable as I had in my own life as of late.

In the morning I followed Linda's orders. The blue-black sky was still littered with stars as I moved toward the three golden Buddha statues in the main hall. I should have felt nervous, but instead I felt lucky. Having the opportunity to be an insider, even for a few hours, was a treat. Moments like this do not come around often, and for most Ohio girls we can comfortably say they never do. It had to mean something that I was here, even if I had sought it out.

Walking past the Beautiful Life Television Studio later on, I asked Linda what had brought her here.

"I just didn't see the point of struggling so much only to come up empty every day. I went to school and I went to work to pay off debt for a place to live and a car to drive. Then I accumulated more debt and worked more hours. It didn't make sense to me. Here, I am part of something bigger. I am in service without the struggle," she told me.

"I can't argue with that," I agreed. "It doesn't make sense when you put it that way. But do you ever wonder if you made the right decision?" There was no way I could leave without asking that question.

"For me, this is the right decision. All my decisions are the right decisions. That's what Buddha teaches us. To second guess that is to second guess Buddha." Her brown eyes took in mine.

So that's how you do it, I thought. You can escape the constant anxiety of making the wrong choices in life if you just don't think about it. I couldn't imagine pulling it off myself, but that didn't mean I thought she was wrong. We just had different ways of being in the world. Mine was to question every single move I made multiple times. If I said I wasn't envious that she could be happy *not* second-guessing her every move, I would be lying.

Linda took me to the top of the hill to see the largest Buddha statue on the premises, along with his collection of little golden followers at the base. The view over the river was beautiful, and the surrounding area was very peaceful—nothing like the noisy crowds of Singapore. I was given the chance to sound the huge gong before I left by swinging a long wooden pole into it. The vibration floated over the entire valley.

Traveling back to Taipei, I tried to make sense of the experience. I didn't want to give up my existence and my life to live in a Buddhist dormitory, but I loved the tranquility the devoted embodied. Of course I couldn't speak to anyone but Linda, but there must be a myriad of reasons one ended up in a place like this. I wondered if it was always a choice.

The gift Fo Guang Shan gave me for my thirty-ninth birthday was the understanding that what I was doing in my everyday life was a *choice*. I was choosing to be unhappy with not finding a job, similar to what I had left behind. I was choosing to call myself a housewife when in fact I could call myself anything. The revelation was that my life was not my external circumstances, only I had believed it was so.

I received one other treasure on my birthday, this one from David. We spent our last few hours visiting the Taipei jade market, which is legendary. I'd been looking for a piece of jade that didn't have that bright-green synthetic look, and here there were over eight hundred stalls to choose from. The sight was staggering and choice overwhelming. David strolled along patiently as I scrutinized each table, even though he didn't understand what was wrong with the hundreds of pieces right in front of us.

Nearly an hour later I found what I was looking for. It was a rectangular pendant with its edges rounded by time. Less than two inches high, it had a carved cornucopia design that the owner said would bring wealth. That was right before he said he would only take cash. My heart sank. We'd been having trouble with bank machines here, and relying on credit cards.

I looked at David who never hesitated. "I'll find one that works," he said in that determined tone which meant business. "How late are you open?"

"Until nine," said the seller, with a small bow of his head.

"Are you sure?" I turned to ask, but he was already gone, leaving me to continue my wandering. It was seven-thirty. I waited for a while before texting that I was returning to the hotel.

"This is the one, right?" David handed me a red drawstring pouch.

I'd already given up hope, as it was just past nine when he came back. Opening it, a smile spread wide across my face. Tears welled up in my eyes. "Thank you so much! I can't believe you got it!"

"I tried three more ATM machines before I got smart enough to take out cash on one of the credit cards. So stupid! I should have done that the first time."

He was oblivious as to how much the gesture meant to me. I'd felt ignored for months, and he had gone so far out of his way to make me happy. He could easily have thrown up his hands and walked away, but he didn't. Perhaps what I had been choosing to believe about us was wrong too.

Fastening the clasp on my new necklace, I made myself a promise.

I had to take back control of my life instead of playing the victim. Life in Asia hadn't worked out as expected, but at the same time, I had a rare opportunity. Understanding Asian ways of life and philosophies, seeing such spectacular locations—many of which I'd never even thought about—and having the time to do anything I wanted. What I wanted was to write. I would stop telling myself I couldn't.

Now that I had it all figured out, I got to work in the weeks before Christmas. The idea to write a book was not new. Ever since landing in the Netherlands, I'd played around with the idea. In my last job in Europe I'd been a program manager, managing project sites across several countries. As I realized how vastly different European cultures were, and how quickly one had to change gears to get things done, the idea took on more and more significance.

On my last trip to Rotterdam, I'd brought with me my journals from my early days of relocating from Cleveland to Heidelberg and then on to Amsterdam. I made a rough outline of the chapters and significant events along the way. The whole idea seemed possible, whereas in the past I'd found every excuse not to get started. What did it matter if I didn't have a regular paycheck when I couldn't get one anyway? And so I wrote.

Pre-dawn meditation at Fo Guang Shan

Chapter 25
Taboo

The Christmas adventure of 2009 had been planned long ago. We were leaving for Cambodia at the end of the month to spend Christmas. Our New Year's celebration would take place in Laos. What I loved was that our adventures were getting bolder. We didn't worry about language barriers, but we did worry about immunizations and comprehensive travel insurance that would get us airlifted out in a life-threatening situation. For China we'd gotten the full series of hepatitis and tuberculosis shots, so we were ready for Cambodia.

Our initial destination was Siem Reap. Truth be told, it was the main reason we wanted to visit Cambodia. The true-life story of the ancient Kingdom of Angkor and its main temple, Angkor Wat, made for compelling reading. These ruins had been rediscovered by a French naturalist in 1860 after they'd been devoured by the jungle centuries earlier. Angelina Jolie's movie *Tomb Raider* had also been filmed here in 2001, giving the city a much needed injection of tourism afterwards. Photos of the massive strangler figs punching through stone temples were too compelling to ignore.

The itinerary for the majority of our days was simple: temples, temples, and more temples. We purchased a package with the hotel for a driver and a guide to help us make the most of the kingdom and I was filled with anticipation. The first day was for us to explore alone, and there was no holding us back from Angkor Wat.

With camera bags and plenty of water, we went directly to the main entrance of the sprawling UNESCO site by taxi. The moment David pulled out his wallet to pay, he was surrounded by tiny Cambodian faces thrusting postcards at him. "You buy? You buy? You buy?" they shouted in unison.

David did a double-take, feeling like he should. "Not right now," he finally said.

"Later? Later? Later?" came the chorus.

"Maybe," he laughed.

They watched us pull out our cameras, and then ran off to find other victims. Laughing, we were both looking at the stone imagery and trying to decipher it. The Angkor designs were like nothing we'd seen in Vietnam or Thailand. Cobras were prevalent, some with many heads and all with very long tails. The beautiful corridors which moved you from one main room to the next were all etched with intricate designs of many-armed Buddhas and dancing spirits.

Other temples we'd visited had mostly been painted and were nowhere near this size. Each time you turned a corner, the sunlight played tricks with the shadows to produce a new view that had to be captured. I snapped pictures of David grinning in front of an orange-robed Buddha carrying a fringed yellow parasol. We explored together and alone, always meeting up along the way.

The afternoon sun was punishing—and it was impossible to stay dry. Sweat poured off of me. I suggested we find something to eat nearby. Given the number of tourists swarming Angkor Wat, I was certain there had to be something we could eat. We couldn't safely drink the water outside of Singapore and street food wasn't an option either. Luckily we found bottled water and grilled chicken skewers with rice. It tasted like chicken anyway.

"What do you want to do after lunch?" I asked David in between gulps of water.

"Take more photos." He answered as though it was the only option.

"Okay. Are you planning to stay here? Or do you want to take a look around?" David had a habit of making plans and neglecting to fill me in on them, expecting me to guess.

"We can look around, but I'm not done with Angkor Wat." He wasn't even looking at me when he spoke. Apparently the rice was more interesting.

"It's just too hot for me to stand around there. I don't feel well. I can walk somewhere else if you want to—it's a little better under the jungle trees." The searing sun was merciless. I tried to find a solution to enjoy our time together.

"I'm not going to leave now. I'll meet you later." He wouldn't budge.

"Okay. I'm going to go into town and write for a while then." My journal was in my backpack and I wanted to capture my impressions from the morning.

"The town isn't that big. I'll find you."

With that, I took my leave. We had three days of temples coming up. I didn't feel I was missing out, and he was trying out new photography techniques. It wasn't a big deal to split up, but why did he have to be so obstinate?

Siem Reap's town is only a few dusty streets with a long strip of places for tourists to eat and drink. The Temple Club was a cool bar decked out in temple artifacts and décor. An Indian restaurant stood out in the mix. Most places were empty during the day while the tourists went temple tromping.

I found a large hotel on the corner where the bar overlooked the street. Ordering a rum and diet Coke, I sat on the verandah with my journal and filled page after page with observations. To get into the protected village of temples, you had to have a visitor pass and your passport information recorded. They even took a photo. Cambodia was so poor that a Vietnamese company ran this operation for them—and Vietnam isn't exactly wealthy either. Multiple international NGO's operated nearby, offering volunteer services and education. It was heartening to see the world working together to protect this ancient wonder.

We ate dinner at Cambodian Kitchen when David showed up. Cambodian home-style cooking is actually quite delicious. Flat rice noodles mixed with vegetables and shrimp hit the spot for me. David tried fish *amok*, traditional fish curry, which had to be magic—it put him in a much better mood.

Over the following days we uncovered the mysteries of the temples with our guide and learned about the Kingdom of Angkor. My favorite was the Bayon, a temple where King Jayavarman VII is believed to have carved his own face in the structure more than two hundred times. Second on the list had to be Phnom Bakheng, the temple we climbed under the last rays of sun to catch her evening bow. We left Siem Reap richer for having experienced it. There was so much to learn that David and I were distracted from our troubles.

Next was Phnom Penh, which was far from beautiful. Cambodia's extreme poverty was blatant in the city, unhidden by the jungle canopy that covers the surroundings of Siem Reap. Everything in Phnom Penh was covered with dirt. Most of the houses and shops in the center looked as though they might collapse at any moment. The Mekong and the Tonle Sap rivers meet at the city's edge, currents stirring up the waters and turning it an awful shade of baby-shit brown. It felt hotter than Singapore, though it was further north.

I never expected Cambodia's capital to be beautiful. Its bloody history has made that impossible. While I was watching Sesame Street safe in my Ohio living room, Cambodians were slaughtered by the millions by a despotic regime called the Khmer Rouge. People were forced from their homes and methodically rounded up to be forced into labor and tortured. It's estimated that twenty-five percent of the population was exterminated between 1975 and 1979. Phnom Penh still bears the scars for all to see.

In 1984, a movie titled *The Killing Fields* caught the world's attention. I was fourteen at the time and had little interest in war and death. I wouldn't have understood it anyway. Today, a museum dedicated to the Cambodian Genocide makes it impossible to misunderstand. S-21, the high school converted to a torture machine, is open to the public. Walking through the classrooms, it is impossible not to imagine yourself sitting at one of the desks. Drops of dried blood on the floor only hint to the rest of the story.

The second part of this war crimes experience takes you to the actual killing fields. Here, a small structure the size of a backyard shed, was crowded full of prisoners every night. The windows, open but covered with bars, allowed them to hear the screams of their friends and neighbors being murdered. Terrified prisoners held indoors didn't know if they would die with them the same night or alone the next. It was only a question of when.

David and I were both ready for a stiff drink after that dose of reality. The Foreign Correspondents' Club has a history of its own along with a wide balcony overlooking the river. It was this balcony that journalists used to capture images and narratives to alert the outside world of what was happening during the genocide and in the turbulent years before.

Now a bar and hotspot for the upscale tourist, I was relieved to hear the whirring bamboo fans overhead and to have a cold gin and tonic in my hand. Intriguing black-and-white photos filled the entryway. My heart skipped a beat just being there. I could practically hear keys clacking in desperation to get a story over the wire. David, on the other hand, merely waited to leave.

Because Cambodia had so recently been opened to tourism, it was difficult to know where to stay. I chose the oldest hotel in the city because I hoped they would know what they were doing and because it looked very grand. The Cambodiana is a massive place. There are restaurants, bars, swimming pools, function rooms—everything you would want in a hotel—amplified by a million watts of everything you wouldn't.

On Christmas Eve, speakers blared in the bar below our room until three o'clock in the morning. Older western men brought their teenage female escorts to the swimming pool and proceeded to fawn over them. Police in the parking lot, presumably to keep the peace, poured drunken guests into their own vehicles and handed them their keys. Cambodia's old-school establishment loved this hotel for every reason I abhorred it.

To get out of the hotel, David and I went for dinner at a restaurant called Romdeng. The owners are well-known for their work with Cambodian children from orphanages and impoverished families. They help teenagers build skills in the catering and hospitality business to make productive lives for themselves. Children in Cambodia are at extreme risk of falling victim to the child sex trade because it is so poverty-stricken. Predators are rampant. The restaurant is also known for its excellent creative cuisine.

"Do you think we should order the crispy tarantulas?" David pulled a face and I laughed out loud. "At least they won't crawl off the plate!" I loved teasing him about his fear of spiders.

"Actually, I was considering the stir-fried red tree ants," he laughed.

"Might not make much of a meal. Perhaps you better order the duck or the pork belly to go along with that."

We didn't order insects but we did enjoy a delicious meal. The place was packed. Obviously we weren't the only tourists who wanted to do something good for the children here. We'd been warned not to buy trinkets from street kids because if they make money that way, they don't see any reason to go to school.

David excused himself to go to the restroom and I watched the other guests. A table of two guys next to us did order the tarantulas. Somehow they didn't look that thrilled when they arrived. Ten minutes later, David arrived at the table carrying a package.

"I bought one of the cookbooks. The recipes are fascinating." He put it down on the table.

"Really? Let me see." I grabbed the brown-paper bag and saw that there were two in it. "Who is the other one for?" I asked.

"I thought Madeline would like it." He answered.

"Oh." I was stunned. Apparently they were buddies even though I had steered clear of her.

I sat in silence trying to make sense of this. David casually mentioned it as though it was nothing. I knew it wasn't. He rarely bought gifts for *anyone*, let alone a co-worker.

"What should we do now?" He asked. "I don't think going back to the hotel is a good idea. That bar noise will be pumping for hours yet."

"Maybe we should ask the staff here if there's a good place to go for a drink nearby." That seemed the logical distraction from the train of thought I was having.

"Good idea. I'll be back in a minute." He left to walk to the hostess at the front.

Everything was spinning. *What does it mean?* Madeline was very single and obviously open to married men propositioning her. She'd already mentioned the herd of men at the project who wanted her. David wouldn't be dumb enough to fall for that. Would he?

"There's an Aussie bar called The Walkabout a few blocks from here. Want to check it out?" David put some *riel* on the table for a tip.

Grateful for the fresh air, I followed him. Maybe it would help clear my head.

The Walkabout looked fine from the outside. It doesn't take long to learn that in Cambodia you never really know what you're getting into until it's too late. Ten to fifteen round wooden tables were at the front of the bar, nearly all occupied by one or two western men. The ages varied, but they all looked rough. Unshaven faces, dirty clothes, and overall gruff in appearance. I'd have guessed the median age to be in the fifties.

There was an edge to the place. None of the men looked around—they all stared forward straight ahead looking at rugby or soccer on the screens in front of them. The women, all Cambodian, were sitting in a line of bar stools around the bar. David and I walked up and took two of the empty seats. I was the only western woman in the bar. All of them stared at me openly.

I ordered a beer and watched the action. David was doing the same, but we didn't discuss it. At least not at first. One by one, women went to each table and talked to the guy they sat down with. Sometimes he bought her a drink and she stayed. Other times she left quickly and was replaced by another woman who might get a drink and an invitation to stay, or might not. Eventually, a pair who had been drinking together left together.

One guy, the ugliest and oldest at the bar, sat at a corner table. David watched him dismiss at least three women before I noticed him and saw another two come and go. What he lacked in teeth he must have made up for in money. He was determined to get what he wanted.

I went to the restroom and just sat for a minute. On the inside of the stall door was a bright-yellow sticker. It said "Child Sex Tourists—Don't Turn Away, Turn Them In!" There was a phone number under it. What

I was witnessing was no doubt disgusting, but the women didn't look underage. It appeared to be a nightly routine in this bar and I had no right to make a scene, even though I wanted to scream.

Phnom Penh wasn't all a horror show. We toured the National Palace with its beautiful intricate design and numerous wats, crafted of silver and gold. Orange-robed monks walked the city streets with the same yellow parasols we saw in Angkor Wat. The people we encountered in the city as well as in the country were incredibly kind and genuinely friendly, not the superficial friendliness that Singaporeans often gave you when they wanted you to buy something.

I couldn't believe that despite the extreme hardship these people had endured, they exuded joy. If they could brightly carry on after the tragedy that had left very few families unaffected, what did I have to cry about? Cambodia forced me to come to grips with myself in a way I hadn't experienced elsewhere. I simply had no right to continue feeling sorry for myself.

* * *

To greet the New Year, we landed in Luang Prabang. The dreamy village feeling was similar to what we experienced in Siem Reap. We had a private villa in a jungle setting overlooking the Mekong. Nearby was an old wooden railway bridge. Its railcar days long over, bikes and pedestrians crossed it to get to the main village. After the Cambodiana, this mountain-protected paradise spoke directly to my soul.

Vientiane may be the capital of Laos, but Luang Prabang is the nation's heart. Fifty thousand people call it home, but you wouldn't know that from cycling the village center. The city has been in existence for over a thousand years. Because of its prime location on the Mekong and Nam Khan Rivers, it has long been fought over. There have been more than sixty temples constructed over the years. Today, there are thirty-two remaining.

On the last night of 2009, we wandered on foot through the center of town. Silver balloon archways marked the pathway to 2010, and revelers were out early. David and I took seats under a massive shrub decorated in empty colored liquor bottles tied to the branches. A young local came by and placed party hats on our heads. David took it in stride, even though he isn't a party hat kind of guy.

Eventually we began talking to Matt and Paul, American and British travelers.

"I'm so glad to be in a peaceful place again after all that ugliness in Cambodia." I remarked.

"Oh, trust me, there's just as much black market shit happening here," Paul corrected me.

"What do you mean? There doesn't look like there's much happening here…" I looked around the bar we currently sat in, to underscore my point. It was New Year's Eve and it was rowdy, but far from obnoxious.

"There are drugs *everywhere* here. You can get ecstasy, meth, pot, probably heroin. There's more going on in this place than you think."

Clearly I was not connected to the Luang Prabang underground. Good thing that didn't interest me in the slightest. "Well, I guess I'd better keep an eye on my stuff then. If those are the kind of people that hang here, I know what kind of hassle comes along with it." I was thinking of Amsterdam where your purse or wallet can disappear in seconds.

"Yeah, it's bad here. We'll still have a good time though. Come with us to Utopia. It's got a good vibe and nice people." Matt weighed in.

"Sounds good to me. Time to change the scenery!" I said to David, who hadn't said a word. I suspected he would just rather go home, but I was having none of it. I took his hand and pulled him up. Fun was desperately needed.

Utopia was indeed cool. It had a huge outdoor beer garden and the tree branches were covered with Christmas lights. It twinkled everywhere. Santa was tending bar tonight and passed me a very strong rum and diet coke. For a second I wondered about the water quality. Then I decided there was enough booze in the glass to kill any bacteria that thought about making me sick. A fire blazed in one corner, warming the cool mountain air. I chatted with people from France, Germany, and Canada. For a while I didn't even know where David was, and I didn't care.

Midnight came and shots came with it. The hippy backpacker crowd I'd been talking to slowly began to migrate elsewhere. Though it had been fun to talk to some new people, I didn't feel like following the party train all night. I asked David if he was ready to leave, knowing full well he'd been ready hours ago. Looking down at the silvery water underneath the pretty bridge, I was glad to see 2009 hit the door. My only concern was what 2010 would bring in its place.

* * *

Laos has magic to offer, within those thirty-two temples and without. The monks walk the streets each morning with empty bowls that are soon filled by locals. The word extraordinary is the only word to describe the temples we visited in Luang Prabang and our next stop Vientiane. The oldest are filled with delicately carved silver guardians and five-headed *nagas*. Many were wooden on the outside making it impossible to predict the richness of the interiors.

I thought I might be bored with temples after having seen so many, but the unique tint of Lao culture on Buddhism fascinated me. What fascinated me more was riding an elephant through the jungle at the edge of the Mekong. David and I each had our own elephant. We climbed up to a platform and the elephant waited below. From there, it's easy to climb onto the wooden seat strapped to the animal's back.

David went first. As his elephant lumbered away, I anxiously awaited my turn. Sitting down, I realized for the first time just *how far down* I would fall if I mismanaged this situation. Looking at the head of an elephant for the first time is somewhat dizzying all on its own. The enormous head isn't quite bald. It has wiry hairs sticking out all over, reminding me of someone's grandpa.

It was a beautiful ride, imagining how royalty and British officers must have felt when they traveled this way in the early days of Asian civilizations and colonialism. Jungle flowers offered up their scents and bright colors to welcome my passing. The scenery—majestic mountains overlooking the Mekong—could not have been more spectacular.

Everything was wonderful until they asked us if we wanted a second ride. This time we would take the elephants for a bath. David was all for it. Swimming was involved and my white shirt wasn't going in, but I was happy to ride to the river. I became a little less happy when I discovered this ride was bareback. No wooden throne for royalty this time, just my legs around the neck of this enormous creature and my hands gripping its ears. It was terrifying. I have the photos to prove it.

David, on the other hand, out-adventured me. He went right into the water to swim with the elephants and help our hosts give them a bath. I stood on the shore taking photos of the five men playing in the water like little boys. Was there no end to Asia's surprises?

Tree vs. temple

Buddha inside Angkor Wat

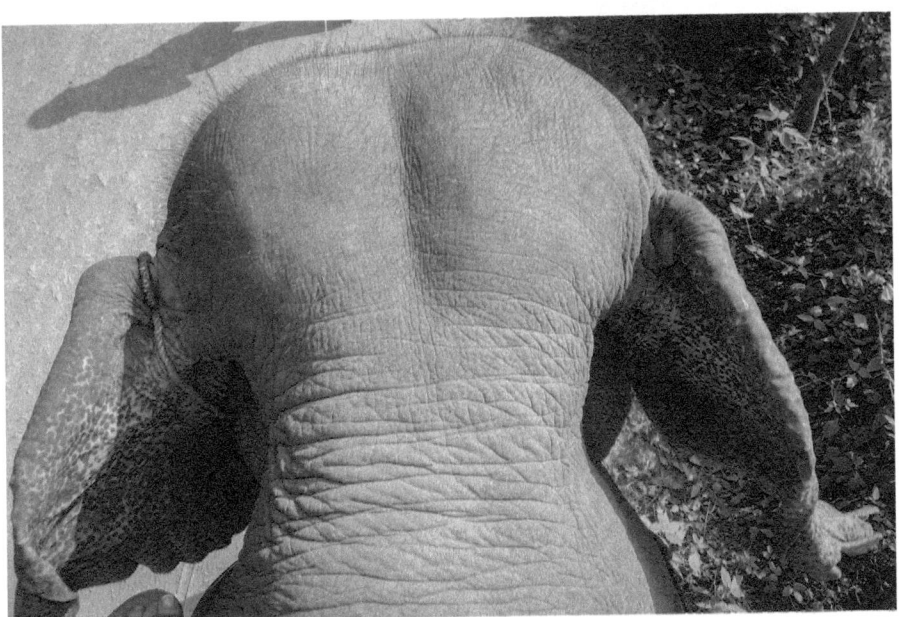

It's a LONG way down!

Our villa beneath the railway bridge in Luang Prabang

Chapter 26
Epiphany

Excitement came to a screeching halt in January 2010. I continued walking to Fort Canning park every morning and swimming as often as possible. The Singapore Supper Club was in swing and we tried a Greek restaurant the next time around. Note to self: Ouzo is not your friend. I also got wind of a screaming deal on martinis every Wednesday afternoon at Morton's, so I rounded up victims to conquer hump day with me. In between drinking and dining appointments, I wrote.

At the end of last year, David had begun biking on the weekends. Considering the fact that he is far from a fitness enthusiast, I encouraged it. It was good for him to release all the stress. My only concern was the Singaporean drivers, many of whom seemed to get their licenses out of a cereal box.

One day he decided to gather up friends for a photography excursion. We had seen the bizarre Indian festival known as Thaipusam once before, and this year he wanted to get closer. I wasn't a fan of watching people torture themselves for the sake of religion, but I didn't want to sit at home on a Saturday either. We met Alexis and a few of David's colleagues at the MRT station for Little India and walked from there to Sri Srinivasa Perumal Temple on Serangoon Road.

Participating in the ritual means self-inflicted pain. The Indian men show their endurance and virility by pushing long skewer-like rods into their skin. The rods are very light-weight, so in order to outdo your competitors, you must add more weight to the rods. The weight comes in many forms. Limes are popular. Feathered golden headdresses flourish. The extremely devout place hooks in their skin to pull the weight behind them, often in the form of small carts–fully loaded. The heavier the load, the greater the offering of devotion.

We walked around watching these men being decorated for the parade, which takes place after everyone is ready. It's sickening to watch. The men are often being shouted at as well, while items are inserted into their skin, told to show off their strength and take it like a man. As if this wasn't enough, I found the flip-flops to be worn by the participants—each one covered with tiny metal spikes to complete the costume.

I took pictures of the men's faces, noticing that a far off stare was often in their eyes. It looked very much like no one was home. I suspected they were using drugs to numb themselves, but who knows—perhaps they are experts at mind control. David, who had been studying digital photography techniques for some time and had a sophisticated Nikon, helped the others to get their best shots. I was on my own.

In the morning I continued reading *The Straits Times*. I didn't rely on it for world news, but it was handy for seeing what was happening locally. The paper seemed to enjoy shaming people, often getting hold of a story and continuing to doggedly report on it daily.

One woman, a Singaporean-Chinese local, was on trial for maid abuse. Sadly, this wasn't the first time I'd read about a case of a Filipina maid being assaulted or verbally harangued by her employer, but the description of the charges was frightening. This woman and her thirty-five year old son had been trying to control their maid with physical punishment. They tried scalding her with boiling water, and when that didn't work to their satisfaction, they used pliers to pull out some of her teeth. Were these people even human?

Another story, this one more of a public service announcement, advised readers that if a team of paramedics arrived in their building to provide emergency assistance to someone, they were to get out of the way immediately. Why was this necessary? Because a man had recently died of a heart attack after a family refused to vacate the elevator needed to get to him. The utter disregard for human life was mind-boggling.

On a Wednesday morning, I floated in the pool after finishing my laps. I closed my eyes and drifted, enjoying the watery silence. My

Epiphany

peace came to an abrupt end when I remembered that Madeline was into cycling. If they were still friends and David was now buying gifts, I could put money on the fact that he was meeting up with her on the weekends when he took his bike out.

I felt sick. There is a kind of knowing where it's no longer just anxiety or fear. It is real and your mind chose not to reveal it earlier to protect you. This was that kind of knowing.

I went upstairs to the condo and doubled over sitting on the couch. Perhaps if I struck a fetal position, I could get that protection back somehow and this would not be happening to me. David and I had met in 2002 and married in 2004. We owned a beautiful home together. He'd helped me through some extremely difficult times of adjustment in Europe. Why would he give up on me now?

It was already late afternoon, so I got dressed for the Morton's martini night and poured myself a glass of wine to get numb. I never even considered not going. I had to get out of the house immediately. Jac showed up first and we praised the humble dirty martini for its strength-inducing properties. She chatted about life at the project, and I told her about my book. The subject of my marriage did not come up.

It took me four days to confront David. I chose the moment he was getting dressed in his cycling clothes.

"When you go out, do you meet Madeline?" Carefully, I watched his face as I said it.

His eyes widened. "Sometimes," was all he said.

"Really? Why didn't you mention it?" My voice shook.

"I didn't think it was relevant. You don't like her, so why would I bring it up?" He tried to hedge the real conversation we were about to have.

"Because you are now buying her gifts and meeting her without telling your wife. I think that's very relevant." I stared at him while my face grew hot. "What exactly is going on here, David? Is there something you want to tell me?"

He sighed. The sigh indicated that he was just so tired of having to deal with me. That was the kind of sigh it was.

"Nothing has happened," was all I got.

"What do you mean "nothing happened"? When did "nothing happen" and under what circumstances are we talking about here, David? This his bullshit!" Now I was pissed.

"We talk sometimes, that's all."

"You talk about *what*? Me? Our marriage? What exactly are you chatting about with someone who acted like a complete asshole in my own home? What you two have in common—like hating me?" I couldn't stop myself. What had gone on in my imagination the past few days demanded to be let loose.

"I told her that I love my wife." He stopped a minute. "And I didn't understand how I now have feelings for her too."

It was a stake through my heart. My head was spinning. No, we hadn't been getting long well as of late, but now it was real. First I was shocked. Then I was angry. Suddenly I remembered her comment about my "marriage problems." This woman had wheedled herself into my life and my relationship because of her own desperate loneliness. She had seen a crack in the door when I brought her to my home in the Netherlands, and she proceeded to kick it open.

Several times David repeated that "nothing happened" and that it was "just talking." I was no longer listening. He had humiliated me by revealing details of our marriage to someone else and I had to get the hell out of Singapore.

Stan offered me a place to stay in Sydney without hesitation. I didn't divulge the reason for my sudden need to escape. I merely told him that I couldn't imagine returning to the US or Europe, and wanted to look for a job in Australia. He was more than happy to help.

As I had no reason to hurry home, I decided it was time to explore New Zealand as well. A friend from my Germany days lived in Auckland, and I emailed her to ask for tips on whether to travel to the North or South Island. Auckland and Wellington were up north, but the largely-uninhabited south was a must. Kate also offered me a stay at her Bay of Islands "bach," Kiwi-speak for beach house. I could not have been more grateful.

Stan had a gorgeous apartment in Potts Point, the perfect location close to the city for job interviews and general entertainment. Not having much money, I didn't do much of the latter, but the former took off like a rocket. Within a week of landing in Sydney, I had three interviews. All three were with large computer hardware and software firms. All three paid very well.

In the times that I wasn't trying to understand the Sydney job market, I was in the State Library writing or analyzing the Aussie way of life. In the evenings I'd get culture lessons from Stan who was well-versed on Australian politics and industry. The more wine we drank, the more honest we both became about the pros and cons of our respective homes.

Stan was generous enough to let me stay with him for a month before I left for New Zealand. I learned that Sydneysiders are extremely forthright about their opinions and seem to be in a hurry all the time, whereas I'd always had the impression that Aussies were so laid back. One of the interviewers was extremely aggressive with me when I touched on a potential flaw in their software, something I've never experienced in an interview anywhere.

Perhaps it was my absence from the job scene that made the experience so abrasive, but I wasn't in a huge hurry to jump back into the corporate rat race. I knew I had to find a way to support myself and my lifestyle, so I might just have to join the lesser evil among them. No matter what happened, the experience was invaluable. There was absolutely no way I was going to move to yet another country without knowing what I was getting into up front.

April was just beginning as I landed in Auckland. Immediately I felt at home. Kiwis are a no-bullshit lot. They get to the point with a lot of wit and sarcasm, but are nothing but friendly. Kate and her boyfriend met me at a city restaurant, and within an hour I was well-prepared for my New Zealand adventure. I knew where to get a local SIM card and phone number, the best place to buy warm clothes for my time on the South Island, and all about New Zealand transport. I couldn't wait to explore.

There was plenty of adventure in the nation's largest city. The best day of my life in months was standing at the helm of an America's Cup yacht sailing in Auckland Harbour. The feeling of power that came from taking control of this ultra-fast racing machine grounded me. I would take back control of my life again no matter what happened. David could play out his "confusion" as long as he wanted, but I wouldn't be waiting around. The cold wind on my face slapped me back to the reality that this is no dress rehearsal.

I didn't just "enjoy" New Zealand. I devoured it. Kate's bach in the Bay of Islands was the perfect hideaway. There was even a writing desk in the bedroom. I used it plenty, in between discovering Maori culture and sailing on that stunning bay of one hundred and forty islands. For the very first time, I saw a penguin flipping his little black tail-feathers in the wild. I climbed the coastal cliffs and learned how critical tide schedules can be. Enormous pods of dolphins roamed the bay.

It was hard to imagine how the South Island could be better than this paradise of the north. Landing in Christchurch put an end to the wondering. As the taxi drove me down the perfectly manicured boulevards and quaint original estates trimmed in roses, it was love at first sight. Home base was a city hotel for two nights as I explored this picturesque village.

In reality, over three hundred and fifty thousand people call Christchurch home, but the city center has an incredible small-town feel. Even the region's name of Canterbury evoked magic and that was before I visited the stunning cathedral and Christ's College—both architectural beauties. The college reminded me of a place Harry Potter would study.

The Botanic Gardens of Christchurch completed a perfect day. Sunny fall weather in the seventies delivered gold-trimmed trees and willows that weeped over the Avon. Small boats and kayaks glided down the river, with no one in a particular hurry. But the best surprise of all waited in the Canterbury Museum. An exhibit honoring the early Antarctic explorers, complete with their original gear, fascinated me. A Methuselah of champagne from 1928 to honor Admiral Byrd's successful expedition bore my favorite date: November 29th. It did not feel like a coincidence.

The real adventure began when I landed in Queenstown. Flying through the Southern Alps to land in this flawless diamond was nothing

Epiphany

short of spectacular. Picking up my rental car took it down a notch. It was my first time driving on the left side of the road, and I was terrified. A white sticker on the dashboard was a diagram of proper turns. Clearly I wasn't the only one who needed a cheat sheet.

A haven for adventure junkies, Queenstown offers it all. Bungy jumping, skiing, snowboarding, kayaking, hiking, camping, and everything else done outdoors. Nestled at the base of the mountains and bordered by the shimmering Lake Wakatipu, I don't think I've ever seen any place more beautiful. My room at the Rydges Hotel was lakeside, complete with a balcony and gorgeous view. It was far too cold to sit outside, but with a glass of Central Otago pinot noir and the pink-purple-hued sunset, it was a dream.

Te Anau was my next stop—the coldest and most remote—which only added to its beauty. On the edges of Lake Te Anau, it is the last piece of civilization before entering Fiordland National Park. There is one main street that includes the usual souvenir shops and restaurants along with an internet kiosk. From here I learned that the park encompasses over a million hectares of land, much of it is so dense that it hasn't been traversed or mapped by humans. That fact made it irresistible.

The two-hour drive to Milford Sound was unlike anything I had seen before. The clouds played hide and seek with the sun, changing the mountain vistas every moment. When I arrived at the first fiord I have ever seen, I thought I must have fallen into the Land of the Lost.

To see the fiord, I had to take a commercial vessel for an afternoon tour. Lit up by the sun, the waterfalls that streamed down the mountainsides created glittering rainbows. When it disappeared, a silvery light covered the water's surface in a spooky supernatural effect. Fur seals lolled on the rocks we passed on the way to the Tasman Sea. The only people were aboard the few boats which cruised the fiord. Here at the bottom of the planet was a heaven that most people didn't know existed.

The road that took me to Mount Cook was the most desolate. I drove for miles without seeing a soul, often wondering if I was driving on the proper side of the road. Without other cars to double-check yourself, it's easy to forget. Mount Cook delivered something new entirely: I touched the smooth glass of an actual glacier for the first time. Cruising in a yellow inflatable boat on a gray lake surrounded by deep-blue ice is otherworldly. This place called New Zealand was nothing short of miraculous.

Navigating the unknown and having the time of my life brought me back to myself. I didn't need to be dependent on anyone to move with confidence in the world. All I needed was my own job and my own money, things that could be easily located in this part of the world. If David wasn't going to continue this adventure called "life" with me, so be it. I would not lie down and die even if my relationship did. The world wouldn't let me.

* * *

Returning to Singapore, I felt stronger than ever. Australia and New Zealand had been an infusion of all that was missing in my life. I'd finished my manuscript and I took control of understanding the publishing world. I also followed up on jobs and had a very promising position within my reach in Auckland.

"We need to decide what we're doing here, or rather you do," I told David when we were both back in the condo with time to talk. "You have mentioned before that there is a possibility for you to transfer to Australia. Are you planning to pursue it? Or are you planning to stay here?" For me, it was that simple.

"I don't know. It's not like I can flip a switch and transfer my job to another continent. It takes time." David was stalling.

"I realize that—I know how corporations work. What I'm asking is what you *want* to do. I've been gone for two months. We've had two months of indecision. I've had enough. You're either in or out of this plan. I'm not giving up my future for *maybe*." All of this was really pissing me off now.

"I will talk to the guys at work about a transfer. I recently read that they have been staffing up in Australia," he said finally, apparently ready to give up on having it both ways.

"Fine. I can put off the interview for another week or two until you see what the situation is, but I can't wait forever." On me, sadness often shows up as anger. I knew I wasn't making myself more adorable with my demands, but I was beyond hurt by his betrayal. I had to prevent it from happening a second time.

Thaipusam

Thaipusam

Land of the Lost
a.k.a.
Milford Sound

Me at the helm
on Auckland
Harbour

Chapter 27
Dreaming in Vietnamese

The summer crawled by. I vacillated between wanting to grab hold of David and never let him go, and wanting to kill him. There were many parties in this situation who had to shoulder blame. My unhappiness with my situation had made me difficult to be around. David's taking another woman into his confidence and acting like he wasn't sure he wanted to stay together was a betrayal. Madeline's maneuvering her way into the position of trusted ally in a storm was opportunistic and sad.

Ultimately I had to decide whether I could trust the person I'd walked down the aisle with or not. We'd been such strong partners even in the worst of times before Singapore that I couldn't imagine it was anything but this place.

One night, during a particularly heated battle of words, David said, "You weren't happy in Holland. You aren't happy here. What makes you think Australia is the answer? Maybe the problem is you."

Ouch. It stung because I had to consider whether he was right or not. Life in The Netherlands had definitely pulled the ground out from under me. I'd been walking a tightrope ever since I gave up my US-based job. The move to Singapore was supposed to be the answer, but I hadn't thought hard enough about how uneven the playing field would be. I couldn't have known that getting a job would be next to impossible, nor predicted the GFC, so I refused to believe it was some inherent "unhappiness" within me.

Aside from the obvious difficulty of managing blame along with another transfer, David and I were doing better than we had in months. Everything was on the table now and we were playing the game with eyes wide open. I didn't hide my dissatisfaction with the ridiculous amount of time he spent at work, and he didn't pretend that the trouble was all down to my state of mind.

Now that I knew my prison sentence would come to an end sooner rather than later, I scoured the map for the places I had to see before I left. The project had another two years to run, but I knew we wouldn't be staying. Whatever time I had left in Asia was going to continue to include a hefty amount of travel. I had no real ties here to be concerned about.

* * *

Halong Bay is a few hours from Hanoi in northern Vietnam. It is World Heritage listed, due to its unique environment and staggering number of rock islets. We would have to fly to Hanoi first, and take a bus from there.

Hanoi is a different world from Saigon. Its French colonial legacy is exceedingly strong, leading to beautifully constructed thoroughfares. Of course, an insane amount of motorbikes still rule the road—but it has a more relaxed feel than its sister to the south. The French façades of the architecture lend it a more sophisticated look, even if it's merely superficial.

Missing its one-thousandth birthday by only a few months, David and I whizzed the Old Quarter streets in *cyclos* and drank cocktails at balcony bars. The night markets left us with more questions than answers, and we determined that the appearance of sophistication does not extend far below the surface. An order of "prawn cakes"—a deep fried dish that Thais excel at—means a pile of dried shrimp with shells and tails in Hanoi. Not wanting to appear rude, we covertly tossed a few into the lake to make it look like we ate some, and hoped no one saw them floating by.

Khanh, our exceptionally friendly desk clerk, arranged the bus trip to Halong Bay. She said that the drive would take four hours, which was a surprise because the distance was around ninety miles. Given the condition of most vehicles in Vietnam, however, we thought it better not to question it.

Dreaming in Vietnamese

The minivan which came to collect us already had a dozen people in it. David and I squeezed in, and the driver told us we had two more stops to make. *Are they going to sit on the roof?* There was hardly any space left as it was.

The erratic driving didn't do much to calm my nerves, nor did the shopping stop that we were forced to take at a tourist scam made up to look like a pearl distributor. That was why the trip was so long. David and I sat for an hour looking over the water, while the others went inside to buy "authentic" pearls.

Finally we reached the bay. The tranquil beauty which had attracted me to Halong Bay to begin with was nowhere in sight. It was a circus. Minivans just like ours, packed to the gills, arrived by the dozen. No less than one hundred colorful junk boats waited at the dock for passengers, with more moored nearby. Vendors sold trinkets on every available inch of sidewalk. This was not what I had in mind.

We waited another hour for the group to be disseminated to their chosen boats and some order to appear from the chaos. Junk boats came in all varieties. Upscale junks with white sails, private cabins, and perfectly manicured teak were at one end of the scale. At the other end, party boats with blaring speakers and underwear drying on clotheslines carried mostly backpackers. Our boat was squarely midrange. We got the largest cabin due to David's "great height" and it came with a private balcony on the back of the boat.

The whole thing was so far from what I'd envisioned that I wasn't feeling very comfortable about spending the night. By this point in my travels, I'd come a long way from expecting perfection, but the amount of people and a complete absence of anything resembling safety regulations made this feel downright dangerous. I was glad this was a one-night trip, because I had considered three.

When we sailed away from the dock, I relaxed a little. The boats were spread out over one hundred and thirty square miles, so we wouldn't be right next to the party boats when we anchored overnight. Reaching the top deck from a small flight of stairs, David and I couldn't help but smile. The rock formations, known in geology as karsts, are magnificent. Surrounded by the calm bay waters, the view is like none other.

The "Bay of the Descending Dragon" got its name from a myth often repeated by the locals. When Vietnam was emerging as a nation, the gods sent a family of dragons to protect it from hostile invaders. The sharp rock islets in the bay are actually the teeth of the dragon. The tale is probably spun so tourists get a romantic notion to take home as a souvenir.

The humidity was oppressive, so I was delighted when we stopped for kayaking and swimming. David and I picked out kayaks carefully, as it was our first time, but found that paddling was easy. There were no guides in the water, just a hand signal to point us in the direction of a large cave. The blue waters were stunning, now that we were free of the garbage-laden dock area. The only other paddlers came from our boat. This was the peace I'd been chasing.

Afterwards, I wasn't ready to leave the water. I dove headfirst from the boat's deck into the glimmering water. Floating on my back, I reflected on the trials of the past year. David and I didn't argue much anymore. We were more careful in the way we spoke to one another. Perhaps this chapter would end well. When I looked up from my reverie, I saw him taking photos of me enjoying the water. I waved and he smiled and waved back.

That night we took more photos from the deck of the purple sunset against the rocks. It was so beautiful that we both smiled more than we had in months. David grabbed my hand and we just stood in silence watching the sun disappear behind the karsts. Nothing needed to be said.

Though I was glad we made the trip, I was extremely uncomfortable on the boat itself and didn't sleep much. Thoughts of potential disaster lurked in the back of my mind after seeing the way tourists were crammed into every available space, to make more money. If safety wasn't a concern on the road, it was unlikely to be a consideration on the boat either. Six months later, one of these boats sank in less than a minute, killing eleven tourists and a Vietnamese guide on board.

Dreaming in Vietnamese

When we returned to Singapore, I emailed the hotel in Hanoi to thank them for making the arrangements for us. I also completed their survey about our stay. Khanh emailed me back, pleased that I had taken the time. "If I can be of any further assistance in Vietnam, please let me know," she wrote.

On a whim I replied "Do you happen to know any magazines looking for native-English writers? I would love to write some articles about the unique places I've visited in Vietnam."

Within two minutes, I had the name and email address of the editor of *The Guide* magazine. Its readers were mostly western tourists. "I can't thank you enough, Khanh! Usually editors are very hard to reach. I will contact her right away."

Many exclamation points and good-luck wishes later, I ended my correspondence with Khanh and wrote to introduce myself to Kim-Ly. Again the response was swift. Yes, she was looking for English writers and would love to have an article on Halong Bay from me to be published in *The Guide*. They would pay one million *dong* for my work. A million of anything sounds better than fifty bucks, but this was the chance of a lifetime. I would be a *published writer*.

Full disclosure: I thought Kim-Ly would appreciate an honest take on a tourist's experience at Halong Bay. As it turns out, honesty is not integral to the Vietnamese tourism business. In typical Asian style, she did not say what needed to be revised in my piece, but I got the picture fairly quickly. Despite my better judgement, I did not write about my concerns. I only documented the good stuff and I disliked myself for doing it—but the desire to be published won.

Once I understood the score, I wanted to write more articles on Vietnam's interesting destinations. Kim-Ly was all for it. As David was still working on his transfer at the higher levels of his company while he continued his project work, I still needed something to do and this was my ticket. Vietnam is incredibly cheap to travel in and my visa was good for another few weeks. I began planning the next stops immediately.

* * *

Hoi An's superpower is its tailors. The city is lined with tailoring shops bursting with beautiful fabrics. I wasn't in the market for red silk covered with yellow dragons, but the electric blue and black linens suited me just fine. I showed the ladies there two shirts and a skirt that I wanted copied several times over. For one hundred US dollars, I would have six new pieces of custom-made clothing in twenty-four hours. Happily I handed over my dollars.

Charm oozes from the pavement of this city. The village streets are original, built as far back as the fifteenth century. Handmade-silk lanterns of fuchsia and chartreuse dance on wooden poles. Street vendors hawk "ancient" Vietnamese golden coins. Clean and pretty tourist restaurants abound.

Most people stay in the center of town, but I opted for a hotel on Cau Dai Beach, and stayed there for the rest of the afternoon after visiting the city. It was too hot not to enjoy the breezes and thatched wooden umbrellas that decorated it. Phattie's seemed like a good place for a writing and cocktail session, so I ordered vodka and orange juice with no ice. As I watched the sun go down, I was primed for adventure in whatever form it came.

Not knowing that train tickets were dirt cheap, I overpaid a "service" to get the ticket for my two-and-a-half-hour ride from Hoi An to Hue. My seat, which had to be second class if there were actually classes, was wooden. The car reminded me of a school bus with one seat on each side of an aisle. The seats would probably hold two people, three if they were Vietnamese, and had windows overhead.

The windows were a blessing for two reasons. First, the Vietnamese coast is more beautiful than I imagined. The sun shone on white sand beaches and small fishing towns that looked idyllic. Conical hats covered tan fisherman casting their nets in the bay. Finding myself on the retail end of the fishing enterprise was the second reason the large windows were handy. A woman walked numerous times up and down the aisles carrying dried fish with an unbelievable stink. The breeze brought occasional welcome relief.

Hue is an unpolished gem. The imperial city for nearly a hundred and fifty years before communism entered the picture, it is the home of striking estates and tombs of the former emperors. Khai Dinh, Tu Duc, and Minh Mang certainly had grand visions of themselves and erected vast memorials to their power, often at the cost and to the detriment of their subjects.

The tomb of Minh Mang is guarded by stone soldiers and elephants in the courtyard before the gate. One must traverse a series of grand archways to reach the place where the former emperor lies buried. The gate which protects his sarcophagus has only been opened once in two hundred years, to place the body in the tomb. He left orders for the guards who carried him to be executed afterward so they could never reveal his true resting place.

The amount in taxes and manual labor that Tu Duc's imperial tomb cost to construct caused a revolt amongst his people. Safe behind his estate walls with his one hundred concubines, Tu Duc was unconcerned with what the populace wanted. He did, however, make sure that a temple was built on his estate to honor his "minor wives."

Khai Dinh's tomb is the last great structure built to memorialize a Vietnamese emperor. During his lifetime, he was greatly influenced by the French and his final resting place displays his affection. The structure is largely European in its opulence. To raise the funding for its completion, Khai Dinh raised taxes on the poor with the help of the French. Needless to say, he was not as well loved as his stunning final resting spot might have you believe.

All the photographs I'd seen and experiences I'd previously had in Vietnam gave no indication of such grandeur. It was an eye-opening experience to discover that here, on the banks of the Perfume River, a powerful family called Nguyen thrived until the end of World War II. The images in my head of jungles, shacks, and villages ravaged by war were far from the complete picture of this country. Hue, even in its dilapidated state, impressed me.

Visitors to Vietnam are not allowed to drive, so renting a car was out of the question. The hotel concierge in Hue set me up with a private driver for the two-hour ride to Ba Na Hills. Ba Na is just outside Da Nang in central Vietnam. The photos online of these mountains and the cable car that takes tourists to the top are incredible. My journey was less so.

The drive along the coast was fantastic. I hadn't known that Vietnam had so many gorgeous beaches. My driver wasn't big on chit-chat, but he happily obliged when I wanted to stop along the way for photos.

When we reached the cable car, the level of fun dropped dramatically.

It began with the ticket booth at the cable car. English wasn't widely spoken here, despite the name "Ba Na Resort" plastered everywhere to attract tourists. He wanted to charge me double what I'd seen quoted for the ride online, and insisted that was for one way. This went on for a few minutes before I simply paid and left. My hotel for the night was at the top of the mountain and my driver was gone. I didn't have a choice.

The ride itself over the lush green mountains was spectacular. Vietnam was so surprisingly beautiful that I couldn't understand why there weren't more tourists around. The hotel was built in the style of a French chateau, and there was some truth in it. French colonists had fled to these mountains to avoid the extreme summer heat, and there are still caves built into the mountainside for wine cellars.

It was demanded that I pay for my room up front, always a worrying sign, and then sit and wait in the lobby. I waited for over an hour before I finally asked them what was going on. Or at least I tried to. Note to self: English is an endangered species off the beaten path in Vietnam. Eventually a small dark-haired man took my bag and motioned me to follow. The hotel lobby was beautifully decorated and very clean, so I never questioned what I was doing.

Even the room itself looked fine on the surface. The little man bowed and smiled, then took off. I put my bag down and tested the internet—which did work. Then I took my camera and went for a walk. Next door, an entire French village was being built, claiming a grand opening in 2012. Looking at the site in August of 2010, I could not see that happening.

I walked up the path behind the hotel, eager for photos from the mountaintop. The villagers or the construction men had been using the paved viewing area as a urinal—for quite some time. It was disgusting. As I turned to leave, the fog that had been building became a curtain. I could barely see five feet ahead of me.

Dreaming in Vietnamese

In my hotel room, I was about to lay down on the bed and sleep the afternoon away, when I discovered several long dark hairs on the pillow. Between the sheets, there were more. I went in the bathroom to wash my hands and found a tile floor that looked as though it had never seen soap. Immediately, I called the desk.

"Someone coming," said the clerk.

"Okay, when is someone coming?" I asked.

"Someone coming!" he said again.

I hung up. I waited. No one was coming. The cable car had already stopped running. There was nowhere to go. I pulled a blanket out of the closet which was hair-free and covered the bed with it. I put my rain jacket over the pillow and kept my clothes on. During the night, I heard a gang of people in the room below me shouting and partying. Then I heard them move to another room. I opened the door and saw a giant ring of keys laying in the hallway, presumably the keys to all the rooms. I lodged a chair in front of the door.

There was no sleep for me, but there was the most beautiful sunrise I had seen in a very long time. Quickly packing, I kept my belongings—but no valuables—in the room while I looked around the rest of the area. Going downhill was better than the path I took the day before. I found a pristine Buddhist temple overlooking the side of the mountain.

A monk and his dog welcomed me with contented smiles and nodded when I asked if I could take photos. Today was proving not to be a total loss after all.

Sitting in Da Nang airport, I watched the other tourists try to communicate with the airport staff with varying levels of success. Though there were no chairs and nothing to eat or drink, I was content to bide my time until the flight. Again I had taken on the unknown and discovered delights I had never dreamt of. Doing it alone was more rewarding too. In the space that created, the authentic feeling of these places moved in, not what a guidebook prepared me to expect. Good or bad, the unexpected was far more appealing than the predictable. I had never felt so alive.

Junk boat on Halong Bay

Hanoi Traffic

Chapter 28
Thai Treats

Singapore had become a pit stop rather than my home. I went there to touch base with David and to get clean clothes. Being there in the early days had made me so unhappy that a gloom hung over the place. I still drank martinis with Jac for happy hour. Alexis now joined in and I'd met another friend named Chloe from Canada. Chloe had been working in Ho Chi Min City as a dentist and recently transferred. Our Wednesday afternoon sessions almost always overflowed into night, but it was one of the few chances I had to socialize in Singapore like a normal person. Putting on a nice outfit and drinking cocktails in a New York-style bar made me feel as though I hadn't lost all of my original American self. Often we ended up at the Mandarin Oriental's fantastic roof bar, lounging on their comfy couches and taking in the skyline over bottles of wine. Vicious hangovers were scheduled for Thursday mornings.

On the knife edge of turning forty, six weeks before, avoidance became impossible. I didn't feel old, but I did wonder what I was doing with my life. Running around Vietnam and soon Thailand for the pure sake of adventure seemed reckless. Shouldn't I have a plan, a fat 401K, and a troop of kids? Okay, forget that last one, but surely the rest should be secured at this age. Apparently I was a late bloomer.

There was no way I was going to spend the momentous occasion of my fortieth birthday in a place I couldn't stand, so I started making plans to celebrate in my favorite city on the planet, New York. So close to Thanksgiving, my birthday is the best time of the year to be in the city. Wanting to make the most of the long flight, David and I rented a cabin in Maine the week before. Along with my friend Jo in New Jersey, we added the Macy's parade to our itinerary. I made sure it would be a trip to remember.

In the weeks before my trip to the States, I wasn't about to sit still. I'd been plugging away at sending inquiry letters to literary agents to get them interested in my book and trying to understand the process of selling a manuscript as a whole. It was far more complicated than I'd expected and I was not tremendously successful. Articulating what the book was about was proving harder than writing it.

So I went to Thailand. Anyone who has ever seen photos of that aquamarine amazingness known as the Andaman Sea knows that its pull is impossible to avoid forever. The islands in the region of Krabi are the nation's treasure chest, and I had to see them before we left for Australia.

My landing point was Ao Nang. I only planned to spend one night on the mainland before heading on to the islands, so I didn't spend much time making a decision about where to stay. It turns out I should have. Thin walls and horny neighbors do not make for a good night's sleep.

The city itself was little more than a strip of beach with a long row of massage huts on one side and bars on the other. I didn't mind kicking back for a bite and a few drinks, but I was glad to move on the next day. Koh Phi Phi Island is legendary, and I was determined to find out why.

I took a ferry there from Ao Nang. Once I landed at the port on Phi Phi, I took another boat to the resort I was staying at. The boat was small and my suitcase too big. The hotel's information didn't mention the arrival by boat, and I had to bribe one of the staff to collect my bag for me.

"Resort" is too big a word for the place I stayed on Phi Phi Island. I'd prefer to call them decorated tree houses. It didn't matter to me where I stayed because at least I got the chance to go there. I was shown to a fantastic tree house on my first night. It was two levels and had a huge bed. Hammocks swung on the balcony overlooking the sea. I couldn't have picked better if I'd tried. Or so I thought.

Venturing into Phi Phi Village was disheartening. It was a maze of dive shops and dive bars with tacky souvenir stores thrown in for good measure. Finding nothing authentic about the place, I had little reason to stick around. Instead, I followed the path past the Reggae Bar that took me to the viewing point on top of the island. The top of the island was hardly the "twenty minute stroll" described by the tourism web site. What I found after climbing the steep stairs up to the top was well worth it, however. I could see the entire shimmering bay.

The tide went out on my way back, and I snapped dozens of photos of the long-tail boats perched in the sand. The sun had started to go down, giving the beach a haunted, empty feeling. This part of the beach, anyway. As I got closer to my hotel, the bass got louder and louder. Bars had filled up and I was now privy to Phi Phi's main attraction, the nightlife. During the day, revelers were out on the water or recovering under beach umbrellas. The place truly came alive only at night.

I passed a spirit house in front of one of the larger restaurants. A spirit house is exactly as it sounds, a miniature house in a prominent spot outside a property. I'd seen them all over Thailand and Cambodia, but rarely had had the chance to stop and take photos. The house is built to offer a resting place for spirits so that they don't cause trouble inside the residence. There is also space for candles and flowers as offerings to keep the spirits in a good mood. It seemed to me that with the amount of debauchery taking place on any given night on Phi Phi, the place could use a whole lot more of these.

Dinner at my hotel was an open buffet of Thai goodness. Mostly vegetarian dishes with some chicken and fish, it was cheap and tasty. The restaurant was dimly lit and I was too tired for people-watching anyway. That hammock on my balcony called my name.

It didn't take me long to fall asleep in it. Parties raged all night, but I managed to tune them out. Around two in the morning, there was a loud banging on my tree house door. Heavy-fisted pounding accompanied by a slurring bellowing male voice scared the hell out of me. My heart raced. I couldn't remember if I'd locked the door or if bamboo even locked. There were no phones. I had to just sit there and wait. It took about thirty minutes before silence came back.

When it did, I ran down to investigate the door, trying not to make a sound. There was a lock and thank God I had remembered to turn it. I crept back upstairs and stared at the ceiling until dawn. Because it was daylight, I felt safe enough to sleep for a few hours before talking to the hotel staff.

"Yes. We have had problems with him before," the woman behind the desk told me.

"Who?"

"The owner's son. He lives in the other side of the house. He is not supposed to bother the guests, but we have heard from several ladies that he tries to get in their room." She was rather matter-of-fact about it. Quite unconcerned.

"I don't want to stay there again," I replied. I can't sleep when I'm worried he'll get in."

"He probably won't. He drinks too much," she said.

A raging drunk probably won't get into your room. That wasn't exactly the reassurance I was looking for. "Do you have another room?"

"Not as nice as that one m'am," She seemed to think room quality was my top concern here.

"That's okay. I'll take it." I didn't care if it was a hut without plumbing and electricity. I would gladly take that over possible rape.

I moved within an hour. It wasn't much better than the hut I'd envisioned, but it was fine for one night. I put down my things, locked my bamboo door and hit the beach. Phi Phi had already provided enough entertainment for me. All I wanted to do was swim in that crystal water and lap up the sunshine without the threat of sexual assault.

The second night I had good reason to be slightly edgier. I had a good bottle of Thai rum take the edge off my anxiety, and I brought my little Samsung notebook onto the beach with me. After one of the most amazing sunsets of my life, I used it to call friends in the US. Talking with them made me feel less alone, but I still had to walk a very dimly lit jungle path back to my hut. When I did, I heard footsteps behind me and broke into a run.

The noises on the second night could have been my spooked imagination, but I'll never know. The only visitor I had that night was a fat orange tabby looking for love. I claimed him as my guard cat.

THAI TREATS

The next day I went to Koh Lanta, relieved to put Phi Phi behind me. My hotel on Lanta was beautiful. I had a private villa with a huge bathtub across the street from the sea. The downside this time around was the angry dark sky that threatened for days.

I felt lucky to have a sanctuary from the nasty weather, but I quickly grew restless. The hotel concierge suggested I rent a moped for the day, and at first I balked. The longer I thought about it, however, the more sense it made. Why sit around indoors when I can explore the entire island?

The island was only twenty miles long, but riding around the empty jungle roads was exhilarating. This was how people truly lived in Thailand, and not what most tourists come to see. The turbulent sea crashed against the cliffs as I sped around hairpin turns. Brand new seaside homes popped up occasionally, as did seafood shacks that served beer and mango *lassi*.

Once I came over a steep hill to find an entire procession heading up the other side. I hadn't been driving fast, as it was a residential area with several houses on stilts, but I slowed further out of respect and curiosity. The leader wore a billowing white tunic and well-worn khakis, while his flock were dressed in a rainbow of color. Some carried drums. Nearly all were smiling. I wanted to ask what the occasion was, but instead I waved and drove on.

Looking for something else to do if the weather stayed ugly, I wrote down the phone number for Roi Thai Cooking School. Learning how to make the incredible food I'd been trying seemed a wise time investment if it wasn't too expensive.

Roi himself taught me the basics of Thai cooking. I de-seeded plump red chilies and ground them along with garlic, lemongrass, and ginger with a dash of sugar to make red curry paste. I made crisp cucumber and papaya salad with toasted peanuts. My crowning achievement was tangy chicken satay with fresh peanut sauce. All of it I ate myself accompanied by ice-cold Singha beer. No, there was absolutely no better way to spend time indoors. My tastebuds sang with delight.

Finally it was time to say farewell to the islands and meet David at Railay Bay. Having someone else around would be a treat after spending my days alone, no matter how much I enjoyed them that way. Railay Bay Resort has a prime location. Its large pool is nestled right at the edge of the beach. The adjoining tiki bar allows you to see all the action. The villas are peaceful with high ceilings and wooden beams. Fresh frangipani flowers line the giant bathtubs.

Arriving was once again by boat—and at least I could warn David not to wear nice shoes. Entering the resort meant walking through knee-high sea water, a small price to pay for this slice of heaven. We dined on the beach the first night he arrived. Though I was now used to this magical place called Krabi, David was clearly enjoying it.

Spicy tom yam soup stuffed with prawns was followed by Massaman beef curry with jasmine rice. The sky was lit with a parade of stars. Finally, the rain had ended. There was no downside here.

We took a private boat tour to explore the inlets and bays unreachable by car. The beaches were by far the most perfect I had seen. Our hosts left us to play in private at the most picturesque bay imaginable. I never wanted to leave.

Lunch was served on a private stretch of beach on a scenic bay, after we swam till we could no longer. The sun was delicious on my wet skin as we sat on blankets to eat salads and fresh watermelon carved into hearts. David officially declared Thai mango the best in the universe, and I had to agree. Even the sea cooperated by staying flat, leaving no reason for David's seasickness to catch up with him. Saying it was the perfect day is cliché, but I could not imagine a better one.

Chapter 29
Bridges

Was it coincidence that as my internal world began to settle into a place of satisfaction and hope, my external world began to comply? My smiles weren't fake anymore. I no longer felt the need to recite my resume to everyone to prove I had once led a successful corporate life. Writing gave me a purpose and I now knew returning to a professional position was possible if I wanted. Only one piece of the puzzle remained.

I flew to Newark in mid-November, slightly ahead of David. I spent the night with Jo and her boyfriend, catching up before the drive to Maine.

"What do you think is going to happen?" Jo asked. "Will you be staying in Singapore?"

"God, I hope not!" I blurted out. Jo knew how I currently felt about my life, but I rarely discussed the depths of my unhappiness with anyone. "We're hoping he can transfer to Australia because that business is growing."

"Wow! *Really?*" her voice was a mix of awe and disbelief. "It's so far away."

"I know. I've thought about that. A lot. The problem is nothing else seems feasible right now, and I don't have any desire to come back here or return to Europe." I tried to explain but it was an odd position to be in.

"I'm coming to visit!" She announced before grabbing the bottle of wine to refill our glasses.

I was relieved we wouldn't have to continue talking about it. Australia was the other side of the planet and I still cared about the people here in the States. It was hard to get that second part across when I was so excited to go Down Under.

Jo only lived thirty minutes from the airport. Two days later we picked up an exhausted David at Newark Airport. I let him get one decent night of sleep before we picked up the rental car and headed north. I felt sorry that he was always getting the short end of the stick in the relaxation department, as he was the one who needed it most. At least there would be plenty of time for that in Acadia National Park.

Initially intimidated to drive out of the city, I knew there was no choice. I couldn't ask David to take the wheel when he could barely function. As my cold hands gripped the wheel, I reminded myself I had recently driven *on the opposite side of the road*. George Washington Bridge? No problem!

David dozed for hours, and I made it to Vermont before I asked him to take over. The drive had actually been peaceful, and we now had less than two hours left before we reached the cabin. The further north we drove, the greener it became. I was so grateful I'd made a stop at Target. Our new thermal underwear was going to come in mighty handy.

The dark gray cabin sat at water's edge on Mount Desert Island. It was square-shaped with two bedrooms and a wraparound balcony. We wouldn't get much use out of the balcony in this weather, but the barbecue grill was a sight for sore eyes. I hadn't been able to grill outside in years.

The place was ultra-comfy, with plush carpet and fluffy furniture. It's waterside position made it inherently peaceful, and it was outside of the tourist high season. The Maine weather was perfect for hiking and enjoying nature's quiet side.

Acadia National Park has miles and miles of trails. Each day we picked a different path, laced up our hiking boots, and loaded our camera bags. After spending several hours in the chilly forest air, we came back to the cabin to build a roaring fire and cook dinner together.

On the day we climbed Cadillac Mountain, I thought I might not make it back. It is the highest point on the US east coast. Dense fog hung over the forest and I slid across the sandstone path several times trying to get my footing. Going up is always easier than descending in a situation like this. Because of the conditions and the lateness of the hour, we contemplated taking the road down, rather than the steep trail. If one of us got hurt, we were very far from help.

David had more guts than me. We knew the shortest path was best, even if it posed the greatest risk. He was patient with my slow climb as I tried to protect myself from re-injuring my lower back that had plagued me for years. He held out his arm for support when I needed it, and we eventually made it past the moss-covered boulders. We were a team for the first time in years.

Another trail took us near Bass Harbor lighthouse. Combined with the dark gray slate of the coastline and a backdrop of tall emerald pines, it was impossible to pass up a photo opportunity. David surprised me with his new toy, a remote control for the camera, so he could take photos from further away after managing the settings. He sat down next to me on the cliff and gave me a kiss while clicking the remote. I felt like we were whole again.

The remote got its second outing on top of Cadillac Mountain at sunset. Recording the setting sun as it descended into Frenchman's Bay was breathtaking, but so was the biting wind. Eventually we left the camera on the tripod and took photos by remote from the heated SUV. Sometimes you need distance to see the full picture.

When we had fully recovered from jet lag and explored Acadia to our satisfaction, it was time to head back to New York for the festivities. My friends were arriving to meet us from all over, and I could barely contain my excitement.

Checking into a gorgeously-decorated Marriott on the east side, I started to feel the specialness of this birthday. The hotel was old-school, not the fanciest place in town but far from the dullest. If you ask me, there is simply nothing like plugging into the New York City air. It sizzles and pops with electricity, and you can't help but succumb. Twenty friends were coming to the city to drink rooftop martinis with me on Madison Avenue, and I could not think of anywhere I'd rather be.

At the crack of Thanksgiving Day dawn on the corner of West 50th Street and 7th Avenue, we stood in a huddle like every other tourist on the scene.

Jo's boyfriend Joe and David went for coffee and breakfast sandwiches, while Jo and I stood our parade ground. Thousands of people arrived to jam every square inch of sidewalk, but they were a friendly crowd. No one pushed or jostled. You felt like you'd want to buy them all a beer if it wasn't six a.m.

The pink Energizer bunny floated by. Spiderman spun his web onto the street below. A group of New York cops stood joking with one another while a giant Hello Kitty approached from behind. It was funny that I no longer cared about this parade in the slightest when it was on television, but standing in the crowd was exhilarating. After eight years outside the States, I didn't even celebrate Thanksgiving anymore. But for this one day, it was great to be a part of something bigger than my worries.

As I was now pursuing my dream life as a writer, The Library Hotel was the perfect place for a party. Dora, my friend from Germany, flew in for the weekend. Allison was there. Richard, one of my oldest friends from Arizona, showed up in his black leather badness. Ohio sent me Barb and Rick to share the joy. Carlo and his wife Juliana brought the Chilean vibe from Santiago. My first best friend and her mother, Nancy and Suzanne, made the trip from Boca Raton. Jeff and Janet, my cousin and his girlfriend from Chicago, celebrated with us too. Jo and Joe brought a killer cake with far too many candles. The room overflowed with love, dirty martinis, and a lot of laughter.

On one end of the bar was the exit onto the roof. Occasionally, I snuck outside to catch a glimpse of the skyline-to-beat-all-skylines.

It felt like being enveloped in a long, black-velvet coat trimmed with diamonds. Hugging myself against the late autumn chill, I realized I already had everything I wanted. Having my book see the light of day rather than sitting in a slush pile on someone's desk and moving to Australia were merely the icing on the cake—not the cake itself.

＊＊

BRIDGES

David went on to Chicago for business and I stayed in the city for another week before flying back to Singapore. The news he came home with was the best birthday gift of all.

"They said yes." He was grinning, but refused to give up the goods in one shot.

"Who are they and yes to what?" I punched him in the arm.

"The leadership in Australia agreed to my transfer. We can move when I am finished in Singapore, but my home office will change in January."

"Oh my God! Are you *serious*? This is really going to happen?" Numbness. Disbelief. I had been carrying a keychain with a little metal shark on it as an Aussie totem for months.

"Yes, *really*. We can choose between Melbourne and Brisbane."

"I can't believe it. I don't know anything about Brisbane. Do you?" I was breathless with excitement.

"Not really, but I was given contact names of people who can help with that. Once we decide which one, the company will pay for a relocation trip to go and check it out."

I bear-hugged him as hard as I could. "Thank you."

The end was now in sight. Our Rotterdam house went on the market immediately. Paying for housing in Australia when his role on the project ended plus paying the Dutch mortgage was the hard slap of reality. Research on the cost of living in both cities made it clear I would need to get a real job again.

Lobbying began immediately as well. David preferred the idea of Melbourne. I wanted to live in Queensland. Even though we had something new to debate, we also had a new chapter ahead of us. For three years, Singapore had felt like purgatory. There was no going back and nothing on the horizon. The horizon was now taking shape and that shape, in either city, was far more appealing than any other we had considered.

I had to get to Rotterdam as soon as possible to start sorting out what would make the trip Down Under and what would be given away or donated. December snowfall was already breaking European records in the first weeks of the month. Hopefully there would be no more drama with the heat. Being there with an eye to the future was far more desirable than sitting in Singapore, no matter how cold it was.

Rotterdam is many things, but I doubt anyone has ever called it beautiful. Wearing a thick blanket of glittering snow, it's as close as it's ever going to get. More inches of white powder piled up daily. I had nowhere to go, so I didn't mind it at first.

Closer to Christmas, the inches became feet and I did begin to mind. David might not be able to fly into Amsterdam if this kept up. The streetlights outside my windows were my measuring stick. Occasionally, even they became hard to see when Holland's famous wind forced a whiteout. I had long since sold my car, so I could only wait and see.

The decision of Melbourne vs. Brisbane was still on the table. As I sat hidden away in my beautiful Rotterdam home, I thought about the fact that I'd never become part of this city. Amsterdam had been the same. I preferred the former because I could blend in so easily in the city on the Maas. With one of the world's largest ports, it was a city of immigrants. Here we came in all shapes and sizes.

My only point of reference for Melbourne was a visit of less than a week. I had enjoyed myself and found it interesting, but I wasn't drawn to it. When I imagined myself living there, I thought of yet another place I would have to fight to be a part of because of its long-standing social circles.

All the recent solo travel had shown me it was a delight to go my own way and part from the crowd. Queensland felt like that to me. If we went to Brisbane, we could also remove "winter" from our lives. Staring at the piles of snow left by racing plows that seemed like a very good idea indeed. Another item in the "pro" column for Brisbane, my friend Stan had recently moved there from Sydney. I would already have a friend.

David arrived the day before they closed the airport. We had to take inventory of our home and contents for the movers. Before that, we had to decide what we were getting rid of. There was family to visit that we rarely had the chance to. It was the busiest Christmas since moving to Singapore three years prior. A sense of déjà vu was in the air, but I had to believe this time would be different. There was no other choice.

After much discussion, Brisbane was elected the winner. David had nothing to compare to, never having visited either, and I felt strongly about living in a smaller city. The current context made us excited to forget about winter. Queensland's economy was thriving on the back of a strong mining industry and the recent discovery of coal seam gas. David's mining experience in Singapore would benefit him there.

After a very quiet New Year's Eve, the last in our Dutch lives, the packing began in earnest. The joy of giving away snow shovels and ice scrapers ranked high on the list of holiday highlights. Seeing all our goods packed into a semi with "Brisbane" marked on every box topped the list. We cleaned the house as best we could and stayed in Amsterdam on our last night in Holland. Only days old, 2011 looked bright already.

Chapter 30
Aftershock

The rush of activity that began with packing up the house didn't let up after it was done. Once our belongings were on their way into storage in Brisbane, I started applying for jobs there. After being out of practice for so long, it was hard to know where to begin. I'd mentally left the technology world behind, but my certification as a project manager was my most profitable skill.

Researching Brisbane's job market from Singapore didn't tell me a lot. At least I had the benefit of interview experience in Sydney to draw from. Every country has its own preferences for resumes and presenting oneself. Stan was a big help where I drew blanks.

I applied to a few of the smaller consulting firms in Brisbane, but they were very technology-driven. I had long since quit calling myself a specialist in any particular software. My interests were on the people side of projects, and those jobs seemed to be eaten up by human resources in the smaller firms.

Along with the other applications I made, I applied to my former US employer. There was an office in Brisbane and I'd resigned on good terms in 2003. Since then, I'd added more skills and experience to my resume. Whether or not it was my preferred place to land, I had to admit it was the quickest way to a paycheck.

Off and on I spoke to Stan to ask questions about where an office was located or what the Australian government process was for something. It had been raining for weeks and his place was on the Brisbane River. The amount of rain that had fallen in Brisbane was "worrying," according to him.

It didn't take long for the worries to come to fruition. Three quarters of Queensland was declared a disaster zone after several of the state's main rivers swelled, the Brisbane River among them. Thousands of houses in the city were flooded and nearly forty people lost their lives. Watching the Australian television coverage from Singapore, I couldn't believe my eyes. We were flying to Brisbane in less than two weeks.

Stan re-lived the saga with us when we arrived. He and his puppy were unscathed after living without power for five days. Many of the apartment complexes were similarly affected, as the power came into the buildings below ground or at ground level.

"It was amazing. I met the entire neighborhood!" he laughed. "Everyone was outside trying to help in whatever way they could. The volunteer team was called the "Mud Army" because of all the disgusting sediment from the river that covered everything after it went down."

"I saw that on the news," I told him. "It was impressive to see that many people helping one another out."

It was true. Stories were still hitting the papers about the selfless acts of the Mud Army in the days and weeks after the floods. Even though we arrived only ten days later, the city was incredibly clean for the disaster that had befallen it. If you had seen it on television as I did, you'd be expecting to land in a war zone.

So many people donning rubber boots and gloves to dig out their neighbor's basement and rescue what was salvageable from the house gave me a positive feeling about my future home. It made me wonder—would Singaporeans react this way in the wake of disaster? Would the Dutch or Americans? Of course it would be a sweeping generalization to say yes or no for an entire nation, but it made me happy to see it in the city we planned to call home.

David had meetings in Brisbane, and I had interviews. We stayed in an apartment in the city to make that easier. It was unfortunate that the most popular night spot in town, Eagle Street Pier, had flood damage, but many of the restaurants remained open. Impossibly, it remained an attractive place even after disaster had struck.

In the remaining time before David had to be back in Singapore, we went further out of the city. Marina had told me that the Gold Coast and the Sunshine Coast were beautiful areas to visit. Stan preferred the more low-key Sunshine Coast, and Noosa in particular.

To get our bearings, we made a mad dash to both. The Sunshine Coast—no highrises allowed!—has a natural feel. It not only has a set of stunning beaches, but a beautiful mountain hinterland to boot. The Gold Coast couldn't be of a contrast. World famous Surfer's Paradise is like Vegas if Vegas was on the ocean.

The old excitement of being in a new foreign country was back. Every detail of this place interested me, and what I didn't know, I was anxious to find out. Brisbane's suburbs each had a distinct character that we had yet to uncover. Stan filled me in on the highlights, but the vision was far from complete when I had to fly back to Singapore.

* * *

I did the best I could to bide my time. The bureaucracy of multinational companies makes them slow-moving beasts, and I've never been known for my patience. February dragged on with a series of interviews over the phone and in person. Though an offer wasn't yet on the table, I expected it would eventually happen.

Penny introduced me to a friend of hers from Perth when she visited in March. While Penny was at the office all day, I played tour guide to Sally. In the weeks before she arrived, I'd been having nightmares. I can't say that I've never had them before, but in general they involve me forgetting to study for a math exam at Ohio State and failing to get my diploma. They have never involved me being terrified of being in a collapsing building.

Sally and I decided one morning to go to Sentosa for the day. She hadn't been before. It's a nice place to spend time outside the city. We were walking through an extremely crowded Harbourfront Mall when I suddenly felt like I was going to pass out.

"Sally... wait." I grabbed her arm. "I have to sit down a minute," *before I fall down* I didn't add.

"Okay, hon. I'll just pop in that store a sec." She was off.

I sat on a bench watching the millions of Singaporeans rushing by. "It's probably because of last night," I told Sally with a wry smile when she came back.

"Yeah, that was a bender all right. I'm surprised I feel as good as I do."

"I'll just grab some water," I said, pointing to a refrigerated display. I didn't feel any better, but I figured I would have to suck it up, because it was likely my own doing.

We took the most picturesque way to Sentosa by cable car. A massive Costa cruise ship below us gave way to the brand new Hard Rock Café and massive Universal Studios. Sally took photos to show her kids, and I took photos of Sally. The blue sky and blazing sun lit up the flowered pathways that led to the mini Merlion. The midday sun started to cook us both.

"Why don't we find a restaurant on the water? That will give us a slight chance at a breeze." My water bottle was empty and it was time to refuel.

"Yeah, all right." Sally agreed. "I could use a bite."

I felt my phone vibrate in my purse and ordered a beer against my better judgement. "What do you feel like?"

"I'm thinking …"

Unzipping my bag, I pulled out my phone. "I just got a text from David," I said before reading it out loud to her. "There's been an earthquake in Japan. It's bad."

"What does that mean?" Sally wanted to know.

"I don't know. He doesn't usually text about things like that. You order. I'm going to call him."

The news was devastating. Japan had suffered an earthquake that hit nine on the Richter scale. A tsunami had resulted. David couldn't even describe to me what he was seeing on television from the office.

"What about my kids?" Sally said when I told her the news.

"I don't know. He said the tsunami warning covers the Australian coast, but I have no idea if that's a precaution or a reality." The only tsunami I was aware of had killed hundreds of thousands of people in Indonesia. I didn't want to think about it.

We both stared at the water that surrounded us. "Do you think we should get out of here?" I said.

"No one else seems to be moving."

AFTERSHOCK

"True. Maybe we should just eat and go back home to see what's on the news. You can call home from there, or you can use my phone now if you want." It was difficult to know what to do.

"I'll call when we know something. They are at school anyway. I don't want to scare them."

"No." They didn't need to feel how we did.

Back at my condo, we flipped on the news. David was right. There are no words to describe what we were seeing. Massive waves bulldozed cars, trees, and buildings. Anything in their path was wiped into oblivion. People were running everywhere. Few could run fast enough. Australia would escape with a heightened surf.

That night I'd made dinner reservation as Ku De Ta, the hip restaurant next to the Sky Bar on top of the Marina Bay Sands Hotel and Casino. The giant boat in the sky, under construction for most of our time in Singapore, finally opened in 2010. I wanted to show Sally the view from this spectacular location, but now that thought was unsettling to say the least.

David and Sally convinced me I was being silly and we went anyway. Canadian Chloe joined us too. There is no comparable view over Singapore and I was glad to introduce it to two newcomers, but I couldn't shake the uneasiness I felt about my nightmares or my lightheaded incident in the mall at the time the earthquake hit. Looking at the bay beneath us, I saw nothing but black.

* * *

There was one Thai city that had eluded me so far. As my Asian time came to a close, I was determined to visit Chiang Mai. It is referred to as the "cultural heart" of Thailand. The collective rave reviews could not all be for nothing. Situated in the northern mountains of the country, it is known for its vast amount of Buddhist temples and efforts toward elephant conservation.

Friends had not misled me. Chiang Mai was as charming as everyone claimed. It felt more like a village than a city, and its gentle people and pace were incredibly appealing. It is also a very easy and welcoming place to wander.

In the heart of the city, where the oldest temples are, there are plaques that speak to the visitors when the monks cannot. "Better an ugly face than an ugly mind." "The wise man is always a good listener." Their common sense made me smile. Another sign advertised "Monk Chat" and gave the daily hours. To me that was an intriguing idea. Here they sought to make Buddism's masters accessible to everyone, tourists and locals alike.

After a day full of temple browsing, I found another advertisement for meditation and monk chat in a tourist brochure at my hotel. Every evening at seven o'clock, the monks hosted interested parties at Wat Phra Singh. The temple's birth in the year 1345 give it a unique appearance and setting in a walled compound surrounded by a moat.

I took a taxi to the temple a bit early to take photos before the sun went down and was greeted by an orange-robed monk named Chiko. Chiko said I was permitted to take all the pictures I wanted, but I was not allowed to enter the silver temple on the grounds. Women were not permitted. Narrowing my eyes, I decided to keep my questions to myself. Chiko seemed nervous enough without my demanding equal rights on his property.

It took a long time for the meditation lesson to begin. Chiko answered a German tourist who wanted to know what led him to the temple by saying he didn't have much choice in the matter. It was a surprise, considering I thought there would be discussion of a "higher calling," but I didn't want to make the man uncomfortable.

Thirty minutes after the posted start time, we entered the temple one by one. Brown square pillows were placed in rows in front of the large golden Buddha statue that was the main focal point of the shrine. Chiko sat down with his back to the statue and indicated that we should sit facing it. Then he told us to close our eyes and breathe deep.

I did as I was told and heard Chiko begin chanting softly. It wasn't so much a lesson as it was a meditation session, but I didn't mind. It was interesting simply to be here.

When I closed my eyes, I began feeling nervous. It wasn't the meditation or the chanting—those things were not new to me. I didn't know where the anxiety was coming from. Because it was so quiet in the room, the voice came through clearly. "Get out," it said. I opened my eyes to see who was talking, but everyone else sat with their eyes closed.

What the hell was that? Since I'd begun this exploration of Asian philosophy and religions, I'd been looking intently for the "inner voice" I was supposed to find. Was this it? I was afraid to question it. I got up and left, walking into the dark evening without a clue where to go.

I found a tuk-tuk to drive me back to my hotel. I'd already eaten, so there wasn't much to do besides watch TV and relax in the room.

The next noise I heard was water—more specifically surf. I had a ground floor room next to the swimming pool and it sounded like there were at least ten people in the pool. I didn't hear any voices, which made the hair on my arms stand up. When I went to the bathroom to look out the window, waves rolled across the swimming pool crashing into one end. There was no one in or near the pool. Everything was shaking.

I grabbed my shoes and ran out the door. All I could imagine was the building coming down on me. The women from the hotel desk were all clustered in a corner of the pool area. I walked toward them.

"Earthquake," said a timid female voice.

"Earthquake," I nodded in response.

"Wait here," she told me. "Safe here. Do not go back inside."

"Okay." I waited.

We stood together for about thirty minutes before everyone went back inside. We met again when an aftershock shook us a second time. My feet bounced on the bed. This time I had my backpack at the door with clean clothes and my passport in it. I had no idea what an earthquake emergency kit contained, but this was better than nothing.

I didn't sleep. The next day I made a trip to the sacred sight of Doi Suthep, an ancient temple in the mountains. Climbing the enormous staircase, I was heartened to see many other people out that day. Perhaps they were all doing what I was, going to receive blessings from a Theravada monk. When I bowed my head and closed my eyes, he said, "May your journey be blessed. I wish you good luck." I hoped that would hold until I reached Australia.

Before I went home, I had one more thing to do. I was going to be a mahout for a day at an elephant sanctuary. The park, a very beautiful farm where the elephants had several miles to roam, allowed visitors to be "elephant owner for a day." There was no way I was passing up this opportunity, no matter how spooked I was about earthquakes.

After changing into a hand-woven shirt and pull-on pants, I was given Mae to take care of. My first job was giving her a bath in the river. Sorry about the pun, but this is no small undertaking. Mae was a full-grown female elephant with an attitude to accompany her size. The experience was nothing less than amazing. I scrubbed her with a brush and poured water over her. She sprayed me with her trunk and rolled in the river. I'm not sure who was happier.

When the time came to start my two-hour ride on Mae through the forest, I was alarmed not to see anything to hold onto. I'd already done this once and wasn't a fan. Not wanting to be a chicken shit, I climbed up the step ladder and got on Mae's back. I was grateful she didn't seem to mind.

The tour came to an end with a visit from the baby elephants we'd seen at the entrance. They behaved adorably, just like puppies. One played in the river while the other stuck close to mom. Neither was steady on his feet yet and they fell into the waves often. Until that day, I didn't know elephants could smile.

* * *

David wanted a last trip too. He never traveled alone the way I did. He was too busy. Once I was offered and accepted the job in Brisbane, we wanted to go somewhere exotic that we might not have the chance to again. We chose Borneo. Simply the name evokes images of headhunters and wildlife. I couldn't imagine what we'd find there.

Knowing that our expenses were about to rise dramatically in Australia, we made the trip inexpensive by staying in Bako National Park. Bungalows could be rented for seven dollars a night. If we wanted to eat there, and there was no other place to go, the cost went to ten dollars. I thought we could manage that.

The ride into the park was unbelievable. The Sarawak Forestry Department provides a boat service for the hour-long ride downriver to Bako. At the jetty, a large sign with *"AWAS"* in bright-red letters and

AFTERSHOCK

"*Berhati-hati, Ada Buaya*" underneath warned of crocodiles. A young boy was tragically taken the week before. I tried to find one with my camera's long zoom lens, but came up empty.

Our small wooden boat carried us down the muddy river past a fishing village and several boats. There was no dock. Boats were tied offshore to long poles, leaving the fisherman to wade or swim back and forth. It was easy to see why crocodiles were a major concern.

Men with tanned, leathery skin cast their nets and waited. In the distance, volcanic mountains overlooked the dense jungle. The rock-faced shoreline made it impossible to see into the forest, but the bird songs and shrill monkey screams left no doubt of the residents. Adrenalin sped up my heart.

I was glad to see a dock at the park's entrance. Adventure was one thing, but crocs roaming through camp was crossing the line. Though I knew to expect very little for a few dollars a day, the accommodation was a tad below "rustic"—but there was a ceiling fan and clean sheets. It could have been worse.

We were inside no more than ten minutes when a face appeared at the window. A monkey peered inside to see what he might abscond with. The second warning sign of the day was near the park office. "*Kera-kera nakal sekeliling anda. Berjaga jaga.*" Beneath that in English, "Naughty monkeys around. Watch out." Naughty monkeys? Check!

Hiking trails snaked throughout the park. The ill-behaved monkeys were macaques. They were everywhere. The real wildlife prize we'd come to see was the proboscis monkey, a rare monkey with an elongated snout. David marked a trail where we were likely to see them and we headed out.

Hours later, our biggest wildlife discovery was an enormous amount of hermit crabs. The walk wasn't exciting, but photographing macaques at sunset on the beach was a rare opportunity. A wild boar sauntered by as well, giving us a moment of panic before we discovered he was the camp's unofficial mascot.

"Did you see that there's a night walk with a guide tonight?" David asked over dinner.

"No, I didn't. Are you interested?" I picked at the beans and rice on my plate.

"Definitely. Who knows what's out there?" David was chewing in a hurry. It was 6:45.

The group was small and diverse. Europeans and people from various Asian countries made a group of ten. "We will take roughly ninety minutes," the guide was saying. "I hope no one is afraid." He had a good laugh to himself while the others were mostly silent.

"Can you see that snake on the tree limb?" The group was stopped directly outside our bungalow. The tree branch hung five or six feet above our front door.

"I can make out the curves. He doesn't look that big." David answered.

"He doesn't need to be. It's a tree viper. *Vely* dangerous." Someone gasped.

"How long has it been there?" I hadn't noticed the deadly snake above my door when I arrived, but now I needed to know what it was up to.

"At least a week. Will probably stay there. As long as he stay there, not to worry. When he gone, worry." The guide laughed again.

Making myself a mental note to check for the killer snake upon entering and leaving my accommodation, I moved out from underneath it.

The next day we chose the longest hike. It went to Tajor Waterfall. The description of the walk said we could go swimming when we got there. Mountain stream? No crocs? Yes, please. Surely we would find the proboscis monkeys if we were out all day in remote areas. That's what we thought, anyway.

It was not to be. What we found was that we were stupidly short on water and dangerously dehydrated. The walk was four hours long and we'd brought one water bottle apiece. The heat of the Malaysian jungle made that amount of water seem like a teaspoon. One portion of the walk left us completely exposed to the burning sun.

"I don't know if I can keep going," I said. My throat was on fire.

"We have to," David stated the obvious. Neither of us knew exactly how far it was to camp.

AFTERSHOCK

We had brought decontamination tablets for purifying stream water, but the water was brown. Dark brown. Even after we put the tablets in, we were both afraid to drink it. It wasn't like one of us could carry the other out of this hilly jungle terrain if it was poisonous.

Eventually we made it to the bench that sat at the top of the steep staircase that led up to the path from camp. The end was in sight. We only had to walk down the stairs and we'd be near the office and the canteen. Getting off that bench took a lot of willpower. Walking down the stone staircase on legs that trembled violently took more.

At the bottom, close to the camp office, there was a large rounded tree covered in plump green leaves. A fat proboscis monkey sat eating them. He even had friends. No more than twenty feet from where our hike began was what we had been searching for the whole time.

Immediately, David dropped onto the ground and started shooting with his Nikon.

Seeing the canteen beyond the tree, I took five or six photos and went for drinks. A bottle of water followed by a can of 7Up and a can of Pepsi went down my throat before I went back to David. He hadn't moved an inch. Handling over liquid relief, I sat down beside him and smiled. Even when things look their worst, a miracle can be right around the corner.

The viper

The elusive proboscis monkey

Giving my friend Mae a bath in Chiang Mai

Author's Note

Dear Reader,

Thank you for picking up this book and thanks again making it all the way to the end! If you had any idea of the number of people who told me that writing about life in other cultures wouldn't interest people, you'd be very surprised to be holding it.

In 2011, I moved to Australia with my husband. Life in the Lucky Country has been interesting to say the least. The scenery has once again changed and now parrots and wallabies cross my path more than anything else–people included! We have a very quiet life in the Queensland bush and I work full-time talking to people and writing about the vital need for greater cultural understanding.

Now, in 2015, I can't imagine going anywhere else. But you know that old expression about never saying never. I'd be the last to predict that this is the end of the line. Frankly, there's an incredible amount of joy in the not-knowingness of it. I fantasize about every place on this wonderful planet. Once I couldn't fathom that I'd visit six continents—now I'm wondering when I'll get to number seven.

Me & a new friend Hue

If you enjoyed this book or *The Devil Wears Clogs*, look me up at www.WorldwisePublications.com or on Facebook at www.fb.me/worldwiseJen. You can also join me on Twitter @JenniferBurge or Instagram at @Jen_Burge to get the latest news on my upcoming book about Australia. Come along with me on my quest to understand the world's people and don't let anyone tell you that it's not worth it.

—Jennifer

www.ingramcontent.com/pod-product-compliance
Lightning Source LLC
Chambersburg PA
CBHW021120300426
44113CB00006B/227